DEC 8 8 2016

Inspired Journeys

Inspired Journeys

Travel Writers in Search of the Muse

Edited by

Brian Bouldrey

The University of Wisconsin Press

The University of Wisconsin Press
1930 Monroe Street, 3rd Floor
Madison, Wisconsin 53711-2059
uwpress.wisc.edu

3 Henrietta Street, Covent Garden
London WC2E 8LU, United Kingdom
eurospanbookstore.com

Printed in the United States of America

This book may be available in a digital edition.

"Golden Friendship Club" by David Stuart MacLean originally appeared in the *Bennington Review* (Spring/Summer 2016), reprinted by permission of the author. "Little Log Houses for You and Me" by Kimberly Meyer originally appeared in *Brain, Child: The Magazine for Thinking Mothers* (September 2009), reprinted by permission of the author. "Driving the Fairy-Tale Road" by Raphael Kadushin originally appeared as "Into the Woods" in *Condé Nast Traveler*, February 2012, reprinted by permission of the publisher. "At the Grave of Sadie Thorpe" by Miles Harvey originally appeared in *New Ohio Review* 15 (Spring 2014), reprinted by permission of the author. "The Chevra" by Goldie Goldbloom, selected as a winner of the Hunger Mountain Creative Nonfiction Prize, originally appeared in *Hunger Mountain: The VCFA Journal of the Arts*, the Prizewinner Issue (2014), reprinted by permission of the publisher.

Library of Congress Cataloging-in-Publication Data

Names: Bouldrey, Brian, editor.
Title: Inspired journeys: travel writers in search of the muse / edited by Brian Bouldrey.
Description: Madison, Wisconsin: The University of Wisconsin Press, [2016]
Identifiers: LCCN 2016013571 | ISBN 9780299309404 (cloth: alk. paper)
Subjects: LCSH: Voyages and travels. | Travelers' writings, American.
Classification: LCC G465 .I58 2016 | DDC 910.4—dc23
LC record available at https://lccn.loc.gov/2016013571

For
the Chapman Folks
With love and devotion

Contents

Part II. Carrying the Bones

Acknowledgments

The editor would like to thank Raphael Kadushin, Russell Scott Valentino, all the contributors, and the editorial staff of the University of Wisconsin Press for their patience and perseverance in the creation of this book.

Inspired Journeys

Introduction

Brian Bouldrey

*T*here are several subgenres of travel narrative—fictive, ekphrastic, adventure, public diary, destination-driven, event-driven. But ironically it is increasingly difficult to get movement in a piece of travel writing. Since we've removed most of the journeying part of travel from the process (get to your gate and knock yourself out with a Xanax for most of the flight), there is only the place to write about. The desire, then, is to lard the paragraphs with detail, details that are meant to give a vivid sense of that place, and all its things. Marco Polo was a traveler, yes, but he was also a merchant, and while he could describe quite well the sumptuous riches he brought home along the Silk Road, there can be some awfully long passages of his *Travels* devoted to lists of goods and livestock, rather than accounts of overcoming treacherous tribes and weather on the road and sea or exciting encounters with the ferocious Khan.

But real travelers move through both time and place and tend to understand real distances of both the "here and there" of "this place and that place," as well as "now and then." And they know that the journey is just as important as the arrival.

Is the term "pilgrim" really another word for "real traveler"? The word has always been used in a fast and loose style; *peregrinus*, the Latin word, was applied to aliens, immigrants, travelers, strangers—

those not to be trusted. The word picked up its religious weight somewhere in the middle ages, when travelers would head for certain shrines in the world in order to venerate (we do this any time we go to the grave of a loved one and place flowers or stones there) and bring back blessed souvenirs. Encountering a pilgrim heading to Rome or Mecca was considered a blessed event and helping such a stranger considered a good deed. But what if the pilgrim's destination was not an established shrine of canon?

The idea of a secular pilgrimage is, in another bit of irony, to venerate someone or some place that may be respected by many but has not yet been recognized as a destination of pilgrimage. Arguably, the godmother of secular pilgrimage is Alice Walker, who, in her essay "Looking for Zora," described her search for the home and grave of the writer Zora Neale Hurston. The essay's satisfactions are many, even as she finds the uncared-for grave deep in weeds. The essay did much for both the shrine of Hurston's grave and her reputation as a writer. It is hoped that the chapters in this book are also full of such pleasures, satisfactions, and elevations. And perhaps, while reading about the journeys, readers will find new inspired journeys for themselves.

When one identifies oneself as a pilgrim, it is not unlike offering the self as a mode more than a person. For nearly a thousand years, pilgrims who made their slow, wandering way to Santiago de Compostela also had to make their slow, wandering way back home. The elation of arriving at Santiago, at celebrating with fellow pilgrims, and perhaps proceeding to the end of the earth in Finisterre has, for modern pilgrims, been capped with a relatively quick plane ride home. And somehow, perhaps because of that quick ride home, we feel as if we should still be on the trail—something feels forever unfinished. So we make a slow, wandering way via the through line of story that knits up our journey. We learn how to transform and braid the strands of physical, spiritual, and emotional experience into a story we can tell ourselves and others. Telling the way within can become the true arrival that medieval pilgrims came to know by walking the long, inspired journey home from a pilgrim shrine.

This is all to say that all the chapters in this book move. They are not just about a place, but about getting to that place. Every writer takes you on an original journey, and brings the story, and the reader, back home. As the wise man Walter Benjamin put it, all storytellers come from two tribes: the mariners and the peasants. We listen to the stories of the sailors for "the lore of faraway places, such as a much-traveled man brings home." We hear the stories of the peasants for "the lore of the past, as it best reveals itself to natives of a place." Is it possible to be both a peasant and a mariner?

There are many paradoxes in pilgrimage and pilgrim narrative: The desire to go someplace else in order to be alive but also to seek a kind of mortal oblivion there. The wish to get lost in order to be found. The desire to make of the self both master and slave—also, not coincidentally, the goal of anorexics and long-distance runners. The journey into wild places in order to become more civilized. Thoreau went into the woods to live in nature. Hegel said we can't live in history and must live in history. The pilgrim lives in both nature and history.

"Religion is for those who fear hell," somebody said somewhere, "and spirituality is for those who have already been there." "Spirituality" is one of those words that seems to cover everything, and therefore covers little. Like the word "eclectic." Or, in food, "fusion." But if pressed to define "spiritual" for the sake of this book—because all of the journeys presented here are deeply spiritual, and eclectic—I would say that it exemplifies a searching. A searching for knowledge, outside the self. The writers I present to you are all knowers, but they are not know-it-alls. Nobody likes a know-it-all.

How does one assemble an anthology of wildly different voices on wildly different subjects, threaded together by this immense and open notion of what a pilgrimage is? Each author addresses that question, and my intention with the order here is to give each of those definitions encouragement, space, and incrementally growing meaning, so that somehow, the reader might believe, now and then, that the whole book is greater than the sum of its parts.

The chapters, then, have been divided into two sorts. Part I, "Chasing the Muse," gathers tales in which authors and artists seek out the birthplaces, death places, and sites of famous moments or works. Kimberly Meyer's love for her own family shines through as she takes her daughters to all the places Laura Ingalls Wilder's family established little houses. Susan Fox Rogers journeys to Antarctica to stand in Scott's huts, while Charles Coe recalls his travel to the now-defunct Soviet Union as a black poet—who, he wonders, is looking at whom? John Beckman risks life and limb while scaling the walls of the Marquis de Sade's castle in LaCoste, France. Trebor Healey follows the footsteps of the ecological exhibitionist Gary Snyder. Marta Maretich finds her own soul reflected in great paintings. David Stuart MacLean travels to California, "the place where people go to die," as his hero Nathanael West described it, making his way to the small town of El Centro, where West himself died before finishing his story about the Golden Friendship Club.

Part II, "Carrying the Bones," describes pilgrimages founded upon the burden of familial death and loss, sometimes immediate, sometimes in an ancestral inquiry, sometimes in legend. Raphael Kadushin follows Germany's Fairy-Tale Road to find his own personal connection to the grimmest of the Grimms' fairy tales, and Sharman Apt Russell contemplates the body and its disintegrations as she hikes the Camino de Santiago across northern Spain. Enjoy Jonathan Monroe Geltner's hilariously disastrous bicycle trip to the writer Wendell Berry's farm, and the discoveries of Russell Scott Valentino while moving through the Azores, where, on one of the islands, a relative is venerated as an unofficial saint. Miles Harvey seeks out a saint of a different sort in his Midwestern reflections at Sadie Thorpe's grave. And in two extraordinarily moving pieces, Jivin Misra and Goldie Goldbloom carry the remains of their parents to two very different remote places, one to Varanasi in India and the other to remote western Australia. Lucy Jane Bledsoe uses the cliff-hanger moment in which a hostile border patrol guard prevents her from entering Slovenia to offer some redemptive thoughts about the challenge and reward of traveling alone, and with a friend. Finally, a new beginning is found at the end of the Mayan calendar as Rachel Jamison Webster heads for Belize to contemplate the endings and beginnings in her own life.

All of these pilgrimages are worthy journeys, redemptive and serious. But they are also built on joy and even fun. "Fun" seems a crass word to use when thinking of burying a loved one in a faraway place, but part of pilgrimage is a suspension of rules, and if you recall anything about Chaucer's Canterbury pilgrims, much fun was had. John Beckman, the novelist and academic you will find here climbing around on the Marquis de Sade's castle, is also the author of a book called *American Fun: Four Centuries of Joyous Revolt*, in which he examines key events in U.S. history when citizens indulged in certain historical phenomena for the sake of fun—the Maypole of Mount Wollaston, hateful to the Puritans; the Boston Tea Party; the hippies and the yippies; the punks—all of which show that a revolt against heavy habit can be joyful and inventive. That too seems to be part of the secular pilgrimages written about here: here are Americans, away from home, in pursuit of enduring happiness.

Part I. Chasing the Muse

"Well, sir, I want to see what whaling is. I want to see the world."

"Want to see what whaling is, eh? Have ye clapped eye on Captain Ahab?"

"Who is Captain Ahab, sir?"

"Aye, aye, I thought so. Captain Ahab is the Captain of this ship . . . ye also want to go in order to see the world? . . . Well then, just step forward there, and take a peep over the weather-bow, and then back to me and tell me what ye see there." . . .

"Not much," I replied—"nothing but water." . . .

"Well, what dost thou think then of seeing the world? Do ye wish to go round Cape Horn to see any more of it, eh? Can't ye see the world where you stand?"

Herman Melville, *Moby-Dick*

Golden Friendship Club

David Stuart MacLean

*T*he Golden Friendship Club is advertised in the back pages of newspapers, among the discrete escorts, the amazing hair-loss supplements, and the miracle weight-loss pills. The Golden Friendship Club is an exciting adventure/opportunity (adventunity?) for people who might have hit a hard patch in making friends. Making friends is hard. It's not like college. No. You move to a city as an adult and find that making friends is impossible. The Golden Friendship Club only accepts the highest caliber of people. The crème de la crème de la crème as it might be, but that doesn't mean anyone is putting on airs. No. There won't be a more down-to-earth, sincere group of people you'll ever meet in your life. The members of the Golden Friendship Club are laid back and are interested in chilling out and being real. Isn't that the hardest thing about finding friends in the city, people who are real? The Golden Friendship Club only meets at the swankiest, hippest joints in town. On your commute, you see the free newspapers and they rave about the hottest new bar? The one *you've* never heard of. And there's that moment when you realize that there is a second world going on concurrently with your own. And that other world is filled with hot bars and Korean tapas fusion food trucks that you track with a secret twitter hashtag, while your world is this commute on the elevated train where you feel lucky to get one of the single forward-facing seats because facing backward makes you nauseous, sitting next to people makes you feel anxious, and standing is out of the question given the state of your lower back. The places the Golden Friendship Club meets at? Well, we get there two weeks before that reporter does.

The Golden Friendship Club has an extensive waitlist but it's going to be waived this week only. The boss told us to do it. The boss wants to make sure that the Golden Friendship Club isn't filled up with a bunch of scenester phonies. The boss only wants real people, sincere people, people looking for an honest connection, people looking to chill. So not only can you side step the waitlist but also this week the Golden Friendship Club is halving our application fee. At this rate, the GFC is never going to make money. But this is where the boss stops and reminds us that the Golden Friendship Club isn't about making money; it's about making friends. And making friends is the only kind of industry he ever wants to be a part of. The Golden Friendship Club is his factory and his factory makes friends. He's Henry Ford, he's Elon Musk. He's totally fictional. The Golden Friendship Club is a scam. As is everything in the back pages of the free newspapers. Your hair won't grow back, you'll stay fat, and escorts are never discrete.

You know what they need to have is microwaves on planes," he said as he turned his ball cap around backward. The hat sported a retro version of the Lakers logo. A basketball team on a baseball hat designed to look frayed fresh from the box.

"Do we have to pay for this?" she answered, flipping through the channels on the seatback TV. She yanked a gauzy, parti-colored scarf from her purse and blew her nose into it.

No one is more famous than the people I sit next to on planes. I like the window seat because I'm scared of flying and looking out the window helps, but I have a smallish bladder. I don't talk to the people I sit next to. I monitor them. Like I'm Dian Fossey.

These two: both youngish and good lookingish. Man and woman both in shorts, tank tops, and flip-flops, dressed more for the beach than for a flight. Both toting grease-creased bags of fast food, bags that emit humid meaty smells even before they're opened.

He's short and muscularly built; he carries himself in a way that the muscles clearly have a causal relationship to his height. He's red-headed and perpetually flushed, giving the impression that he's furious at all times.

She's in that beachy Stevie Nicks slot. Blonde highlights in her long brown hair. Bra, camisole, something else: she's got so many straps on her shoulders I'm reminded of the nest of cables behind my parents' TV. It must take her half the night to disconnect them all.

When they sit down they unpack immediately. Reams of stuff emerge—magazines, neck pillows, pill bottles, phones, iPods, head-phones, sweatshirts, eye drops, hand cream, antibacterial gel, glasses—and are secreted in the front seatback pocket, draped across their laps, and stuffed behind their heads. They encamp like pioneers, the aisle laden heavy with their necessaries.

I'm not going to get to the bathroom on this 11 p.m. flight from Chicago to LAX.

The writer Nathanael West said that people travel to California to die. That once life's possibilities back home had become exhausted, the promise of orange trees and the prospect of being fame-adjacent lured them from the Midwest. But then a person gets to the very edge of the country, finds the orange juice cloying, the celebrities disap-pointing and short. The person then stares out at the wide expanse of the ocean: an incomprehensible amount of undrinkable water. And then these late pioneers just wait to die, finding any possible titillating distraction they can as they wait.

I'm going to California to see where Nathanael West died.

The rental car line is a long scar of boredom. It's an hour of slow shuffling before I'm waved to Betty's station. Betty is famous to me. More famous than that couple on the flight, who I've now forgotten completely. Betty is upset that the coffee she just drank did nothing for her and that it's going to be a while before someone brews another pot. In five seconds at her station, I know all of this about the coffee and Betty, and she hasn't even asked me for my name. She talks to the people behind her, flirting with the men who run in and out with the keys. Betty is bad at her job, which, as sins go, isn't an unforgivable one. She's vaguely proud of how bad she is at her job. I am an annoyance to her. But there are so many other annoyances piled up in the line behind me there's no real motivation for her to get me on the road. There's a little smile tucked behind her disdain, like she's draining pleasure out of the minutes she can squeeze out of my day. It's power. All of the cars that my reservation fits don't exist at this Avis. Betty is upset that I don't want to upgrade to the manager's special. We stand off for forty-five minutes before she decides she can give me a Mazda at the promised rate.

Nathanael West is my favorite writer. He wrote four novels, two of which aren't very good. The other two are so good they scare me. He's acerbic and unsentimental, and I started reading him when I was sentimental about exactly those attributes. He was also young, brilliant, and wildly unsuccessful, about which I am still sentimental.

After a life of inconsequential affairs, trips to whorehouses, and trips to the doctor to remedy his STDs, he got married at thirty-seven to a woman more famous than he was. Her sister had written a Broadway play. The play was called *My Sister Eileen*. West married Eileen. She had a son—a five-year-old named Tommy—from a previous marriage. West had a wife and child. In a snap, his youth was over.

I'm driving southeast through Palm Springs and Desert Shores—the great brown boulder landscape of lower California. I realize too late that I'm doing it wrong. That I should've taken the ocean route by San Diego down to El Centro and the lake route up 86 back home. If I wanted to really re-create West's last trip, that's what I should have done. But I'm tired, and it's hot, and I'm a little afraid of the land that I'm traveling through. It's all giant rocks and then flat desert. I am in danger of either dehydrating or being smooshed.

Vijay runs the hotel I'm staying at. He gives me a room on the second floor. It's the kind of place where every room opens out onto the parking lot. The kind of place I assume is for people looking to cook meth with a minimum of hassle. Outside pushing the maid cart is an Indian woman who stabs glances at the front office. Her stares identify her as Vijay's wife. She cleans the rooms; he sits in the office. Her stare also states that she is not happy about this arrangement.

Vijay asks me what business brings me to town. The framing of the question is important. It must be business that has brought me, the question says, because no one comes to El Centro for pleasure.

I tell him I'm here because of a writer who died nearby.

"Did he die recently?" Vijay asks.

"No. In 1940. December 22. His wife died too." But not his dog, Julie, I keep myself from telling him. His dog survived the accident and eyewitness accounts say that after the accident Julie kept trying to jump back into West's crumpled station wagon.

"Is this for a movie?" he asks, sliding me my keycard.

"He wrote for the movies. Nothing anybody would know though."

"He lived here?"

"No. He ran a stop sign over at the intersection of S80 and 111. He was coming up from Calexico." I trail off. Both he and I realize how dumb it is for me to be here. A writer mostly no one has heard of ran a stop sign and died over seventy years ago. This town just happened to be the town he was passing through when he died.

Vijay passes me the credit slip to sign.

Nathanael West clipped the front of a white Pontiac traveling east, spinning his station wagon. The people in the Pontiac were injured but lived. West had been down in Calexico and Mexicali on a hunting trip. He'd been married a month. He was thirty-seven. His wife, Eileen McKenney, was twenty-six.

West was not famous, but he was friends with people who were. Writers mostly. Just the week before he'd had Dorothy Parker, Sheilah Graham the gossip columnist, and her live-in boyfriend F. Scott Fitzgerald over to his new house. When West had been a hotel clerk in New York City, he'd spotted a free room to Dashiell Hammett for a few weeks. He'd even started a magazine once with William Carlos Williams. West was lousy with literary connections, but of any tangible literary success he was innocent. His four books combined hadn't made much over three thousand dollars for him.

Before he died, he had been doing work with Columbia and RKO pictures and was making the best money of his life. His last novel, *The Day of the Locust*, had been a flop, but all of his novels were flops. One of his books had a print run of three thousand. Two thousand were remaindered and pulped.

Failure didn't stop him. He was working on a new novel that he had sold on proposal to Random House. He, McKenney, and Tommy moved into a house in North Hollywood.

I have a new baby. She is six months old. I don't teach in the summer, so I've been taking care of her. It's August. I need to get away from her. Nothing has consumed my life in the way that she has. I haven't been to a movie in months. I get angry at stores for not being open at 7 a.m., seeing how I've already been up for two hours. I go to the grocery store and don't recognize any of the celebrities smiling on the tabloids at the register. My wife works a job she doesn't love but that gives us health insurance.

It's 107 degrees in El Centro. The heat is dry but it's doing things to my stomach. The wavy lines you see coming off the pavement on hot days seem to be inside of my belly. I go to a restaurant with a big parking lot, jam myself into a booth, and order the carne asada tacos. Families start to flood the place. Tables are shoved together to fit whole tracts of family. I order a beer. Someone behind me tests a microphone by tapping it against his pants. A skinny fifteen-year-old girl with dyed orange hair at a table next to me explains to her parents that what she really wants is to find a real man.

A man starts singing. The playback tape is saccharine strings and syrupy horns. The man with his wireless mic prowls the restaurant floor singing Spanish ballads. He's in a mariachi's short fitted jacket and high-waisted pants. His hair is brushed back into a dry pompadour. The families all ignore the singer. It's almost as if they're a little ashamed of him, and because it's a small town they exude that sense of being used to being ashamed of him.

I can't help thinking that I'm seeing the world like West would. Like his death left an aura or lost spirit or gateway or invisible dome that lets his disciples tap into his vision of the world. Silly absurd people! How wonderful! How awful!

I got married at thirty-seven as well. It's weird to get married so much later in life than everyone else. Some of my friends were on their second marriage by the time I got my first. One of the hardest things about marriage was that it really intruded on my loneliness.

I drive around in my rented Mazda. El Centro is the county seat of Imperial County. It's a mess, hit hard by a recession that never seemed to stop. The glory years of the area were decades ago. The downtown strip is gutted. The discount shops with mannequins tilted over, pressing against the windows. The hollow storefronts. Not just empty but gray, cluttered, dead. It's like when you get a root canal and the endodontist kills the nerve and the rest of your life you carry a little chunk of dead tissue around with you. These empty storefronts look like dead tissue.

I picked up West's collected works at a used bookstore when I was backpacking alone through India in 1998. In Delhi I booked a train ride to the southernmost state of India. The train ride was three days long, which I passed drinking train station chai and reading all of West's novels.

Riding the second-class sleeper trains in India, I felt independent. Or more likely I mistook isolation for independence. I didn't speak the languages of any of the areas I traveled through, so I watched people talk to each other, eavesdropping without comprehension, intuiting content through the gestures and facial expressions of strangers. In my journal, I catalogued all the ways I saw people use their hands in a day. The next day I just wrote down different kinds of postures. The next day, every hairstyle I saw. This is how I occupied myself. It was a sketchbook of sorts. I was alone and couldn't stop thinking about other people.

West became the author with whom I identified those days of isolation. In the foreword of the book, I discovered that West and I both worked the late-night shift at a hotel. There's something about that job that teaches a tolerance for boredom and its possibilities for sudden immediate wildness. The emptiness, the seconds that felt like hours, punctuated by a passel of drunks clamoring for cut-rates on rooms, two of them dry-humping on the lobby sofa. The confidences you keep for strangers. The ringside seat to squalor. I felt a bond with West.

I head out east on S80. It's a few miles outside of town. It's an intersection. A nondescript desert intersection with a scrap metal plant on one corner and a trucking company on another, a Shell station tucked away on a frontage road. I don't pull over. There's stoplights now where there used to be a four-way stop sign back in 1940. Highway 111 is the bigger road, with a speed limit so fast that the northbound cars strobe by in the heat. The light changes and I pull through the intersection and drive east for a while. I make a U-turn and head back to the intersection. I drive through it three more times before I realize that I'm driving the Pontiac's route, not West's. I'm doing it all wrong. I'm not West. I'm the car he hit.

I go to the hotel and immerse myself in a Denzel Washington marathon. We don't have cable at my house so TV has become something to swallow in enormous hunks, like the garlic bread at an Olive Garden.

My wife video calls me. She holds our daughter by the armpits and waggles her at the camera. I ask our baby questions that my wife answers in a singsongy voice. I miss them and I tell them as much.

West's last book, *The Day of the Locust*, was about Hollywood, but not about the stars. Instead the book featured the marginal people of the movie industry. The people that populate and construct the backgrounds of the movies are West's subjects: extras, chorus girls, scene painters, stage mothers, little people, the out of work, the out of fashion, the out of sorts, all the peripheral people in a town dominated by stars. One of the main characters is Homer Simpson, a dopey hotel bookkeeper from Iowa who comes to Hollywood for his health. He spends each morning with his enormous hands submerged in ice water in an attempt to wake them up. He then sits in his backyard and watches a lizard stalk flies. Homer cheers for the flies.

The next morning, I head south to Calexico.

West and McKenney stayed at the Hotel de Anza in Calexico, crossing into Mexico to do some hunting. West was born and raised in Manhattan, but he loved to hunt. At some point nature became an obsession for him, a place of beauty and rest. You can see it in his books. In *Miss Lonelyhearts*, the only peace the narrator experiences is at a cabin in the woods. In *The Day of the Locust*, the only passages that are purely beautiful are those describing the birds calling in the scrub bushes.

The drive to Calexico is quick. It's ten a.m. and it's already boiling hot. I cruise down First Street. First Street is the last street in America. There are lines ten people deep for the ATMs on First Street. The Bank of America has installed three on the sidewalk and each one has a line. The street is full of people squinting in the sunshine.

The Hotel de Anza is still standing. It's a mammoth white building, taking up an entire city block. It was built in four months in 1931 and was a locus for Hollywood types during Prohibition for people crossing into Mexico to gamble. When it was built, it had three dance floors, an early air-conditioning setup, and a system to pipe ice water into the rooms. It's a retirement home now.

When I pull up there are two men in cowboy hats sitting in the sweetheart arch. Both are older and Christ-thin, their jeans hanging off of their bony hips. Both give my Mazda a once over and continue their quiet conversation.

On December 22, 1940, West got a telegram at the Hotel de Anza that F. Scott Fitzgerald had died the day before of a heart attack in Sheilah Graham's apartment. West and McKenney and their dog, Julie, got in the car and headed north on 111. He ran the stop sign at the intersection of S80 and hit the white Pontiac. West, McKenney, and Julie were all thrown from the car. West and McKenney bled out onto the pavement. Julie, the dog, was injured but kept trying to jump back into the wrecked vehicle.

When we were bringing our daughter home from the hospital, I was so exhausted from the three days of barely sleeping that I couldn't believe that more was expected of me. We'd inherited a car seat from family friends and I couldn't get the straps to work. I couldn't get them tight enough to protect her. The nurse, a skinny Kirsten Dunst look-alike, was frustrated with me. She told me to call her back when I'd figured it out.

When we got home the baby screamed all of the time and when she wasn't screaming I worried she was dead. She was so tiny; it seemed improbable that she could survive, impossible that I was one of the people in charge of helping her to survive. Asleep in her bassinet, I'd poke her tiny foot until she moved.

I travel up 111, now doing it correctly, really retracing West's route. The whole reason for this trip would be done here in a few minutes. The book West was working on when he died focused on the back pages of magazines and newspapers. The little scams set in the classified ads, promising people nights of camaraderie and laughter. His book was going to focus on the Golden Friendship Club, a Ponzi scheme zeroing in on the lonely and brokenhearted. All those people left on the edge of California glutted with orange juice and glimpses of Gary Cooper staring into the vast expanse of salt water could find solace in this special social club where they'd promptly be scammed out of their life savings. But since it's a West book, the lonely people would probably stay in the club even when they know it's draining them dry. It sounds like the perfect West project.

And then Fitzgerald's heart stops working.

Looking north on 111, it was all indeterminate landscape. Behind me were the Sierra de los Cucapah mountains, ahead of me a blurry blankness. And it's nothing. Absolutely nothing. An anonymous intersection some dead writer I liked died while running a stop sign to go to the funeral of a dead writer he liked. He killed his wife. Left his new son an orphan. Chasing a dead writer.

And I realize the sin I've committed—not unforgivable as long as I drove safely the rest of the way and the plane didn't crash, but a mistake nonetheless. I left my wife and my daughter, traveled across the country, so that I could stand at this nothing intersection. What do I get from standing here? It's not nothing, but it's not something either.

It's a sucker's game: reading. Makes you think you have real relationships. With strangers. Dead strangers. It's a scam. I needed to get home to my wife and baby girl.

After the moment at the intersection, I pulled into the Shell station off the frontage road. The clerk was a compact woman in her forties dusting the open boxes of candy bars. Her hair was pulled back and tucked into a meticulous bun. The creases on the pants of her uniform were so sharp they could slice tomatoes. She was methodical, moving down the row of candy and then coming back on the lower row, like she was mowing a lawn. I stood at the counter with my apple juice waiting for her to finish the entire rack because it was clear there was no interrupting her.

I watch her with West's eyes: so absurd, so lovely.

Little Log Houses for You and Me

Kimberly Meyer

> There seemed to be nothing to see; no fences, no creeks
> or trees, no hills or fields. If there was a road, I could not
> make it out in the faint starlight. There was nothing but
> land: not a country at all, but the material out of which
> countries are made.
>
> Willa Cather, *My Antonia*

Little House on the Prairie

The summer we went searching out the little houses of Laura Ingalls
with our daughters, we were trying to remember things that had
been lost a long time ago. We were traveling to try to preserve things
too that we knew were disappearing, things perishable, the present
turning into the past, and we helpless to stop it.

We'd passed through Oklahoma in the heat of that first day on
the open road: congregations of cows flicking their tails; a truck full
of melons on the side of the road; the skeleton of a weathered gray
barn; a rusted out school bus in a field; hand-painted signs that said
things like "Fresh Produce Right Here" and "You call it Abortion.
God calls it Murder"; barbed wire fences; telephone lines.

We arrived in Kansas at sunset and camped at a lake near the Little House on the Prairie. In the tent that night, the air motionless and the big moon almost bright enough to see by, I read to the girls from my childhood copy of the book that was set there, with its pale yellow cover and brittle pages and Garth Williams illustrations. My grandmother had sent it to me when I was in kindergarten, before I could read, about the age that my Sabine, four, and Mary Martha, six, were that summer. I told the girls, though it's entirely possible that I invented this out of a desire for it to be true, that looking at the indecipherable characters on the pages of *Little House on the Prairie* is what made me want to learn how to read. That night in the tent I chose "Camp on the High Prairie"—the chapter after the perilous crossing of the Verdigris River when the Ingalls family's covered wagon nearly gets swept away in the swollen creek and Jack, their trusty brindle bulldog, disappears. "While they were eating supper the purple shadows closed around the camp fire," I read, pausing for effect, hoping the girls would see the connection between us and them. "The vast prairie was dark and still. Only the wind moved stealthily through the grass, and the large, low stars hung glittering from the great sky."

To breathe life into inert words, to make what once existed alive again within us—this was my intent. In one of the earliest recorded narratives of a pilgrimage to Jerusalem, Egeria, a woman most likely from Galicia, writes of her travels through the Holy Land and across the Sinai Desert into Egypt from the years 379 to 388 AD. On Mount Horeb, she notes:

This is that Horeb where was the holy prophet Elijah when he fled from the face of King Ahab, where God spake to him saying, "What doest thou here Elijah?" as it is written in the book of Kings. For the cave where holy Elijah hid is shown to this day before the door of the church which is there; the stone altar is also shown which holy Elijah built that he might offer sacrifice to God. All things the holy men deigned to show us. There we offered an oblation and an earnest prayer, and the passage from the book of Kings was read; for we always especially desired that when we came to any place the corresponding passage from the book should be read.

If my husband, Terry, and my daughters and I were on a pilgrimage ourselves of sorts, then the words I read to the girls that night in the tent—*for we always especially desired that when we came to any place the corresponding passage from the book should be read*—were those of the saint whose shrines we were seeking.

Since her death, Laura Ingalls Wilder, author of eight books about her childhood on the frontier (and a ninth, *Farmer Boy*, about her husband, Almanzo's, as well), had become a bonnet-clad icon, and all the little log houses she'd lived in, or even just the land itself, had been preserved and memorialized by devotees, among whom I numbered myself. When I say that as a child I was a Laura Ingalls devotee, let me clarify. I was obsessed. I read all nine volumes in order, over and over again. I wanted to be Laura. Every day I plaited my long brown hair into two straight braids. My mother sewed me a muslin frock with a dark green calico apron and matching calico sunbonnet, which I wore for several Halloweens and as often as I could get away with it otherwise. I took quilting classes. I taught myself embroidery and needlepoint. Despite our living in Houston, I fantasized about making candy by drizzling hot molasses over milk pans filled with snow. I watched the television show starring Melissa Gilbert as Laura and Michael Landon as Pa every Monday night on NBC after my bath, not caring how drastically it diverged from the books. When I found out, in reading a biography of Laura Ingalls Wilder that my parents gave me for Christmas one year, that our birthdays were the same, it seemed somehow predestined, written in the prairie's infinite stars.

And when I say that my grandmother *sent* me *Little House on the Prairie*, this is because the summer before my kindergarten year, my parents, who had both been raised in St. Louis by parents who had themselves grown up in St. Louis, packed up a U-Haul and left behind their brothers and sisters and nieces and nephews and the small Missouri town where my father had been coaching football and wrestling and teaching driver's ed on the side to make ends meet and headed south to Texas to try to make a better life for their children than they were likely to find in the Midwest, which was dying. Along with other "pioneer families," as the first one hundred were literally called, we settled in a new development north of the city of Houston called the Woodlands, on land in the Piney Woods once part of a large logging operation. Before that, native Atakapan tribes had ranged through the area, hunting and gathering and smearing their bodies with alligator grease to protect them from mosquitoes. But they were all gone by the time settlers began arriving in the early 1800s so that *there was nothing but land: not a country at all, but the material out of which countries were made.* We drove up in our U-Haul in 1974, at the beginning of a regional population boom. In the Woodlands, whose marketing campaign declared it "A Real Hometown," my father, not unlike Pa Ingalls, eventually made a life for himself and our family building houses. It never occurred to me at the time, but I see now that I didn't need the sunbonnet or the braids to be like Laura Ingalls. I too grew up on a frontier. I too was party to creation through destruction.

And now I was reading the Little House books to my daughters. I had passed on my pioneer dress and sunbonnet to them. I taught them to knit and to sew. We baked bread together and, every once in a while, made butter by shaking a mason jar filled with cream. In the playhouse Terry built out back, the girls would travel in their imaginary covered wagon, put out imaginary prairie fires, and shiver through imaginary long winters while I cooked dinner or folded laundry or swept the back porch. But they were growing—Ellie, the oldest, especially, who was ten and thinking of boys and wearing black nail polish and reading Harry Potter the way I'd read Laura Ingalls, insatiably. And Terry and I knew, I suppose, in the way that you're always aware as a parent of how quickly time alters your children irrevocably, that we only had a short window of opportunity left to us during which we might convince our daughters that a three-thousand-mile road trip in a Volvo station wagon to visit little log houses that a small girl in a sunbonnet lived in many years ago might be fun. Though I believe we actually even said to each other that the trip would be educational, Terry and I really just wanted to have our daughters all to ourselves in a little tent on the prairie, to try, for a moment, to still the traveling hands of time.

❖

The next morning, on our way to the Little House on the Prairie, we stopped at a gas station for some drinks and to get directions. When the cashier, a young man sporting a thin black mustache and a camouflage cap, heard where we were headed, he told me his Aunt Ruth owned the land that the replica log cabin sat on. Trying either to impress me or to shock me, I'm not sure which, he said, "We used to drink beer in the covered wagon in the front yard there."

This was initially all I could think about as we stood before the Little House on the Prairie, as nearly perfect a reproduction as the owners of the property could muster from the scant evidence of the one-room, squared-log, mud-chinked cabin Charles Ingalls built there. Inside was the china shepherdess on the mantle, a replica of the one Ma always carefully unpacked after each wagon journey to say that they were settled; the cornhusk mattress on the corner bedstead; the red-checked tablecloth on the hand-hewn table.

The August 1870 census for Montgomery County, Kansas, lists one C. P. Ingles, a thirty-four-year-old carpenter born in New York State, and his wife, Caroline, thirty, born in Wisconsin. Mary was five, Laura three, Carrie a newborn. The Ingalls family moved to this land near Independence in September 1869 during a land rush that began the year before. They probably had heard that the Osage Diminished Reserve would soon be opened for settlement, after the Osage Indians signed a treaty selling their land to the U.S. government and agreeing to move to their new reservation—later Osage County, Oklahoma. But while those details were being negotiated, the Ingallses, along with thousands of other settlers, and at the encouragement of various formal settler groups, actually began squatting illegally on Osage lands—"Little Squatter on the Osage Diminished Reserve," as the scholar Frances Kaye puts it. The Leavenworth, Lawrence, and Galveston Railroad had managed to negotiate a draft treaty with the Osage that would have allowed it to purchase a large part of the Osage Reserve for twenty cents an acre over fifteen years—a steal in every sense of the word. Though confirmation of this treaty was eventually blocked in the Senate, by persuading settlers to move onto Osage land before a legitimate treaty was enacted, settler groups hoped to ensure that farmers—not businessmen or other railroads—would be the beneficiaries once the Osage left.

And so at the end of *Little House on the Prairie*, when the Ingalls family must leave behind the cabin and the hand-dug well and the newly planted garden just beginning to sprout and the field of grain and the plow that furrowed it, Pa blames the federal government for misleading the settlers. But Pa is wrong. He had settled his family on land that did not belong to them. The trees they felled to build their house were not theirs. The water from the creek, the grasses on which their horses fed—all of it was owned by the Osage.

While she may fudge on this issue—consciously or not—Wilder as author does seem to recognize the complicated and contradictory nature of her family's place on the prairie. While Ma—gentle, refined Ma!—always speaks of the "savages" in the Indian camp near their cabin, Laura is particularly keen to see the exotic natives when they move to Indian Territory, and she even wants Pa to get her a papoose, whose black eyes she meets one day and whose gaze she cannot shake. She cries and cries for it. Pa tells her, "Hush, Laura. The Indian woman wants to keep her baby," signaling an awareness in the adult Wilder that now she knows better, though I still find this scene chilling.

And even though we know that Pa does not believe that "the only good Indian is a dead Indian," he most certainly would have agreed with their neighbor Mrs. Scott, who declares to Ma, "Treaties or no treaties, the land belongs to folks that'll farm it. That's only common sense and justice." One evening, playing his fiddle, Pa sings of an "Indian maid, Bright Alfarata," who roams the banks and, in her canoe, plies the waters of the Juniata River singing of her warrior lover. But the song also mourns the fleeting years that have "borne away the voice of Alfarata." After Pa stops playing, Laura asks, "But please tell me where the voice of Alfarata went?" and Ma replies, "Oh I suppose she went west. . . . That's what the Indians do." But Laura, in a scene every parent will recognize, keeps pestering. "Why do they go west?" she asks. Ma tells her that they have to. "Why do they have to?" "The government makes them, Laura," Pa says. "Now go to sleep." But she's still not satisfied. "Will the government make these Indians go west?" she asks.

> "Yes," Pa said. "When white settlers come into a country, the Indians have to move on. The government is going to move these

Indians farther west, any time now. That's why we're here, Laura. White people are going to settle all this country, and we get the best land because we get here first and take our pick. Now do you understand?"

"Yes, Pa," Laura said. "But, Pa, I thought this was Indian Territory. Won't it make the Indians mad to have to—"

"No more questions, Laura," Pa said, firmly. "Go to sleep."

Just two or three years after the Ingallses arrived in Kansas and began illegally squatting on Osage tribal lands, John Gast painted *American Progress* (1872), an allegorical representation of Manifest Destiny in which Columbia, a personification of the United States in flowing white toga, leads farmers and frontiersmen, oxen and horses westward, holding a school primer in one hand and stringing telegraph line with the other. Native Americans and wild animals flee before her advance.

One of the final chapters in *Little House on the Prairie* acknowledges this particular ruin in which the Ingalls family, however unwittingly, took part. The Osage are leaving their ancestral lands, pushed west by the government that makes them go, though the Ingalls don't seem to know that yet. Laura and Mary and Carrie, Pa and Ma, stand in the doorway of their little log cabin watching. Pa tells Laura, "Look at the Indians, Laura. Look west, and then look east, and see what you see." Laura looks:

As far as she could see to the west and as far as she could see to the east there were Indians. There was no end to that long, long line. . . . It was dinner-time, and no one thought of dinner. Indian ponies were still going by, carrying bundles of skins and tent-poles and dangling baskets and cooking pots. There were a few more women and a few more naked Indian children. Then the very last pony went by. But Pa and Ma and Laura and Mary still stayed in the doorway, looking, till that long line of Indians slowly pulled itself over the western edge of the world. And nothing was left but silence and emptiness. All the world seemed very quiet and lonely.

"Every act of creation," said Pablo Picasso, "is first of all an act of destruction."

After the girls had grown bored with sitting on the corncob mattress and pretending to eat puffed up vanity cakes at the table, we wandered over to the gift shop in a white clapboard farmhouse nearby. The girls, our giddy little consumers, had been chattering in the dark tent the night before about what they might buy with the money we'd given each of them to spend on the trip. Ellie ended up purchasing some books written by Rose Wilder Lane, Laura's daughter, a novelist and journalist herself and the one who encouraged her mother to write down the stories from her childhood, and who even collaborated to some extent in the writing itself. Sabine chose a tin cup with a peppermint stick and a penny taped down inside, a replica of the present Mr. Edwards carried for Laura and Mary in a bundle on top of his head across the icy Verdigris River that Christmas on the prairie. Mary Martha bought a calico Barbie dress with sunbonnet and white, lace-edged apron, in which Enchanted Evening Barbie looked entirely ill at ease. As the girls were taking out their crumpled bills from their Hello Kitty wallets, I chatted with the woman at the register about why she thought people come from all over to see this little house where Laura lived. She told me, "I think, even though we know life was harder then, it seemed simpler somehow."

I was trying to decide what I thought about this theory outside the gift shop, while the girls ran around in the sun and Terry and I sat on a bale of hay beneath a shade tree. We struck up a conversation with Norma, an older woman from Independence with carefully arranged, abundantly sprayed hair, and her two teenaged grand-daughters. Norma told us about growing up nearby, about how she remembered churning butter in the days before electricity and tele-vision, when horse-drawn plows still tilled the fields. She knew that life was harder then, she told us, but she thought families were closer too. She glanced at her granddaughters, dressed in nylon football jerseys and tight jeans. When I asked them if they'd come here because they liked the Little House books or because their grandmother made them, they sort of laughed and looked away.

Later, on our drive north, we stopped for lunch. Terry and I share an affinity for these Midwestern towns passed over by the inter-state or hollowed out when Walmart moved in. Their worn storefronts housing video stores and Family Dollar shops or nothing at all remind us, perhaps, of what is always passing, what has passed. We ended up at a Pizza Hut because the local café was closed down. As we were waiting for our food to arrive, we bribed the girls with quarters for the jukebox so that we could talk in peace. Terry said to me then, "I think out here, we're seeing the last effects of the Industrial Revolu-tion." When I asked him what he meant, he said, "What made life easier ended that old way of life." He paused for a moment. "But you know, even if life was harder then, those girls we met don't have it easy. They don't have the connection to the land that the older genera-tion does. And they're just stuck in these dead-end towns." I remem-bered the open field of soybeans we'd snapped pictures in front of. The big blue sky. In an odd mirroring of what Pa says when that endless line of Osage pass before the Ingalls cabin, there had been a sign along the fence behind the Little House on the Prairie that read, "Stand here and imagine a line of wagons heading as far west as the eye can see." I recalled how strangely moved by this I'd been—perhaps because of all the hope and desperation it took to drive a wagon that far into what was, to the settlers, nowhere. It was *not a country at all, but the material out of which countries are made*. Perhaps because of the inevitable devastation it would lead to.

Little Town on the Prairie

Nebraska, late afternoon. The Sand Hills like dunes rolling and rising to the horizon, grasses clinging to them. Cattle huddled together in each other's shade. Windmills. Round steel tubs beneath them half-filled with water. Railroad tracks, but no train.

In the old black-and-white photos, the women stand with babies on their hips in the big bluestem grasses of the prairie, which come up to their shoulders. Driving across these plains, I could picture them as the sea the settlers often compared them to. I could begin to imagine how insignificant one might feel against such vastness. Heading west in their wagon toward Silver Lake in the Dakota Territory, Laura says,

> The farther they went . . . the smaller they seemed, and the less they seemed to be going anywhere. The wind blew the grass always with the same endless rippling, the horses' feet and the wheels going over the grass made always the same sound. The jiggling of the board seat was always the same jiggling. Laura thought they might go on forever, yet always be in this same changeless place, that would not even know they were there.

I wondered, driving across the Sand Hills of Nebraska as the sun pooled in the western sky, did this feeling of smallness inspire a sort of humility that can hardly exist anymore? And wasn't that a more accurate version, really, of existence? Isn't all civilization—that effort, whatever form it takes, to tame the wilderness—merely an attempt to make ourselves feel less inconsequential? And—*always in this same changeless place, that does not even know we are here*—aren't we just fooling ourselves?

Nebraska also made me wonder: if this terrain had once inspired humility, did our hubris explain what had subsequently become of it? How could we have ever thought we'd need all that land? And was this seeking of fresh starts in wide open spaces always doomed to end in strip malls and fast food restaurants, Walmarts and KMarts and Targets, miles and miles of concrete? In the books that chronicle Wilder's years in Dakota Territory—*By the Shores of Silver Lake, The Long Winter, Little Town on the Prairie, These Happy Golden Years*— I see the beginnings of an American narrative of sprawl. Traveling to Silver Lake, where Pa has gotten a job as timekeeper and storekeeper for the Chicago and Northwestern Railroad as it pushes west, Laura sees the grooves of old Indian trails and buffalo wallows, grassed over now. Then she watches as a town, with its false-fronted, stove-piped buildings, springs up in weeks where nothing had been before. In this town, she attends sociables and literaries and a revival. She makes friends. But later she says, *The town was like a sore on the beautiful, wild prairie.* Strangers move in. Then they move on, some farther west, some back east. Pa says, *They come and they go.*

The Book of Genesis is in part the story of a series of covenants God makes with various Chosen Ones—Adam, Noah, Lot, Abraham. Again and again, the Lord creates a world and then watches as his creatures destroy it. So he wipes the slate clean—banishment and flood and fire and brimstone—and begins again. It's an optimistic story in a way—drawn forward always by the possibility of eventual perfection. It's the American Story too. As Nick Carraway looks out over the waters of Long Island Sound at the end of *The Great Gatsby*, he imagines the continent as it must have looked to the Dutch sailors who first settled there, their wonder in beholding it. And he thinks of Gatsby's wonder when he first saw the green light at the end of Daisy's dock. "Gatsby believed in the green light, the orgastic future that year by year recedes before us. It eluded us then, but that's no matter—tomorrow we will run faster, stretch out our arms farther. . . . And one fine morning—So we beat on, boats against the current, borne back ceaselessly into the past."

Over and over again in America, we have wanted, like God, to make something more perfect, to finally get it right. *And the earth was without form, and void. There was nothing but land: not a country at all, but the material out of which countries are made.* Over and over again, from Puritans to pioneers to suburbanites, we have forsaken what we made when it became corrupted, abandoned it for the next Eden, for the newer world washed clean of the iniquity of the old. *The town was like a sore on the beautiful, wild prairie.* But what a mess we continue to make.

❖

We camped in the Black Hills of South Dakota for a few days on our way to DeSmet, the Little Town on the Prairie. That first evening, we set up our tent in the last light of an August night, sweating. I wiped the girls' arms and legs with a wet cloth to help cool them so they could sleep. Sometime in the night, a windstorm swept through the canyon we were camped in, and for hours our tent filled like a lung, then emptied, and filled again.

In the morning, the heat and haze of the previous day had been erased, so that the world seemed to have crystallized around us, come into sharper focus. The girls picked wildflowers and we put the bouquet in an empty tin can on the picnic table, which I'd covered with a red-checked vinyl cloth. I made coffee in our blue speckleware percolator and pancakes on the camp stove, and thought of Ma, who always made do, but made life lovely as well—the pie of green pumpkins that would have otherwise gone to waste, the bright button lamp fueled by axle grease, white muslin curtains trimmed with remnants of Laura and Mary's calico dresses. I looked at the table and the flowers and the stack of pancakes I had made by adding water to a packaged mix and felt unjustifiably but inordinately pleased with myself.

✦

"It's everybody's story," Tim Sullivan told us as we stood in a barn on the actual Ingalls Homestead in South Dakota, now a living history museum comprised of a series of replica buildings—Ma's Little House, the Burvee Shanty, the Dugout, the Little Prairie School.

"It's everybody's story," Sullivan, the owner of the Homestead, said again. "It was bigger than just the Ingalls family." I thought about the grassed over Indian trails and buffalo wallows and supposed it was, in a way, everybody's story. Playing his fiddle, Pa had often sung,

> O come to this country
> And don't you feel alarm,
> For Uncle Sam is rich enough
> To give us all a farm.

Those farms were provided by the terms of the Homestead Act of 1862, which essentially said that any citizen of the United States, or any immigrant who intended to become a citizen, could claim 160 acres of land as long as a 12 × 14 foot home was built on it, the land was cultivated, and someone lived on the claim at least six months every year. If all these conditions were met for a total of five years, the land was given to the claimant—free. Charles Ingalls filed his claim on these 160 acres southeast of the town of De Smet on which my daughters and I now stood in February 1880. Six years later, he proved up on the land and it was his.

"You know what a hay twist is?" Sullivan asked the girls. I was so relieved that the night before I'd chosen to read to them this exact chapter from *The Long Winter*. Ellie told him, "It's what they had to burn instead of wood." "Okay. It's December of 1880," he began the story of that desperate season, "and the town is snowed in. Trains can't get in or out to deliver the coal and food supplies, see. And remember, there were no trees here when the settlers first came. This was all prairie. So they didn't have wood to burn." He grabbed a handful of hay from a bin behind him. "Now you know what this is, don't you?" The girls looked at him, blinking. "This is slough hay. I'm going to teach you how to make a hay twist. Do you remember how many twists they had to make to boil water for a pot of tea?" he asks. "About seven?" Ellie answered. "Yes!" I thought when Sullivan nodded.

Sullivan sat with the girls and began to twist the slough hay, turning and turning until it coiled in on itself, golden flecks of straw clinging to his shirt. But this was summer. And just for fun. There was no blizzard raging. We weren't starving. We would never have to do this day in and day out for months on end to keep from freezing. "Their hands were red and swollen," Laura writes of that endless chore she and Pa performed, "the skin was cold and covered with cuts made by the sharp slough hay. The hay was cutting away the cloth of their coats on the left side and along the underneath of their left coat sleeves. Ma patched the worn places, but the hay cut away the patches."

Standing there in the barn, I realized that part of the reason I had wanted to make this trip in the first place had something to do with the lesson Sullivan was, in effect, teaching. I wanted my daughters to understand how difficult life had been for these pioneers they like to pretend to be. When I was little, I'd often thought to myself, "I want to live in the olden days!" Which meant I wanted to wear calico dresses and knit woolen socks and satisfy my inexplicable and persistent yearning to churn butter and make cheese. Now my girls had taken up the refrain. "The new-en days are boring!" they would chime, their sunbonneted faces upturned. But there was something in me, some perversity, perhaps, that wanted them to see that life wasn't so simple back then. I remembered what the woman in the gift shop at the Little House on the Prairie had told me—people are drawn to these stories because they describe a simpler life. But was it more simple? Look at the photographs, the faces creased with worry and work, I now wanted to argue. Look at the houses, I wanted to point out to the girls, how small and dark and cramped! Look at the chores they had to do, even when they were very young! Look, I wanted to say to my increasingly sassy tweenager, at that rule about no speaking unless spoken to! Look at how few gifts they got at Christmas— mittens! oranges! a peppermint stick!

At the homestead gift shop, Ellie bought a corncob doll kit (corncob, scrap of calico, ribbon)—a replica of Laura's first doll. Sabine purchased a stuffed Jack the Brindle Bulldog. Mary Martha found a new calico bonnet, which she would go on to wear continuously for the rest of our trip, even to bed. I bought tapes of pioneer songs played on Pa's actual fiddle: "Swanee River," "Captain Jinks," "Buffalo Gals," "My Old Kentucky Home." But I was beginning to worry: Why did we need to validate our experience through buying?

The twelfth-century *Pilgrim's Guide to Santiago de Compostela* describes what would have been a familiar sight to pilgrims arriving at that shrine in northern Spain, where the body of St. James, brother and apostle to Jesus, was said to reside: "Behind the fountain, as we have mentioned, there is the parvis [the open space before a church], all of it paved out with stones. It is there that scallop shells, the insignia of Santiago, are sold to the pilgrims; and one sells there also wine-skins, shoes, knapsacks of deer-skin, side-bags, leather straps, belts, all sort of medicinal herbs no less than sundry drugs and many more things." As at the little houses, an entire industry sprang up in the Middle Ages catering to pilgrims. Medieval churches licensed merchants to sell sacred keepsakes: candles, badges, boxes of earth from which God fashioned Adam, models and paintings of various holy sites, ampullae of clay or silver filled with water from the Jordan or the diluted blood of a martyr. Pilgrims were the first tourists and the mementos they brought home were the earliest tacky souvenirs. But their souvenirs could work miracles. I wondered again about my daughters and me in the gift shops at the Little Houses. Were we buying the trinkets of a saint? Was this our feeble attempt to get nearer to Our Lady of the Prairie? If so, what saving miracle did we seek?

At the northern edge of the Ingalls Homestead, just below a slight swale in the land, the five cottonwood trees that Pa planted, one each for his wife and four daughters, still shivered in the late afternoon breeze. While Terry looked at the map in the station wagon to check on directions for our drive to Minnesota, my own daughters and I stood among them for a long time. We watched the light spangle and weave. We listened to the leaves rustle against each other like silk dresses. We wondered about departed spirits. We tried to hear what they said from that other world.

On the Banks of Plum Creek

In the tent that night at a campground on the banks of Plum Creek just outside Walnut Grove, Minnesota, Ellie lay with her corncob doll, whom she had named Charlotte—the name of a doll of Laura's. "I wouldn't know how it is to love a corncob doll since I don't have one," Mary Martha said. "But I would like to know how to love a corncob doll," she added when she saw Ellie taking offense. "I think having a corncob doll is kind of weird," Sabine continued, oblivious, "because corncobs are what you eat and eating is good but hugging something you ate is yucky." When Ellie blurted out some rant against this great injustice, I heard myself saying to her, "Do you think Laura would have talked to her sisters that way?" In the moonlight through the windows of our tent Terry and I caught each other's eye. "WWLD," he mouthed. When I looked questioningly back at him, he whispered, "What Would Laura Do?"

Outside the tent, the insects' pulsing call to each other in the dark was like a giant heartbeat. Their voices now seemed oracular, since this was the site of the grasshopper plague that nearly ruined the Ingalls family. In early 1874, Pa traded his team of horses for a small farm near Walnut Grove. With no trees nearby for a log cabin and no money yet for lumber, they lived at first in a dugout in the creek bank with a front wall and roof made of sod. Instead of glass, they had oiled paper windows. Pa plowed and sowed his fields and, eventually, with his fine crop of wheat nearly ripe, he built a house of sawed boards on credit.

But in the dry late summer of 1874, farmers across the Midwest began to report strange glittering clouds in the sky. The millions and millions of grasshoppers that made up these clouds descended to earth and ate everything—crops, of course, but also every green leaf on every living plant, the sheets and cloths laid over vegetable plots in futile attempts to save them, human hair and skin, even each other. "The whole prairie had changed," Laura says in *On the Banks of Plum Creek*. "The grasses did not wave; they had fallen in ridges. The rising sun made all the prairie rough with shadows where the tall grasses had sunk against each other. The willow trees were bare. In the plum thickets only a few plum pits hung to the leafless branches. The nipping, clicking, gnawing sound of the grasshoppers' eating was still going on." Scientists aren't fully certain what caused the grasshopper pestilence, though they suspect that, in part, it may have been the clearing of land for farming itself.

One Sunday, in the midst of this pestilence, Laura recalls how Ma read to them from *Exodus* about the plague of locusts: "For they covered the face of the whole earth, so that the land was darkened; and they did eat every herb of the land, and all the fruits of the trees which the hail had left; and there remained not any green thing on the trees, or in the herbs of the field, through all the land of Egypt." Then Ma reads of the promise God makes to bring his people "unto a land flowing with milk and honey." This confuses Laura and Mary. How could land flow with milk and honey? Wouldn't that be sticky? "Well, Laura," explains Ma, "if good milch cows were eating grass all over this land, they would give a great deal of milk, and then the land would be flowing with milk. Bees would get honey out of all the wild flowers that grow out of the land, and then the land would be flowing with honey." Ma says that Pa thinks the Promised Land is right there in Minnesota.

There were two successive years of grasshopper plagues, two successive years of crop failures. In November 1875 the Ingallses had a son, Charles Frederick. Freddie, they called him. By the following summer, he was dead. In 1876 a daughter, Grace, was born. Perhaps her name signified a frail hope that their afflictions were at an end. Then Mary fell ill. Pa shaved her head close because of the fever. She still went blind. After that, they left for South Dakota.

❖

Walnut Grove was a sad little town of railroad tracks and grain silos holding fast to its tenuous link to Laura Ingalls. In the museum we saw a sewing basket that *resembled* Laura's and a quilt *believed* to have been sewn by her. The building also housed memorabilia connected to the television show, which was located in a highly fictionalized version of the town. Here was the mantel from the set; here, a plate collection with scenes from the series; here, panty hose worn by Allison Arngrim, who played Nellie Oleson; here, a scale model of the show's house built out of 32,700 toothpicks. Down the road at the Little Café on the Prairie, where we stopped afterward to get something to eat, the girls begged us to buy them "Laura's Lunch Pail"—essentially an empty paint can with PB&J, an apple, and some licorice—all for $8.95. We couldn't bring ourselves to do it, though. In the bathroom of the restaurant, a sign hanging above the toilet read, as if responding to my thoughts, "So what if this isn't Home Sweet Home. Adjust."

After lunch, we drove out to the actual site of the Ingalls dugout. What was once their homestead is now owned by the Gordon family. To get to the home site, you put three dollars into a mailbox near their big white farmhouse and red barn, then drive past fields of corn and soy beans and swathes of prairie grasses to Plum Creek, which is hidden from view by thick vines and brush. We climbed a sandy bank to the site of the dugout. Now there was only a wooden sign marking the spot. "The Charles Ingalls Family's dugout home was located here in the 1870s," it informed us. "This depression is all that remains since the roof caved in years ago. The prairie grasses and flowers here grow much as they did in Laura's time and the spring flows nearby."

The girls were disappointed and began to pout. They liked the replicas, liked being able to lie in a cornhusk bed even if it wasn't

Laura's cornhusk bed, liked riding in a covered wagon even if teen-agers used to get drunk in it. For them, she became real only through the imagined. And for them, no home here on the Banks of Plum Creek was an offensive waste of their time.

But I found myself inexplicably moved. All along the bank, wild plum trees were growing in lush strands—maybe, I thought indul-gently, grown from the seeds of trees Laura and Mary and Carrie picked from, seeds Ma discarded as she lay the fruit on clean sheets to dry in the sun. "The shade of the plum thickets was a thick shade," Laura says of this exact spot (*for we always especially desired that when we came to any place the corresponding passage from the book should be read*). "Sunshine flickered between the narrow leaves overhead. The little branches sagged with their weight of plums, and plums had fallen and rolled together between drifts of long grass underfoot."

Terry and the girls and I climbed up to the top of the bank and looked out over the open prairie of the tableland. Slender footpaths led among the trees and through the grasses, and the girls darted off along them. I could see their small backs disappearing into the brush. Mary Martha's sunbonnet hung between her tiny shoulder blades.

Unlike at the museums we'd been to, the replica houses, here there were no reproductions, no attempts to preserve time, to annul time, to reverse it. Time had, in fact, gone on, had ravaged this site and erased all evidence of human habitation. Which was in its way pitiless, and thus just right. There was something honest about this wall of collapsed earth in a way that all the facsimiles we'd visited were lies. Here, on the banks of Plum Creek, all that had endured and thrived, continuously, as the sign said, from the Ingallses' days to ours, had been the natural world—trees and grasses, water and sand.

Little House in the Big Woods

"I don't think I would like to live back then anymore," Ellie was saying, "because it just seems too hard and there were a lot of ways you could die—like of sicknesses. And doctors didn't know what to do about them." We were sitting on camp chairs around our fire in Wisconsin, near the town of Pepin, the girls debating the advantages and drawbacks of living in the olden days. Mary Martha, holding her blanket and sucking her thumb, agreed: "I think it would be hard to do all those chores," she said, taking her thumb out of her mouth just long enough to make her statement. "And in the winter and stuff. From doing all those hay twists, my hands would get really, really sore." "Yeah, and people, they have to wear long dresses and that's very hot in summer," piped in Sabine, who was curled up like a little kitten in my lap.

I looked up at the stars, which were near to me and clear against the darkness, little pinholes of light. The sky was so wide and open it seemed I could see from rim to rim. I felt dizzy and thought I could sense the spinning earth beneath me. I was almost afraid if I stood up, I might fall off.

"The great, dark trees of the Big Woods stood all around the house," Laura says in the beginning of her first book, "and beyond them were other trees and beyond them were more trees. As far as a man could go to the north in a day, or a week, or a whole month, there was nothing but woods. There were no houses. There were no roads. There were no people. There were only trees and wild animals who had their homes among them." But the Big Woods and much of its wildness were gone now, most of it converted to pastureland. To get here, we'd driven along the Laura Ingalls Wilder Memorial Highway, through green hills and valleys, past big red barns with stone foundations, Holstein cows with heavy, swaying udders, spruce trees, fields and fields of corn. We'd seen a facsimile of the Little House in the Big Woods, where Laura was born. At the museum in town, the woman behind the desk, who gave us directions to the homesite, told us that the first log house the town built had to be reconstructed because people had stolen the chinking to take home as souvenirs. Relics of the saints, I'd thought, remembering that as early as 385 AD, armed deacons had to surround the True Cross in Jerusalem, which, like the Little House in the Big Woods, was certainly a reproduction, in order to prevent pilgrims from kissing it and taking a splinter away with their teeth.

Back in De Smet, South Dakota, I'd asked one of the tour guides why she thought so many people were drawn to the Little House books and to making this pilgrimage to see the homes Laura had lived in. "I think it's the writing," she'd said to me. "Remember, when Mary went blind, after she was struck by scarlet fever, Laura became Mary's eyes. She had to see for Mary, and I think that's where she learned to describe the land so beautifully." If she did nothing else, Laura Ingalls Wilder preserved that land and that time—the clear creek, the prairie grasses, the slough, the big blue sky, the near stars. Maybe I love these little houses, these small towns, these wide prairies because they are so rapidly disappearing. Maybe I love them because they are vulnerable. And there is something about the vulnerability of the land that moves me in the same way as does the vulnerability of my children—both are changing and moving continuously toward some inexorable end.

The Holler

I have an uncle who lives in Dent County in the Missouri Ozarks, not far at all from where Laura and Almanzo eventually settled with their daughter, Rose. On our way to see this last little house in

Mansfield, Missouri, we stopped to see him. Uncle Bob lives with Larry, his "roommate"—as my grandmother prefers to say—of more than thirty years. They share an apartment above an old general store in the town square. Larry is a self-described country lawyer. His offices are where the store used to be. My uncle keeps the books and gardens and has managed to learn Italian by listening to satellite television stations broadcast from Italy.

We had arrived the evening before and camped by the Black River, down the road from their place. In the morning, my uncle took us to see the Holler. In 1971, just a few years before my parents left the Midwest for the Woodlands, Bob and Larry and a small group of friends from St. Louis tried to found a new life, away from the city, away from modernity—reverse pioneering—on sixty-five wooded acres they called "Hippie Holler." For centuries this forest had been the hunting grounds of the Osage, who had villages nearby with gardens where they grew their squash and corn and beans. These would have been the same Osage Laura watched leaving from the doorway of her Little House on the Prairie.

For three years, Uncle Bob and Larry lived in a tipi that they had sewn themselves while they and the others built a house and put in a garden and tried to subsist. When I asked Uncle Bob as we drove through the forested hills if he was influenced more by the Native Americans, who once lived here, or by the homesteaders, who pushed them out, he told me, "Both. We just thought it was essential to know how to do things ourselves. We were trying to preserve arts that would be lost."

When we arrived at the Holler, the sun was high and the cicadas frantic in the heat. We pushed through dense undergrowth as we climbed up toward the house. On our way, Uncle Bob pointed out the spring where they used to keep a stoneware crock for their—here I experienced a wave of unmitigated envy—butter and milk and homemade goat cheese. We passed the outhouse, which at one time had sported a stained glass window from an old church. Just beyond, through the trees, he said, was the stone chicken coop he'd mortared together himself one summer.

Though in a state of disrepair, the house Uncle Bob and Larry and their friends built was stunning. Arched doors lined the front and back of the house, made of stones collected from the land and paneled inside with walnut wood from trees on the property. A massive rock fireplace anchored one end of the cavernous space. It had the feel of a desolate medieval hall whose inhabitants had died ages and ages ago. "This is only half of what the house was imagined to be," Uncle Bob told us as we stared, amazed at the craftsmanship, amazed that anyone living today could make—would bother to make—something so beautiful with only their own hands and some simple tools. "The kitchen was through that arch," he explained, "and that other arch was going to open to a library. We had a player piano. There used to be a deck. We were going to build a greenhouse."

In the end, though, this self-reliant life was impossible, as my uncle puts it, "for 1970s suburban thirty-year-olds." One of the couples who were part of the core group divorced and left the Holler. Eventually the others followed. And Larry had to move to town when he was elected prosecuting attorney or risk getting snowed in. Winter was coming on, my uncle told us, and it all just fell apart. "I couldn't go back to the Holler for years and years because it was so depressing, the failure. And I can still sit up on a hillside there and hear all the noise it took to build it, what little there is."

These Happy Golden Years

These Happy Golden Years ends on the day Laura marries Almanzo Wilder, as the couple lingers in their own little house, built by Almanzo, after their first meal together. "It's a wonderful night,"

Almanzo says to Laura, and she replies, "It is a beautiful world." In her mind, she hears the voice of Pa's fiddle and the echo of a song: *Golden years are passing by*, it goes. *These happy, golden years.*

Hardly. Farming was no easier on Almanzo and Laura than it had been on Pa and Ma. Drought and hail storms ruined their crops and kept them in debt. Diphtheria crippled Almanzo—he walked with a cane for the rest of his life. They had a daughter, Rose, in 1886, but their second child, a son, died of convulsions two weeks after his birth. Their house burned down. In a manuscript composed during the Great Depression for the Federal Writers' Project, Rose Wilder Lane, by then a middle-aged woman, tells the story of her parents' leaving South Dakota, where "it was a saying . . . that the Government bet a quarter section against fifteen dollars and five years' hard work that the land would starve a man out in less than five years. My father won the bet," she says. "It took seven successive years of complete crop failure, with work, weather and sickness that wrecked his health permanently, and interest rates of 36 percent on money borrowed to buy food, to dislodge us from that land. I was then seven years old."

Rose tells of their journey to the Missouri Ozarks in 1894, during the worst economic depression the United States had yet experienced, when twenty percent of the workforce was out of a job and commodity prices for farmers were plummeting. Transients clogged the roads and byways. "The whole country is just full of emigrants, going and coming," Laura recorded in a journal of that trip by covered wagon. When they arrived in Missouri, Rose recalled, "It was strange not to hear the wind any more. My parents had great good fortune; with their last hoarded dollar, they were able to buy a piece of poor ridge land, uncleared with a log cabin and a heavy mortgage on it." In time and with achingly hard work and frugality, this land became Rocky Ridge Farm: two hundred acres in meadow, pasture, field, and wood lot; three houses with central heating, modern plumbing, refrigerators, electric ranges; garages for three cars. The American Dream.

When we pulled into Mansfield, the small town near Rocky Ridge, we were greeted by a sign that reminded us, "Seven Days Without Prayer Makes One Weak." Because there was no campground to be found, we stayed near the highway at the Little House Inn, with its thin sheets and an air conditioner that rattled all through the warm night. We slept restlessly. In the morning we ate next door at the Little House Diner. We wished we were home. We couldn't stand to see one more artifact loosely tied to Laura's life, one more commemorative spoon in one more gift shop. Even the girls seemed exhausted. But like Pa and Ma, we forged ahead, cheerfully and without complaint. We took the tour of the white, rambling farmhouse on the hill that slopes down through trees to open pasture, where horses were grazing. We heard how Almanzo built the kitchen on a smaller scale to suit Laura's tiny build. We walked through the bedroom where they slept in separate twin beds. The girls looked up at me questioningly. We saw the desk where Laura wrote the Little House books. We looked out the picture window that she wanted instead of art, a view that framed the hills. We viewed Pa's fiddle, childhood books of Ma's, Mary's Braille slate, Laura's sewing basket, Laura's shawl, Laura's iron, Laura's Bible. Afterward, we sat outside in the grass beneath some shade trees. It was noon. None of us had anything to say. But I was thinking that the plenitude of Rocky Ridge is a happy ending, at least.

Laura began writing the Little House books in 1930, when she was sixty-three years old. Pa and Ma and Mary were all gone by then. Carrie and Grace lived far away. At the end of *Little House in the Big Woods*, Laura lies in bed listening to Pa's fiddle playing softly, to the lonely wind.

She looked at Pa sitting on the bench by the hearth, the firelight gleaming on his brown hair and beard and glistening on the honey-brown fiddle. She looked at Ma, gently rocking and knitting.

She thought to herself, "This is now."

She was glad that the cozy house, and Pa and Ma and the firelight and the music, were now. They could not be forgotten, she thought, because now is now. It can never be a long time ago.

The Little House books were written in nostalgia and longing for a time that was gone. They were written, perhaps, in an attempt to give life again, through memory, to what no longer remained. Sitting there on that grassy hillside with my children surrounding me, little wildflowers, I recalled the photographs of the Ingalls girls in their own youth, which we'd seen in the museums, how they had died years and years before my daughters were even born. "This is now," I told myself. And I tried to hold on to the picture of my daughter's faces, flecked by sunlight and shadow, before they got restless and stood up to walk away.

The Way of the White Clouds

Trebor Healey

Alone I wander for a thousand miles . . . and I ask my
way from the white clouds.

Maitreya Buddha

In western civilization, our elders are books.

Gary Snyder

Books mean a lot to me, and that question of *what is their
source?* has launched many a pilgrimage. I've been to Thomas
Wolfe's house in Asheville, North Carolina, and Ben Bulben
in County Sligo, Ireland, in search of Yeats's vision. I once visited
Tom Spanbuaer's Dangerous Writing workshop in Portland, Oregon,
fascinated with his unique voice, and in Santiago de Chile I even tried
unsuccessfully to meet Pedro Lemebel, the author of the sweetest and
most politically intelligent gay love story I know, *My Tender Matador*.
But before all that, it begins—and essentially continues—with Jack
Kerouac, who sent me high up into California's High Sierra, hiking
in just a jockstrap up Matterhorn Peak in eastern Yosemite Park with

my buddy Frank, following the path that Japhy Ryder and Ray Smith took in *Dharma Bums*.

And yeah, I kid you not, that's what Gary Snyder (Japhy Ryder) used to wear hiking as recounted in the book—*and who was Jack Kerouac (Ray Smith) to suggest otherwise?* He always "shambled" after those who were "mad to live." And yeah, full disclosure, I kind of had the hots for Frank—and I'm sure Jack did for Gary—but this is before I came out and long before I suspected Jack or read Ellis Amburn's revelatory *Subterranean Kerouac*, where it all became clear.

Of course, you didn't have to be queer and conflicted about it to be carried away by Kerouac. The insipidness and deadening sleep of American consumer culture was enough. And I'd always been something of an escapist. I lived through books after all, and had thus spent more time in Tolkien's Mirkwood, Zola's Paris slums, the Tibetan plateau, and Tolstoy's Russian countryside than I had in most parts of my own country. And as college wound down, and the scepter of my inescapable homosexuality threatened to exile me for good, I longed to set out, to keep moving, to stay one step ahead of a fate I couldn't or wouldn't accept. I wasn't looking for another home or a refuge, some place where I'd fit in. No, I wanted to revel in belonging nowhere. The freedom I wanted—or the only one I could imagine then—was the freedom of a hobo.

Kerouac's *On the Road* came to me like many books have—by chance and yet with a hint of auspiciousness. There it was on my brother's desk, the little orange Signet paperback with its depiction of a blazing late afternoon sun glowing yellow below that unique and otherworldly name in bold black, "Kerouac."

"What's this about?" I asked my brother.

"Oh, that's about the beatniks, back in the '50s. It's for my post-war American history class. It's all right. You can have it, if you want, when I'm done with it." My brother was majoring in history and

loved Dos Passos, Studs Terkel, and Steinbeck. We were the two intellectual kids in the family—he of the left brain, me of the right—and
we agreed on less and less as the years passed. Kerouac would be no
different.

I forgot about the book until he handed it to me a few months
later. They'd been difficult months, in which I'd made my first hesi-
tant and ultimately failed attempts at coming out while battling an
incapacitating depression and also introducing myself to Buddhism
in a desperate effort to make an end run around the spiritual crisis
engendered by my Catholic upbringing. But I wasn't really ready for
being gay, being depressed, or being Buddhist. Jack Kerouac, on the
other hand, was what I was ready for.

I read the book in just a few days, blown away by Kerouac's can-
didness, the honesty, the completely free-spilling prose, the sparks of
joy wrested from the dark night of despair, the very familiar mystical
Celtic Catholicism that led straight into Buddhism, the improvisa-
tional jazz of his poetic prose—as if anything could happen. And
yet, *On the Road*, like all Kerouac's books, is haunted by the fact
that nothing ever really does. *Vanity of vanities, and all is vanity*—my
thoughts exactly, and apparently Kerouac's, inspiring the title of his
last, and what he considered his best, novel, *Vanity of Duluoz*. I'd
read my Hemingway and reread Ecclesiastes. I wasn't put off by
Kerouac's sorrow—"go thou and moan for man"—because I always
thought—and still do, for better or worse—that there's great wisdom
in sorrow.

I left school and began to wander. Into the mountains mostly,
where it was simple, primordial, free of all the social pressures I was
unable to cope with back home. But I also frequented Portland,
Oregon, which in the '80s still had a very gloomy and beat feel to it,
so well rendered in Gus Van Sant's *Mala Noche*, which also captured
the state of my self-esteem and hobbled sexuality as portrayed by the
lovelorn protagonist.

My brother's favorite history professor at Berkeley told him once when he'd related that I was on a Kerouac bender and had shunned gainful employment for long, aimless cross-country jaunts and Mexican sojourns that "no good can come of that."

My brother was interning for an insurance company by then and letting—as I saw it anyway—his intellectual future dissipate under the spell of Mammon. He'd quoted the professor to hurt me, and I probably retorted with some harsh remark about the gilded cage of worthless academia, but I kept the professor's comment in my back pocket all the same, suspecting and fearing that perhaps he was right. Well so be it, I thought then—bring it on.

Because I was in love with tragedy, having decided I was one (you take self-love however you can get it?). Like a million other young Hamlets with a college degree but no interest in being an adult, I felt like I was living an impossible quandary. I was just lucky that I wasn't a real prince I suppose. I could hit the road and do nothing in motion, which is slightly more bearable—or at least provides the requisite distraction from endlessly ruminating on the hopeless dilemma, whatever it might be—than being stuck in some castle with a whole kingdom to consider. Was I being self-indulgent? Well, certainly—but what young man isn't? I look back now on who I was then and I feel a profound compassion, bordering on pity, for that poor guy. And yet, something in me smiles too. If there was nothing left to do but run, good for him that he ran. If he couldn't find a way out, he was going to have a good look around before cashing in.

And in the process, I read everything Kerouac wrote, gluttonously feasting on all of it (which I've only done twice since—with Tom Spanbauer and Roberto Bolaño), from *Subterraneans* and *Lonesome Traveler*, to *Visions of Cody*, *Satori in Paris*, *Desolation Angels*, *Tristessa*, *Doctor Sax*, and *Maggie Cassidy*—and of course, *Dharma Bums*, where it all came together in one beautiful little journey up a mountain.

In *Dharma Bums*, Kerouac displays the thrill of "beginners mind" as the Buddhists call it, when you discover the poetic beauty and liberation of the Buddhist path. He's introduced to it by yet another great character he's discovered through the world of poetry and travel—Japhy Ryder, who is clearly a proxy for Gary Snyder. Kerouac projects the full glory of the wandering Buddhist beggar monk (bhikku) of legend onto Japhy—the lonely Northwest childhood, hiking alone among the high peaks, his interest in anarchism and Native American myths and culture, the trips to Japan to study with real Buddhist monks! Jack's got a crush on Gary. And this was clearly a big part of my enthusiasm for Kerouac too. He was crushing out on these guys, the beginners mind of falling in love with someone, but from the relative safety of a straight identity.

I was doing something similar and had had a series of backpacking buddies since I began to spend time in the California wilderness. It's not for everyone and takes a certain kind of adventurous spirit who isn't bothered by sudden weather changes, and a lack of shelter, bathrooms, food, company, and everything else civilization has to offer. But most of all, they've got to be athletic and physically hearty and almost masochistic. Frank was just such a guy and grinned ear to ear when I ran into him back in San Francisco. He agreed to go packing with me the next weekend, and I gave him my copy of *Dharma Bums*, knowing full well he'd know what I was getting at, when I said: "Read this."

Frank gobbled up the book in true Neal Cassady style and was full of enthusiasm, calling me up to tell me he'd already run out to purchase a jockstrap at the local sports store.

We set out at dawn, but not before tying one on the night before as we readied our packs to the accompaniment of Billie Holiday and Thelonius Monk, quoting from the novel and toasting to dear dead Jack and the still-living Gary Snyder—who incidentally I'd run into one afternoon years and years later at 11,000 feet going over Bishop Pass. But Gary Snyder wasn't real to me then—he was Japhy Ryder, a magical bodhisattva of the wilderness that Ray had discovered reading haiku or some such at the legendary Six Gallery in San Francisco.

Journeys that begin in the dark have a thrill to them that all romantics know. We drove east and watched the line of the horizon slowly fade from black to gray and then "ahh" like one of Kerouac's roman candles, the sun came up and we laughed because the city was long gone behind us, part of some other day, way back there on the other side of that darkness that the sun now erased. It was gone and *we* were gone.

It was a long drive through the Sacramento Valley and then up into the foothills and all the little gold country towns with their flickering, nostalgic lights, finally reaching Yosemite National Park, which we had to cross through completely and reenter from the other side. Matterhorn Peak was hard to get to, and we wondered why they'd chosen it. Well, Gary Snyder had probably been everywhere else, and Frank and I had covered most of the Sierras by then too—certainly the western parts of Yosemite. The trail's remoteness made it all the more special and unique. We parked my crappy old '69 sky-blue Dodge Dart (a vehicle worthy of Neal Cassady if there ever was one) and pulled off our shirts. Frank looked at me and laughed. "This is insane."

"Are we angel-headed hipsters or are we not?" was all I could think to say, winking back at him. And down went our pants. In just our jockstraps, we hoisted on our packs and were on the trail by 9 a.m., thankful we'd been the only people at the trailhead.

The firs towered, the pines and high peaks beckoning from farther up the canyon, and we began to see all the things Kerouac had recounted in the story—the blue lupine and red poppies in the meadows, the snag bridges over streams made of fallen fir and pine.

We rock-hopped through the scree. And all the while we snacked on the same peanuts and raisins and dried prunes and apricots. We camped under the same thirty-foot-high overhanging rock that night, marveling at the once gray peaks now glowing purple and pink all around us. We made the same bulgur and vegetable stew, followed by chocolate pudding, and then tea on my little stove, drinking it just like Japhy had instructed us to: "the first sip is joy, the second is gladness, the third is serenity, the fourth is madness, the fifth is ecstasy." We liked that idea, but probably only made it to step 3 to be completely honest. We laid out our sleeping bags and stared at the ribbons of stars and talked about our insignificance and the amazing vastness of existence.

We hopped up the next morning bright and early, made coffee and oatmeal on the stove, and got organized to get moving for the second and final leg of the trip up to the top of the peak. "I ain't wearing that jockstrap in this cold," Frank announced.

"Ah, come on, Frank. We gotta do this right."

"It's too cold!" he barked back. "You can wear yours. I'll wear mine, but it's gonna be under a warm pair of pants." I didn't want to be a fool all alone, so I took Frank's cue and relented. And wouldn't you know it, an hour up the trail we ran into two guys coming down—in jockstraps! We high-fived them, and I pulled down the top of my pants to flash the band of my jock.

"That doesn't count!" they shouted as off they went.

It got colder and colder as clouds gathered and we kept our pants on, adding our fleece jackets. By the time we were approaching the peak, the rocks were getting slipperier and dangerous as rain was beginning to fall. Frank and I had been in these situations before and knew it was stupid to keep climbing now that lightning was likely. But, like I say, Frank was always game. I was usually the cautious one, but in this case, I was on a pilgrimage, and if it killed me, I was going all the way to the top.

I could see it didn't mean as much to Frank. Frank was fun, Frank was game, but he wasn't the lost or tragic soul I was just then. Frank could take it or leave it.

We hurried. We passed a tiny lake—they'd called it a pond in the book—surrounded by mossy clumps of bunch grass, and I knew we were close. There were no trees at all up there, approaching 12,000 feet. Just rock and water and snow. Everything misty among the clouds. Quiet except the wind, which blew with a hollow sound from the west, cooling our sweaty clothes and giving us a chill. And then the peak appeared before us momentarily from out of the dense fog and we scrambled up over the last one hundred yards of giant boulders, smiling big as we reached the top and hugging one another and shouting into the void. And there was a little canister there, tucked among the stones, as there often is. Inside was a little notebook in which hikers leave their thoughts or quotations. I didn't know what to say. There were excerpts from *Dharma Bums* in the notebook, of course ("A mountain is a Buddha. Think of the patience, hundreds of thousands of years just sitting there bein' perfectly silent and like praying for all living creatures in that silence and just waiting for us to stop all our frettin' and foolin'," and "There's nothing wrong with you Ray, your only trouble is you never learned to get out to spots like this, you've let the world drown you in its horseshit and you've been vexed"). I remember thinking then that the book was almost thirty years old. I just wrote, "Thanks Jack." As if he'd come along one day and read it. But that's what I felt. *Thanks Jack, for being a great writer who loves the mountains and is trying to be a Buddhist and is kind of lost and searching, and . . . I guess, just thank god there was once somebody out there a lot like me to tell me exactly what I needed to know right then at that time in my confused life.* I suppose I write to this day for no other reason than to reach that person who I'll likely never know, but whose life somehow echoes my own and will benefit from the story as I tell it.

We hurried down, and the thunder and lightning came—fortunately not until we got back under the tree line where we could huddle among the big pines and wait for the storm to pass.

❖

Years went by, and Frank fell in love and Frank got married and had three kids, and Frank and I didn't hike anymore together. And I traveled around some more—cross-country on a bike, all through the Northwest and Mexico and Patagonia, living for a while in Chile and Argentina. And now, when I'm back in California, I often go to the mountains alone. But I've never returned to Matterhorn Peak, although I think of that trip every time I'm in the Sierras and I do what Ray and Japhy did when they left their campsite. I drop to one knee and cross myself, thanking the little campsite for housing me. And so, in that way, I'm still climbing Matterhorn Peak following Jack; I'm still a dharma bum, I'm still a bit of a lost soul. And like Jack, I'm a sorry Buddhist and still a Catholic. All through South America, I frequented churches to bless myself, light candles, and try to connect to the sacred part of things. Me and Jack. Like family.

Because, of course, I can't tell this story with any real justice to its profundity for me without sharing the dream I had once while I riffed on Kerouac all those years. I had purposely read Kerouac's work chronologically, and so I slowly learned what became of him (as if I'd been saving it, as if I didn't want to know early on, though of course I knew). I wanted to savor *his* unfolding as a story too, woven through each of his stories, which in a sense, it clearly is as his work is highly autobiographical, arguably not fiction at all. In *Visions of Cody*, the road starts to feel tired and one watches Neal drift out of his grasp, and in *Desolation Angels*, he seems to lose Japhy Ryder too, along with his beginners mind. In *Big Sur*, one feels the full weight of his alcoholism, his fatigue, and self-destructiveness. After that, he seemed to withdraw and wrote mostly about Lowell and his childhood—*Doctor Sax*, *Vanity of Duluoz*, *Visions of Gerard*, among others—reverting in a sense to his Catholic childhood self, no longer on the road at all.

There were endless films about the beats, and having read all the books, I watched all the movies. I saw the famous clip of Kerouac reading from *On the Road* on the Steve Allen show, when his success was just beginning to bloom. And how fleeting. Because there were the other clips, like the one from the William F. Buckley show where he murmured and argued, often incoherently, drunk, defensive, and stubborn, looking like a complete mental and physical wreck.

And then I had the dream. A vivid lucid dream about Jack that made me realize just how connected to him I felt. A corny dream really, as dreams often are, but clear as a bell in how I'd psychologically performed a kind of transference from my own emotionally distant father to Kerouac. Oh brother!

We were in Kentucky, at a lodge out in the woods. I was sitting with my mother and three brothers at a large table in the dining area of this lodge that seemed to be a kind of hotel that looked like one I'd visited on my bike journey when I was in West Virginia. It was all wood beams with views of the surrounding snow-covered mountains, so I knew it was winter. Christmas? I can't be sure, but some special occasion, and my mother's ire was up. She was correcting us as she had when we were children. "Don't balance your butter knife on the plate like that, don't put your elbows on the table, sit up straight" ad infinitum. She was upset as well because there was an empty seat where my father should have been sitting. I understood then that my mother had husband-swapped and Dad was gone—for how long was uncertain. In Dad's place was the guy coming across the dining room. And turning to look—lo and behold, it was Jack Kerouac himself! I was elated of course and stood up. My mother furrowed her brow and asked me to please sit down just as Jack arrived and squeezed into his seat. She then began to harangue him with a litany of questions along the lines of "Where have you been? How could you? You're late. This is inexcusable." Jack said nothing as we boys stared down at our plates, terrified to say a word, knowing Mother would pounce on us. Jack never looked at my mother either, but just down at his own plate and napkin. Then he stood up and walked back the way he had come. I remember glaring at my mother. *How could you treat him like that?* I got up and followed Jack, and she said nothing as I did so. I found him in the entryway, putting on his overcoat and boots.

"Where you going, Jack?"

"On the road" was his answer. I warned you it was corny. Predictably I asked, "Can I go with you?"

He looked me right in the eye and said just as predictably, "No. You gotta find your own road."

I already knew that, but appreciated Jack being explicit about it, especially as a writer. I couldn't write like him either. I had to follow my own road in more ways than one. Because I'd had it bad and had even gone so far as to look into the Merchant Marine. But it wasn't the '40s anymore and the whole shipping industry had become a completely different ballgame with advances in technology that had reduced crews to just a handful. What's more, you had to go to school for a couple years to get a degree that would make you competitive. You couldn't just ship out, as I soon learned when I went into the Seamen's Hall with dreams of world wandering. Hopping trains was more difficult as well, and though I dated a beautiful Neal Cassady-like junkie for several years who hopped lots of trains, I never joined him after hearing all his tales of beatings, and of friends losing limbs. I did park cars for a while in a downtown lot but was never as good at it as the way Jack described Neal's car-parking prowess in the car lots of New York City in *On the Road*. I even worked as a park ranger one summer since fire lookouts were now automated and there were few if any positions left for that.

And though I was from a long line of Irish drinkers and even brought along port and Madeira on backpacking trips in honor of hobo Jack, I kept my drinking in check; if for no other reason, I eventually did come out and was terrified of "slipping up" with a sex partner during those dark years of the plague—or as the years progressed, getting that bloated look of the boozer, which would curtail my ability to be the successful slut I was quickly becoming. And there was no way I was ever going to live with my mother, nor was I ever going to be a famous writer who changed American culture.

Then again, maybe I didn't have my own road so much as that I took another fork while traveling down the same one. Or maybe, since many, if not all, of Kerouac's cross-country jaunts took place along Route 66, that road didn't even exist anymore, at least not as one contiguous highway.

The dream was an ending of sorts. I've had lots of dreams like this, and though whenever I tell this particular one, eyes roll, still I'd found myself crying when I'd awoken, because in some very basic movie-of-the-week way, it had set me free. Jack was my dad, I loved him, I wanted to be like him, and he did the right thing and said *You gotta live your own life, be your own writer. Don't follow me.* My own private Oedipus complex, resolved like a little haiku. I didn't have to kill my father; he fell on his sword right there in front of me.

Thanks Jack. Because he sort of laid it out for me. *Here's your situation*: his books. Then he ends with the dream, which basically says: *Figure it out yourself.* A Buddhist koan, straight up. His life and mine, and everyone else's. Or at least those of us who wander. Pilgrims. A certain kind of traveler who is never specifically going anywhere.

Because he ended up in Florida and I've ended up in Los Angeles. Enough said. It isn't really about *where* or Jack Kerouac or his story. It is the voice. Because the voice is the journey, is the thing between the source and the story. The only thing one writer has to teach to another. The song of it. How to climb the mountain. How to do it with your whole heart—yours and nobody else's—like it's the last thing you'll ever do.

Hill of Dreams

Charles Coe

I sat sprawled in a chair, drunk as a freshman at a fraternity mixer, on the outdoor deck of Baku International Airport, watching jet after jet emblazoned with the classic Aeroflot hammer-and-sickle logo make an endless series of butter-smooth take-offs and landings. The planes themselves didn't inspire the greatest confidence from a mechanical standpoint, but the pilots were a different story. Most were Soviet air force reservists, and since an Aeroflot gig was much coveted, only the best of the best made the cut—just a click below cosmonaut material. Watching them was like watching an aerial ballet.

I was sitting outside in hopes that a little fresh air might clear my head; my alcohol haze was courtesy of the local gentleman roaming the Baku airport like a one-man welcome wagon—a wineskin of booze hanging on a rope around his neck like a chunk of hip-hop bling.

I'd been escorting two of the teens in my group on an errand to another part of the terminal when he accosted us with two paper cups full of brandy. (I never saw anyone in the Soviet Union pay the slightest attention to the fact that twenty-one was the legal drinking age.) I didn't want to offend him but wasn't willing to let our kids drink, so I returned his 100-watt smile, deftly grabbed and chugged both cups, tossed a quick "Spasibo ("thanks" in Russian), and hustled the kids along.

It was the kind of brandy that could blast the plaque off your teeth, along with a good bit of enamel. Soon, to the kids' amusement, I was so jacked up I think the twelve-foot-high poster of Gorbachev hanging from the terminal ceiling winked as I passed. Somehow I got the kids back to our group and then sloped out onto the deck to "relax and meditate."

This experience reenforced something I'd learned already in my short time in the Soviet Union: when it came to drinking, the locals were in a completely different weight class. Go to a party or a dinner, or just hang out at the hotel and soon the booze is flying; you need to surrender any fantasy that you could match your hosts drink for drink. Just give a humble smile, sip your vodka, and acknowledge that you're a wimpy Amerikanskiy. Better to sacrifice a little pride than to wake the next morning in a drainage ditch with your head swollen to twice its normal size.

It was September 1988, three years before the collapse of the Soviet Union. I was part of a group of thirty American artists— musicians, writers, dancers, theater people, and photographers— touring that part of the world as part of an exchange program. We were there for a month, giving performances and doing collaborative projects with the locals. I was along as a singer, working with local jazz musicians and the American musicians on the trip.

Things had started out a little rough: my luggage never arrived and no one in Moscow or New York had any idea where it was. Maybe stolen, or sitting in the dark in some forgotten back room. Or maybe some guy in Sheboygan was enjoying my BVDs. I never found out. I had a couple extra pairs of undies, my toiletries, and a few other odds and ends in my carry-on luggage, and I wound up doing laundry just about every night in my hotel room sink.

Our travels took us to Moscow, to Tbilisi in Georgia, and Baku in Azerbaijan. Moscow and Tbilisi were fascinating places, but I found Baku the most interesting—maybe because 150 miles from the Iranian border it was the most exotic. For a fellow born and raised in Indiana it seemed like another planet; I was fascinated by the Muslim markets with men in turbans sitting behind beautifully arranged piles of produce, gutted goats and chickens hanging like Christmas ornaments. A mosque in one block and an Armenian Christian church in the next. And a dizzy-making polyglot. Everyone spoke Azerbaijani, a language of complicated lineage distantly related to Persian, and Russian—the common language of the Soviet Union. There was also Armenian and a basketful of Muslim dialects.

Everywhere were reminders that Azerbaijan was a Soviet state. There were political slogans painted on walls in foot-high Cyrillic script and posters and paintings of Gorbachev—often side by side with the Azerbaijani prime minister. Most major intersections featured massive, brutally ugly Soviet Realist sculptures of some proud peasant, scythe in hand, his wife (and maybe an ox) at his side, everyone gazing into the distance at the glorious socialist future.

Baku is the largest city on the Caspian Sea; from the balcony of my hotel room (where my underwear hung to dry) I could look out across the water to the distant, spidery shapes of oil rigs out on the horizon. Ena, our guide, explained that drilling for oil had long been a cornerstone of the Ajer economy. Alfred Nobel, who invented dynamite, made another huge chunk of the family fortune in the oil fields of Baku; about 10 percent of the money that established the Nobel Prize was drawn from his share in the Nobel Brother's Petroleum Company there.

Ena was indispensable; we couldn't have made our way across the Soviet Union without her as our translator and guide. But her presence was also nonnegotiable; tour groups weren't allowed to roam the Soviet Union unescorted. Everyone was assigned a guide whose job it was to keep us from nosing around anything we had no business seeing. Intourist, her employer, was the state tourist agency founded by Stalin in 1929 and run at the time of our visit by the KGB. (It's since been privatized.) There was another less sinister reason Intourist guides tended to be very controlling: they were proud of their homeland and wanted to show it in as positive a light as possible.

I met Ena the first day of the trip when she greeted us at (rescued us from) the airport in Moscow. I was introduced as the person she'd be working with on our group's logistics and planning, and she gave me a polite handshake and a little bow, as if I were a middle-level diplomat. We'd get together every day to go over the next day's schedule and iron out any kinks. She was extremely efficient and placed high value on that trait in others. When she realized I could be counted on to hold up my end of things, she loosened up enough for me to start joking around with her. "Ena, I'm sure a visit to the People's Museum of Tractor Gear Parts is an awesome and inspiring experience," I said one day. "But I was wondering if we could spend a couple of hours tomorrow without any plans? Maybe find a café in the afternoon to have some tea and chat with the locals?"

When I asked her about life in Baku, she said, "Everyone gets along fine." It was only later that I realized she'd fed me the chamber of commerce version.

As much as she suggested that everything in Baku was hunky-dory, nothing could have been further from the truth. Animosity toward the Armenian minority was strong and getting stronger; it was only a couple of years later in 1990, on what became known as Black Friday, that a seven-day pogrom broke out against the Armenian population. Thousands were beaten, tortured, murdered, and thrown out of the city. The violence got so bad that the Soviet Army intervened—the only time during Perestroika that military force was used against a civilian population.

I have no desire to romanticize the Soviet era—one of the most depressing, antihuman periods in modern history—but you have to give the commissars their due in one respect; there was very little of the kind of violence between ethnic groups that's been a staple of the post-Soviet world. The simple explanation is that people feared the government and the army more than they hated each other.

It had always been a major propaganda claim of Soviet socialism that their culture was free of the kind of racial and ethnic tensions that plagued the capitalist world. As a black person that aspect of life in the Soviet Union was of particular interest to me. When I got back to the States and people would ask how the locals had responded to me, I'd tell them it depended on where I was at the time. In Moscow I'd get the occasional curious glance, but big-city Russians were used to seeing black entertainers, athletes, students, diplomats, and the like.

In the hinterlands it was often a very different story. In Baku I was quite a novelty; one time we visited an orphanage outside the city, and when I got off the bus I was surrounded by a crowd of children shouting, "Michael Jackson! Michael Jackson." I asked Ena to explain that I wasn't actually Michael, but that we were good friends and he asked me to say hello.

Another time I was sitting on a park bench near our hotel, reading a book and sipping a bottle of apple juice. A man sat down right next to me though I was surrounded by empty benches, crossed his legs, and just stared. I tried my "dobryj dyen" (good afternoon) but he didn't respond—just kept staring; I realized he didn't want to talk; he just wanted to look. I was tempted to say "screw this" and get up and walk away but decided instead to stay put and keep reading. I was curious to see how long he'd sit there gawking. After a few minutes, he got up and without a word or another glance went on his way. I told Ena about this later and she just nodded, as if this kind of thing happened all the time. "Yes," she said. "Like you are animal in the zoo. Do not take personally."

But at the time I was clueless about Baku's real problems. All I knew was what I was told, and what I could put together from the images that flashed before me. I'm always skeptical when a writer parachutes into some new place, pokes around for a week or two, then cranks out an assured description of "The Way Things Are Around Here" that's laid out as neat and tidy as the grid lines on a city map. When I talk about my time in Baku, I'm a blind man trying to describe an elephant from the parts I could touch. I look back on that time and it's all just a series of snapshots.

But one set of images remains sharp and clear: my memories of Ena . . . I remember how our meetings in the hotel lobby turned into kaffe klatches, then lunches, then dinners. Our conversations started going beyond which museums to visit and how many buses we'd need and began to edge into the personal. We started meeting in her hotel room or mine over a bottle of wine. I remember the moment she was writing something down and brushed the hair from her face in that particular way I had come to enjoy watching. She looked up and something about my expression made her put down her notebook. I remember reaching out to touch her face . . . and a little later realizing that there are times when if you really care about someone you have to step back from the edge of the pool when every cell in your body wants to dive.

As I walked back to my room my lizard brain kept screaming that I was a complete idiot, that someday I'd kick myself. But twenty-five years later I realize that in fact the opposite is true. I've done things in my life I'm not proud of, but when I look back on that night I'm proud of something I *didn't* do.

We never talked about it. There were no more late-night hotel-room planning sessions. A week later in Moscow at the airport, the last time we'd ever see each other, she gave me a hug and a peck on the cheek. I wrote her a long letter when I got back to the States, but never heard back. Maybe my letter got lost in the famously sketchy Soviet postal system. Or maybe she just decided, for whatever reason, not to respond. Wherever she is now, whatever she's doing, I wish her the best.

I'd signed on for the trip because I'd needed to yank my feet out of the grooves they'd worn in the map. Needed to crawl out of bed to take a piss in the middle of the night and fumble for the familiar light switch, half asleep, until I remembered why it wasn't there. I needed to put myself in situations where my usual moves wouldn't get it done. I'd gotten what I'd come for, and now it was time to go.

I wish the best to all the good people I played music with and yakked with until oh-dark hundred, drinking vodka and solving the world's problems. It saddens me to recall how excited they were about the coming of democracy and to realize that what they wound up with wasn't democracy, or even capitalism. It's a kind of feral, Darwinian gangsterism. For many of them life was actually better under communism.

One night in Tbilisi I was having dinner on the deck of a musician's apartment and listening to his hopes and fears for his country's future. He pointed at a distant hillside covered with large, beautiful houses—their lighted windows aglow in the night. "Many poor people like me fantasize about one day living up there when things are different in my country," he said. "We call that the Hill of Dreams." I hope my friend is dreaming still, and that the old republics can somehow, someday leave behind the hatred and violence that for too many people seem to have become a permanent way of life.

The day before we left Baku I was waylaid in my hotel by a guy walking down the hall in the opposite direction whose eyes opened wide when he saw me. "American?" When I smiled and said yes, he took my arm and said, "Come, come, we drink and talk! I will practice the English." I was tempted for a moment to ask if he was related to Welcome Wagon Guy at the airport but kept my peace and went with the flow. He steered me down the hall into a room where two other men were sitting around drinking vodka and noshing from a platter of meat and cheese. An old black-and-white TV was showing old Tom and Jerry cartoons, which were extremely popular in the Soviet Union. There's no dialogue (hence no language barrier) and they're extremely violent; when I walked in, Jerry the mouse was sticking Tom the cat's tail into a wall socket.

We hung out for an hour or so while they peppered me with questions about life in America and told me about their lives in Azerbaijan. When despite their protests I had to leave, my host filled everyone's glass once more and insisted on a final toast, rising to his feet as we all followed suit. He suddenly became somber and paused a moment to collect his thoughts in English.

Finally, he raised his glass. "I hope always there is peace in Azerbaijan and peace between your country and mine," he said. "Everybody eat, everybody sleep, everybody make love. Why fight?"

In the Huts

Susan Fox Rogers

From a distance, Robert Falcon Scott's 1901 Discovery Hut looks like a shelter in a park, a low-lying bungalow where you would find a barbecue pit and a picnic table huddled under the wide, sloping roof. Designed in Australia, the hut looks out of place perched there at the tip of Hut Point on Ross Island, the tropical wood whitened by wind, sand, and time.

The distance I looked from was McMurdo, the largest base on the continent and the hub for the elaborate United States Antarctic Program. Scott describes first arriving in McMurdo Sound at eight in the morning on January 22, 1902: "A few miles separated us from the spot where we were ultimately to take up our winter quarters, and as we got to know this scene so well it is interesting to recall some extracts from what I wrote when first we gazed on it: 'To the right is a lofty range of mountains with one very high peak far inland, and to the south a peculiar conical mountain, seemingly ending the coastline in this direction; on the left is Mount Erebus, its foothills, and a glimpse of Mount Terror." It is a straightforward description, void of emotion. It is a description that endures.

Scott was not the first to enter the Sound. James Clark Ross arrived in 1841, naming McMurdo for Lieutenant Archibald McMurdo. But Scott lays claim to enduring the first winter at latitude 77 degrees

40 minutes. Since then, this spot has been a stopping point for many expeditions, including Scott's later Terra Nova expedition (1910–13), Shackleton's Nimrod expedition (1907–9), and for the Ross Sea party of Shackleton's dramatic Endurance expedition (1914–17). Historically, it is one of the richest locations on the continent; I hungered for McMurdo, imagining I would walk into—breathe— that past.

When I landed in McMurdo, the romantic in me fainted. McMurdo looks like a sprawling mining camp, aesthetics be damned. All of the buildings are hiked up on stilts and the dorms are colored a dreadful otter brown. Everything rests above ground: sewage and water lines, fuel lines and tanks, so it's as if you are looking at the guts of a factory. Rows upon rows of supplies surround the station, like an endless Home Depot of the south. And the noise of trucks backing up or the hum of the shuttle, Ivan the Terra Bus, or the enormous Deltas that can navigate ice and snow never ceases.

My impressions on December 16, 2004, the day after my arrival: "Here I am in a large, airy room, a row of computers to my left and farther over wide windows looking out onto McMurdo Bay. In the distance loafs Mount Discovery, and somewhere, about thirteen hundred miles farther south, the South Pole. McMurdo Sound looks patchy, the sea ice melting (though it's still twelve feet thick). Behind me stands Mount Erebus, which spewed great smoke yesterday. There's a TV screen in the hall outside my office that shows the activity inside the volcano—there is a camera attached to the rim." Another description void of emotion. In the space between what I saw and Scott's description a sadness ballooned. How many years, miles, computer screens, and helicopters separated Scott and me?

Ten days passed. In that time I visited New Harbor, a field camp at the mouth of the Taylor Valley in the Dry Valleys; climbed

Observation Hill where a cross remembers Scott, Oates, Wilson, Bowers, and Evans with a Tennyson quote: *to strive, to seek, to find, and not to yield*; flew to the South Pole for a day where I cross-country skied onto the polar plateau; skied to and from Williams Ice Field several times; hiked the loop to Castle Rock. I had fallen in love.

I have fallen in love with places before: Cape Cod; the south-west of France; Patagonia; Tucson, Arizona; Tuolumne Meadows. By falling in love I mean that the places changed me. All of these loves are a bit masochistic, for the place can only give back so much, my love unrequited. But this love of the Antarctic was the most masochistic of all as the ice returned my love with wind and cold, and a silence that ripped me open. A heartbreaking time limit haunted this affair as I had but six weeks on the ice on my National Science Foundation grant. Aware that "this is it!" I grasped at trips to remote camps, helicopter rides, stories in the coffee house, people.

I had put off visiting Scott's hut, though it stood there, not more than a ten-minute walk from town. I do not want to be overly dramatic, but I was afraid of entering the hut. All of my outings and experiences had unzipped my senses, leaving me dizzy, disoriented, elated. I was overstimulated, running on a cold, ecstatic adrenalin. The hut might be my undoing.

And yet I had to go. The walk took me toward the dock where a U.S. Coast Guard icebreaker wormed its way into an ice pier that had been under construction for weeks. For forty-five minutes I watched the icebreaker crash forward, then retreat, churning the Ross Sea of McMurdo Sound, ice and water billowing up in a mad froth.

And I wondered what Scott would think of this community of thirteen hundred souls huddled at the edge of the Ross Ice Shelf. Would he be stunned by the computers connecting workers to the web or the TVs that blared from darkened rooms? Who knows. But Scott would have used bulldozers and would have given anything for that icebreaker. He brought every imaginable form of transportation: skis, dogs, a balloon, sledges, and on his second expedition he added ponies complete with snowshoes and a snow machine in the hopes that something would work efficiently on this impenetrable terrain. He was curious and imaginative, ready to experiment. This and his moodiness are why I love him.

I approached the hut and ducked under the overhanging eaves of the pyramidal roof. In the four feet that stretch beneath the eaves lay a pile of hundred-year-old seals, blackened with time, and waiting to be used for oil, to light the stove, and to offer heat and light. Why had Scott's men not used these seals through their two cold winters?

Unceremoniously, I unlocked the door and was assaulted by the smell of seal blubber. Smells are few on a frozen continent, so it took a moment to adjust to the sting of this lurking, one-hundred-year-old odor. At the end of the narrow entranceway a pile of straw scattered across the floor, and to the left of that in a small room hung some mutton. I turned into the main room, an expansive space, thirty-six by thirty-six feet, to find a few beds, a table, and a kitchen with a frying pan ready to go. Random tins of baking powder or okra or beans remained on the shelves. In one corner rested a wooden chest marked Special Dog Biscuits. These details of daily life intrigued me, but mostly I was struck by the sense the hut felt hollow, empty.

As I wandered through the hut, I did not swoon or weep. I felt no connection to the past; Scott was not there to greet me. My own experiences—skiing out from the South Pole into a relentless white sea, or stepping into ice tunnels cold to negative 57 degrees, or digging ditches at New Harbor, or dancing with Jules in the heavy shop on

Christmas Eve had all moved me more than this pull to the past. Oddly relieved, I left the hut.

I stood outside, watching the icebreaker now resting at the pier. Why did the hut feel so lifeless? One reason might be that Scott and his men did not really live in the Discovery Hut in the winter. They lived on the ship, anchored in Arrival Bay and set in ice two hundred yards away. The hut proved a bit useless, as they could not keep a working temperature inside. Mostly, it formed "the most pretentious theatre that has ever been seen in Polar Regions," as Scott described it in his journal. Their life work and sweat did not coat the walls of that bungalow.

Just outside the hut and up a small hill rests one of the many crosses that mark this landscape. Here, Able Seaman George T. Vince died. Scott describes his quick, unexpected death: "Another step would have taken him [Wild] over the edge; he sprang back with a cry of warning, and those behind him, hearing it, dug their heels instinctively into the slippery surface, and with one exception all succeeded in stopping. What followed was over in an instant. Before his horror-stricken companions had time to think, poor Vince, unable to check himself with his soft fur boots, had shot from amongst them, flashed past the leader, and disappeared." Where he disappeared was over the edge of a cliff, with a plunge into the sea ice below. The cross appeared lonely, stuck out on a promontory, with a view to the busyness of McMurdo. The starkness hit me; tears inched a frozen path down my cheeks.

Did Vince know what he was getting himself into? Yes and no. The polar motto was *safe return unlikely*. And no one ends up in the Antarctic by accident. You have to want it, to be willing to give up spouses and children, careers. There were PhDs in linguistics washing

Susan Fox Rogers

78

dishes and dentists fixing snowmobiles. Everyone I met had their story of what brought them south. Love, money, adventure.

Many had headed south following his or her hero. The Amundsen people were organized, unemotional; Shackleton fans relied on luck and high jinks. We Scott followers were the ones who thought it wonderful Scott had named his son Peter, for his friend J. M. Barrie's creation, Peter Pan.

My father, a novelist and exuberant storyteller, introduced me to Scott. Dinnertime involved tales of our Rogers family from Kentucky, of uncles with shotguns and syphilis, or the Montegut side of the family from the Southwest of France. And then there was this fellow Scott, to me a distant cousin, who went to the South Pole and died so tragically on his return. I was ten when my father embarked on his polar obsession and so grew up with these stories of man-hauling sledges, and of tents lost in blizzards thinking that this too was family. I did not like imagining the men eating the ponies, but I thought it pretty swell to have such a brave relative. I had undertaken this trip to the ice, with my father at my shoulder. His daily e-mails revealed his knowledge of the land. "The Discovery Hut must be very close," he commented when I first arrived, and I could tell his impatience at getting a view of the hut. I knew my report would disappoint him.

"It's not magical," I said, the phone line eerily clear from the Antarctic to Central Pennsylvania. I'd arrived at my Compostela and had felt no spiritual lift. This is the pilgrim's biggest fear: to walk for days and not be transformed, to return as she left.

Roald Amundsen, who was the first to the South Pole, writes, "Oddly enough it was the sufferings that Sir John [Franklin] and his men had to go through which attracted me most in his narrative." I understand this pull to suffer. When a storm kept me grounded at

Cape Royds for eight days, our food dwindling, I was elated. I had journeyed out wanting to be plucked from the earth and roughed up by the wind; to suffer physically is to give the soul its due expression. Set in this vast landscape it took on a magnificent scale. It was possible, fighting the cold and wind, to really love life.

Scott and his men pushed through all manner of suffering from food shortages to frozen toes, noses, fingers. In the magnificent *Worst Journey in the World*, Apsley Cherry-Garrard writes of a cold so intense his teeth split. Then there is the suffering of the mind. I think of the dark polar nights and how that might take me if I wavered. But Scott and his men had their theater, their Thursday and Sunday lectures, their work that kept them focused. Cherry-Garrard was never as happy as he was those two years on the ice.

Where I come from, to be happy is to be comatose to the world. Anger is a sign of intelligence, moodiness the indicator of the true artist. Yet to be moody in the face of the storm that surrounded me would be folly; the storm would surely win. To be angry through the darkness of a polar winter is suicide. Happiness is armor in this landscape, and it must be genuine.

Just before my departure from the ice, Monika, the capable woman in charge of helicopters, called me. "Make a wish," she said. At the start of my trip, I would have, without hesitation, asked to visit the hut at Cape Evans, which was used during Scott's final expedition. But the Discovery Hut had been such a bust that I waivered. Also, Cherry-Garrard didn't make Cape Evans sound that wonderful: "It is uninteresting, as only a low-lying spit of black lava covered for the most part with snow, and swept constantly by high winds and drift, can be uninteresting."

I felt my father's voice emerge from me as I said, "Cape Evans."

"Second choice?" Monika asked, all business. It wasn't easy to get me there, she explained. But two days later, as I climbed onto the helicopter for Cape Evans, she smiled. "You owe me one, missy."

The young helo pilot dropped low over the flanks of Erebus so I could peer down into the crevasses where seals hid. And then he flew over the hut, a gray dot in a vast landscape. It looked so small, so overshadowed by the continent that cradled it. The helo landed about two hundred yards from the hut. I clambered out, and the metal bird vanished into the taut blue sky.

I was not alone. In the distance, I could hear banging of hammers and the drone of a generator. This was not going to be a solo, spiritual moment in the hut. But as soon as I met the five Kiwis at work restoring and maintaining the hut I was taken by their good cheer and generosity. Historic carpenters and an archaeologist were focused on shoring up the stables and removing the ice that had built up on the south side of the hut. This is where Birdie Bowers stored a large part of their food—the crates are there, coming undone but still filled with provisions. The south side of the hut was always a problem, and this year, water had leached into the hut and frozen to the floor. Cherry-Garrard writes of digging out the south side of the hut—and it was as if, almost one hundred years later, that work continued. The clang of jackhammers and the sure thump of hammers made the hut alive; the banging cheered me.

I visited the stables first, noting the names of the ponies (Beegum, Gulab, Abdullah—they came from India) tacked on plaques across from the stalls, and there on the wall hung those ridiculous tiny snowshoes they had crafted for the horses. Inside one of the stalls rested the boxes that held their butter, which all came from New Zealand. Each company designed a special box for the expedition—Penguin butter my favorite. That day in the stalls the archaeologist found a face mask for the horses, a food bag, and also a knapsack.

They have never thoroughly cleared out the stalls because a lot of horse poop remains, but also when Shackleton and his men used the hut, they were too lazy to walk out to the latrines, and so availed themselves of the first stall. This waste, frozen for all time, remains.

When I walked inside the main hut, the sense that the men had just left, their beds intact, and the kitchen ready, knocked me flat. Cans of kale or cabbage lined the shelves, and a case of champagne from Reims with one corked bottle waited to pop for the next celebration. Mugs hung from little hooks, and plates were neatly stacked and clean. I found Cherry-Garrard's bunk, just below that of Birdie Bowers. I touched his pillow; *his head rested here*. In the back far corner stood Wilson's bed, the chief of scientific staff, and over it a small shelf held bottles of medicines, the pills waiting. Every bed had a small shelf above it, some with a cup and toothbrush.

The photographer Ponting's darkroom takes up a square room in the back (he slept there as well) and next to that was an area filled with beakers, and other equipment ready for research. I stood in the hut for over an hour, not wanting to miss any detail. I could feel the busyness of life in this hut. I could see and feel both the hardship and the happiness in Scott's pillow.

It was all so ordinary. Scott, my imagined cousin, wreathed in a heroic halo, had slept here. And I realized that that is life: we sleep, we eat, we poop. Isn't this what the pilgrim learns, that it's so very simple, just one step after another? And then you are there, at your hut.

I had to step outside, to let the hut sink into my bones. A short distance from the hut, crates of food remain and up on the hill a spooky, sad sight, one of the dogs, still chained, the metal collar around the bones of its neck, the head bare, and the bullet casings nearby. They shot the remaining dogs before returning.

I wandered the land around the hut, looking south to Big and Little Razorback Islands, Inaccessible and Tent Islands, North to the

Barne Glacier. Behind the hut: Erebus, alternately clear then cloud-covered, and across the sound the magnificent mountains of the Dry Valleys.

In 1984 I walked from the Tour Saint-Jacques in Paris to Chartres with four thousand other people, the first leg of one of the pilgrimage routes that weaves through France then heads across northern Spain. One hundred of us slept in a barn the first night, and the next day we rose before dawn to walk. Other walkers, emerging from their own nearby barns, fell into line with us. All held a candle, lighting the way as we skirted the edge of farmers' fields. The lights were like fireflies, flickering into the distance. And then someone started to sing a hymn. All joined in; the sound of hundreds of voices in the dark rose as if from the earth itself.

Looking out at the beauty of the Antarctic land, the silence of the ice entered me; that silence became a hymn, one of solitude and communion. I listened to that silent, roaring hymn as I waited to be plucked from this spit of land and returned to the comfort of McMurdo. Safe return assured.

Physically safe, yes. But my return did not feel safe. The journey out had been long and the return so fast, snatched from the hut at one thirty by a Coast Guard helicopter flown by a woman pilot and copilot. I sat on the floor in the back, looking down on the ice, a patchwork of green and blue and white. I had seen Scott's bed, touched his sleeping bag. What difference did that make? None and all.

The hard part is the return, not a simple backtrack. A few days later I climbed onto that LC-130 cargo plane on Willy Field bound for Christchurch. I looked out of the tiny window onto the shrinking ice, tears running down my cheeks. I looked around at all of the other people strapped into the jump seats, wearing their government-issue white bunny boots. Everyone was crying, eyes wet, cheeks wet. All I could hear through the earplugs was the roar of the plane.

I called my father when I got to Christchurch. "You were right, the hut at Cape Evans." I paused, didn't know how to describe it.

From thousands of miles away, I could hear him laugh. "Tell me all," he said.

At Home and Abroad
with the Marquis de Sade

John Beckman

*T*he first secular pilgrim to the castle Lacoste (the Marquis de Sade's brutish medieval fortress gouged from a rock high above the Vaucluse) was probably Anne-Prospère de Launay, the criminal proprietor's nineteen-year-old sister-in-law. She arrived there in November 1771, on convalescent leave from a Benedictine priory, where she had been a "secular" canoness, sequestered by her mother from the cake-engorged orgy that was Louis XV Parisian society. Destined neither to be a nun nor, as it would turn out, a wife, Mademoiselle de Launay, as I like to imagine her, bivouacked in those hedgerows of thorny secularity that divide the pastures of open piety from the bare-faced cliffs of sheer obscenity. Arriving by carriage in the habits of her order, she warmed right up to her sister's husband's advances.

Lacoste, during those months, was like the secular Chapel Perilous. The thirty-one-year-old marquis, recently sprung from debtors' prison (Fort L'Evêque), stocked his larders, wardrobes, and bookshelves with unaffordable luxuries. He enlisted his wife and house servants and townsfolk to perform in his lavishly amateur theater festival. Amid his drafty stone halls and refurbished apartments, he kept his pretty sister-in-law close at hand; she maintained his personal linens, she served as his private secretary, she traveled with him and Latour (his lascivious valet) between his theater at Lacoste and his remoter one at Mazan: for she was also stage acting under his direction—under the direction, that is to say, of eighteenth-century Europe's nastiest thinker. But Sade himself, during this period, was just getting started, just testing his powers, and this forbidden young canoness must have played a specular role in his own secular catechism: both were just learning the limits of badness. Undoubtedly, as their love affair played itself out, they were rough-drafting even the newest-fangled taboos that would soak the pages of *Philosophy in the Bedroom, Justine, Juliette,* who knows? maybe even *120 Days of Sodom.* For their common interest, from all we can tell, was transgression, *tout court.*

Things got interesting that next summer. In late June, Sade and Latour caused criminal mischief in Marseilles—hiring several young prostitutes over a series of days and forcing them into humiliating and life-threatening acts. In brief, although all of them claimed to have refused to perform the capitally punishable act of sodomy (leaving Sade and Latour to sodomize each other), the prostitutes were made to ingest poisonous quantities of Spanish fly pastilles, enough to keep one of them vomiting for days. (Another of them whipped Sade's bare backside a tallied 859 times with a heathery broom.) By September (to skip ahead), while Sade and Latour were being tried and convicted and then beheaded and burned (all in effigy) on Aix's Place des Prêcheurs, the real Sade was absconding with the real Mademoiselle de Launay on a Bonnie-and-Clyde holiday in Venice. What began for her in nun's dress on the drawbridge to Lacoste had blossomed in less than a year into international intrigue along the Grand Canal, where she lived fully alive with a legal relation (young, dashing, witty, brilliant) who was in the process of being immortalized by *la mort civile.*

It's unfair, you may say, to call Anne-Prospère a pilgrim. Only some marginalia in her coy-mistress voice, as well as the circumstances of her on-the-lam affair, and possibly uncle l'Abbé de Sade's own exasperated replies to her apparently palpitating (but now irretrievable) letters, stand as evidence of her budding psyche. Who knows what perils, if any at all, she hoped to find at Lacoste? Maybe Sade coerced her or even *kidnapped* her. Maybe I too in calling her a pilgrim am literarily kidnapping her after Sade's own example, which is to say fashioning her into another iteration of Justine (Sade's iconic ingénue) whose religiosity propels her, as if by unseen forces—to be sure, by *narrative* forces—into the darkest of secular maws. Maybe I just want her to have been a secular pilgrim. Maybe I just want the company. If so, then where am *I* coming from? And why did I make my own secular pilgrimage to Lacoste, which has stood in ruins since it was ransacked by villagers late in Sade's infamous lifetime? Why?

I wasn't raised in a convent, but almost. I grew up crookedly in the 1970s and 1980s in the overwhelmingly Roman Catholic town of Dubuque, Iowa, a hilly, bluffy Mississippi River town whose heyday was over before the twentieth century hit. The smartass son of two psychologists, I lovingly studied its law's brocade borders, keen to the daintiest whorls of transgression. A schoolboy who stored *Hustler* magazines in his cello case; an altar boy who, drunk whenever possible on sacrificial wine, tripped over his cassock during daybreak liturgies; a "five-dollar boy" in the seamy, rice-steamy Red Dragon kitchen who flirted with hiring the mouthy prep cook (she boasted of moonlighting as a prostitute); an inextinguishable class clown who burned twelve years of Catholic school with the singular purpose of pranking priests and nuns (such low-hanging fruit, such meager rewards); a mostly harmless bad boy among much badder boys in a witlessly socially conservative town, I found little use, except gross transgression, for the rules, creeds, formularies, doctrines, and (in retrospect) wonderfully prissy rituals that thoroughly embroidered my tender consciousness. I scoffed at "sin" and the crude threat of "Hell." I skipped Mass, when I could, at Mr. Donut. In high school religion class I composed jejune arguments in support of atheism. Only superstition—the superego that governed Dubuque's sprawling archdiocese—made any material sense to me, since it added a thrill to all of my transgressions, which is probably why, when given the chance, sometime during my sixth-grade year, I chose for my confirmation name the mythic word "Job," much to the startled Archbishop's amazement. *"Joe?"* he clarified right there at the altar. "No, Job." I suspected on some level that I was courting disaster.

It was under the secular shade trees of university that I first encountered the Marquis de Sade, by way of his *120 Days of Sodom.* What a lark! Like some kind of punk rock Madeleine, it hurled me back, *splat,* to my middle school misbehavior. It coked my Nietzsche-softened undergrad mind as edgily and effervescently as the Dead Kennedy's *Fresh Fruit for Rotting Vegetables* had coked my *Mad* magazine–tenderized sixth-grade mind. Like the DKs, like *Motel Hell* or *The Texas Chainsaw Massacre,* it struck me as a profoundly giddy joke, which is to say it overwhelmed me, sent me looking for its ever-receding punch line. It made me laugh, and my laughter made me sick. Its horror penetrated deeper than "horror." It intended, with a panzer division's single-minded purpose, to blast the sacred at its roots—the holy, the delicate, the innocent, the beautiful—to lock them in irons and torture them silly; to insult, to devour, to mutilate, to blaspheme, and ultimately to murder them. It shocked me to have to ask the question "How could such a book exist?" when I also felt that it *had* to exist.

The book's gallows humor, deliberate or not, derives from its physical impossibilities and its bizarrely compounded lists of abstractions. It's a legible record of the author's own mania. Like my lovingly built list of 143 obscenities that Sister Henrice confiscated in fifth grade, like the tallied 859 blows on the young marquis's buttocks, *120 Days* is numerically abstracted, manically clinical—composed of lists of gruesome crimes that the author totted up while locked in the Bastille. At the same time, for all of its nauseating comedy, *120 Days* was my first encounter with *grown-up* horror, *grown-up* punk, with a grown-up shock value that didn't threaten my sense of safety but punctured my intellectual skin, pummeled me in my ethical organs. Amused as I may have been by his tamer criminals—by, for one, the puckish libertine who enjoys deflowering brides in that tufted moment between the marriage rite and consummation—I was really reading in awe of the "Divine Marquis" himself, who made Dante's Hell look like Waldorf School. À la billionaire director James Cameron, Sade blew his fortune on a Jules Verneian submarine for exploring the imagination's Marianas Trench, a black moral hole where, for example, "a notorious sodomist, seeking new ways to combine that crime with blasphemy, incest, murder, rape, and adultery, first shits on a consecrated Host; he then rams this up his arse and has it tamped-in by his son's cock; with the son's cock still in place he rapes his newly wed daughter, beating the groom to her maidenhead, then tops it all off by pulverizing his niece with a battering ram." Once Sade reached those ugliest depths it appears he never wanted to leave. In his books he lingers there still, some Phoenician sailor, bobbing in the grimmest chambers of the sea.

By July 1999, when I took my first pilgrimage to Lacoste, Sade's undersea trench had undergone a sea change. No longer, for me, just one man's fancy, it had become an inverted, Sistine Chapel–sized fresco illustrating the barbarity of millennial power and privilege. Halfway through a two-year teaching gig at the Université de Bordeaux III, living in an airy eighteenth-century flat that owed its horrid splendor to the triangular slave trade, I spackled the gaps in my loosely lived southwestern French lifestyle with notes and daydreams for my second novel, *Justine*. Over the previous six years, I had had occasion to view several Disney Princess vehicles—*Snow White*, *Sleeping Beauty*, *Beauty and the Beast*, and so on, so many times over that all I saw was their monocultural road map. These motherless princesses, these feisty ingénues, looking very pretty and fighting quite blindly in service of fatherlands no one expected them to understand, suddenly, at some point, coalesced in my mind with Sade's haplessly brazen heroine Justine. This much-abused orphan, who wandered the French countryside defending her virtue—only to be battered down the social ladder (by aristocrats, doctors, lawyers, monks), was the shadow self of Snow White's ilk. Justine was their purest vulnerability—and force. *Justine*, as my novel intended to demonstrate, was the missing Disney Princess flick, the one that would make sense of Disney itself. My only fear was that Disney would get to it first.

My *hermano* Gustavo came over from Berkeley with our mutual friend Wensday. They humored me for needing to touch Lacoste's stony ruins: Sade's toxic writings, not unlike sacred texts, demanded of those who took them seriously the eerie closure that only *presence* conveys. There had to be a *place* attached. So the three of us took a road trip down to the Vaucluse.

We emerged from traffic two days later in the airy Roman town of Arles. In the turquoise dusk light, guided by mango *tabac* signs beyond its stone amphitheater and area, crowding with tourists into the purple-black squares (their faces orange, yellow, and green under the tin-hooded midcentury lamps), we too sported the goopy Fauvist colors of the town's most notable historic denizen, Van Gogh: Gustavo's ginger-yellow Tintin bangs were a paintbrush tipped with a blob of pink; Wensday's iridescent straight blonde hair shone like a drive-in movie screen. To be sure, our no-star hotel, where Wensday retired early that night, occupied the site of his erstwhile studio, where his butterscotch bed had worn a vermillion couverture and where he may have, for all we knew, severed his celebrated ear. Late that night, when the colors were gone, drunk and awake and freed from the road, Gustavo and I trekked past the *préfecture de police*, stumbled down a fine-gravel *allée* of trees, and seeing no other way around it, climbed a tall, spiky iron fence and dropped ourselves down into Les Alyscamps, a sprawling and pitch-black Roman necropolis that only grew darker as our eyes adjusted. Lumpy stone figures. A monastery's silhouette. The high, hulking shoulders of cypress trees. What had attracted us there, arranged like rows of deep stone bathtubs along this death-town's main thoroughfare, were a series of ancient above-ground tombs, some still capped, some smashed in, some gaping invitingly open and vacant. Starlight illuminated a fine pine duff collected in the open ones. We exchanged a look, faces blank in the dark. Each of us chose a tomb of his own; each committed his own private crime. Lowering myself down and lying on my back in the intimate quarters of some stranger's death, I passed through the petty joy of irreverence into some place I haven't been since. Silenced by the tomb's heavy walls, seen through a passage in the overhanging trees, the starry sky gave nothing back at all.

Early the next day Wensday stayed on in Arles, while Gustavo and I took our day trip up to the Vaucluse, a mountainous region due east from Avignon, where Lacoste wasn't labeled on any of our maps or even mentioned in our primitive guidebook. Like Kafka's castle, it was a geographical cypher; like Joseph K., we went anyway. Hungover, and having visited death's blank space, the reluctant pilgrim and the reluctant driver kept quiet on D99 to Cavaillon, where we recaffeinated in a Géant convenience store. As we began to come to, and as long purple mountains broke from the smoky sky high above the nut-tree groves, I navigated for Gustavo from our one cicerone, a paperback biography of de Sade that offered maddeningly abstract clues. Gordes, it appeared, was the nearest town. When we got there, by winding up switchback roads to a rich little village atop a rocky perch, we learned, like Joseph K., from a suspicious local, a pretty blonde *madame d'un certain âge* in Day-Glo trainers and a beige linen pants suit, that our castle was the jagged horn of stone jutting from the crest of the facing mountain. How to get there, through the murky green valley below, was entirely up to us. So we followed our pilgrims' intuition.

We drove with open windows in the late-morning heat, straining to keep the mountain in sight while we curved through the valley's dry olive groves. Intuition itself gave a sickening feeling, for the main roads were determined to keep us off the mountain, either directing us up the Bonnieux Valley toward Apt or down it, whence we came, back to Cavaillon. My rash curiosity took us up snakier roads, all of them dead-ending at private metal grates. Gustavo, a Californian with an easier temperament, drummed the wheel and laughed at our failures, but I wasn't so cool. Welling in me was that Catholic-boy orneriness that made this thing a pilgrimage to begin with. Lacoste's rude facticity badgered me. Hidden from maps, removed from view, Lacoste itself, so close, so stubborn, resuscitated my outraged delight in the man for whom the castle was ransacked and ruined. So when at length we happened upon an official white road sign, rimmed in red, naming the place in all innocence, I guess I felt my first disappointment. And when our bubble-car climbed the skinny hairpin roads that brought its ugly angles into view, then out of view, then up close and looming high, their chalky gray stones scraping the powder-blue sky, my excitement was hampered by the nag of realism and, upon parking in its mountaintop parking lot, even by a needle-poke of betrayal: how dare it all be so banal? Along its neatly swept medieval streets, just wide enough for an ox cart to pass, Provençal flowers poured from window boxes. The white-face clock in the crumbling bell tower was accurate and gleaming. A quaint wooden shingle above a rustic doorway advertised, *helàs*, the Café de Sade. We ordered espressos from a clean-cut French boy, the only human to be seen on the mount, and went out to have a look around.

I can't know if Anne-Prospère, arriving there centuries before, had detected the obscenity dwelling inside—or maybe was she bringing it with her? Or bringing her own matching shard of pottery like a mystery-cult member's tessera? Maybe I was magnetized by my own inner obscenity. But as we combed the rocky premises that hot clear July morning, its serrated walls and narrow ledges roaring with winds from the oceanic valleys, I experienced a keen and mounting frustration that we couldn't so much as peep inside. The twee, Taos-like surroundings notwithstanding, the fact remained that here were the rooms—the theater, chapel, boudoirs, and cuisine, the locked three-chamber "Laboratoire du Sadisme"—where he lived and frolicked and thought during what may have been his freest days. All of them, it appeared, were open to the sky, their obscenity visible to helicopters and God. Somewhere, inside, in some closet or corridor, was that vanishing point of obscene plenitude into which all of pornography goes, absent and present, reactionary yet justified, a transcendental signified. But how the fuck could I get *in* there? A steel drawbridge over a gouged-out mote stopped at an immovable, riveted steel door. A barred basement window behind a mulberry bush offered only a cold, musty smell. Gustavo humored me as I prodded and poked and stood back to survey the high window frames through which, from one stingy angle, you could barely descry naked roof beams.

But one mean aperture, situated halfway up the castle's windward face, looked almost reachable. I was already going for it when Gustavo protested. No practiced climber, no urban explorer, I flattened my body to the uneven rocks and edged my way upward and to the left. My smooth and tender scholarly fingers searched the masonic crevices for holds. My side-splayed feet, in Adidas Rod Lavers, poorly made do with the merest of outcroppings as I lunged myself farther and higher from safety—and gradually nearer the wind-whistling window that promised a glimpse of my interior world. For that, as I recall it, is what propelled me and possibly had been propelling me for decades: a positive look at the immoral blankness that had goaded my misbehavior, such as it was, since childhood. I must have known there was nothing there to see, that there *couldn't* have been anything. Still, like a black hole its gravity was immense. Only when I had touched the stone window frame did Gustavo call me to my senses. "Don't look down," he said with concern.

I didn't. I couldn't. No new footholds presented themselves. I could stretch no further toward the window. Turning back looked just as futile. Clutching the stones, risking my life, I enjoyed a moment of sheer concentration. On the other side of that ruined wall, I felt Sade's story roar for a moment and then echo away into the tittering of laughter.

Afterward, when I had picked my way back down, we had our lunch of baguette and pâté de campagne on a grassy ledge beneath the castle. We drank a Languedoc from paper cups. The dry green valleys were vast and serene. The Luberon mountains lay far to the south. The whole scene called for Hemingway syntax. Alone on earth, we were startled by voices, *American* voices, coming up over the ledge. Peering down, we saw people our own age arranged in chairs around a terrace. They were looking at stapled manuscripts. A grizzled fellow spoke with authority. As veterans of an American writing program, we knew in an instant what they were doing and regarded each other in dismay. I recall poking fun at the "banality of evil," but we knew the rudest joke was on us.

Years later I went back alone, wanting another look around. The ruins had been bought in the intervening years by the fashion mogul

Pierre Cardin, but they hadn't changed at all in appearance, and apparently the public still wasn't let in. The Café de Sade was still in operation, and I lingered over my espresso. I wandered around the castle's perimeter and marveled at my path up the wall. That path, like a pulse on an EKG, was one in a series of dangerous acts that had patterned that tumultuous stage of my life. My late twenties had been a period of serial monogamy, promiscuity, binge drinking, drug experiences, perpetual travel, luxuriant friendships, intellectual adventure, high-pitched emotion, grueling work, and much risky play. It had been an age when the abyss—seen from a tomb, felt through a wall, plunging beneath my tightrope tricks—had twinkled with lovely positivity. The abyss had been an actual thing, if without a bottom. Now I could only wonder at it. I was glad I hadn't fallen in.

More compelling to me that day, however, was the Fontaine de Vaucluse. Four or five snaky kilometers from Lacoste, one of the world's most forceful natural springs surges from the base of a 230-meter cliff. Francesco Petrarca, the twelfth-century Italian progenitor of the sonnet, imagined Laura de Noves, his beautiful young virginal muse, skinny-dipping in the wide green crystal pool that is lavishly fed by the spring. For Petrarch, Laura became the fountain itself, along which he lived in monkish solitude, "a delightful place," as he called it, where he could live in pursuit of sheer imagination, not bothered by "vulgar concerns" like "fortune or fame." Fittingly, he may never even have met this woman. In real life she married Hugues de Sade and centuries later became the Marquis de Sade's most cherished ancestor—and another probable source for his pristine Justine. While Sade was imprisoned in the Château de Vincennes, she appeared in a dream and promised to relieve his suffering, had he only the "courage to follow" her. Sade sobbed and cried, "Oh! My Mother," but woke in pain, unable to join her sect of purity.

That warm afternoon when I arrived at the fountain, where the soaring bluffs and coursing rapids easily outdid the tourist-trap squalor, I discovered I was extremely thirsty. As usual, I had drunk nothing but coffee all day. Too thrilled, too distracted to buy a drink, I hurried up the path along the stream, following signs to the legendary pool. The sunlight dappling the loud whitewater seemed to usher me toward the source, a drumming, a beating, then an expanding quiet where the rays shone cleanly through the emerald-green water, onto the smooth white rocky bottom. The path rose high above the pool, and an old iron rail drew a clear prohibition, but my curiosity, or something much stronger than that, propelled me to duck down under the rail, despite the looks of my fellow tourists; to clutch my way down the dirt drop-off; and to crouch on the rocks at the edge of the pool. I don't know what I was looking for, what besides water, exquisite water. I studied the sunlight's underwater show, and my thirst returned with extra strength. But it wasn't until I had been gazing for a while that I realized all of this water, enough to fill a Motel 6 swimming pool, was fresh and pure, *potable*. I could *drink* it. Crouching down deep to keep my balance, I lowered my hands into the icy water and helped myself to a generous mouthful. The flavor was pure, and bright, and weird, as if it had taken on the sunlight itself. I drank and kept drinking, paying close attention to the water's sunny taste, until I felt something change in my mind—not in my brain, but in my mind. Surprised, delighted, that's when I stopped. I stood up and experienced an astonishing effect.

I refuse to describe the effect for two reasons. First, because I risk sounding like a fool. (Everyone knows secular voids are way cooler than fantasies of holy plenitude.) Second, because I wouldn't want the Fontaine de Vaucluse, already overrun by tourists, to be splashing and muddied with zealous pilgrims—least of all unruly writers.

The Terriblest Poet

Brian Bouldrey

His autobiography begins, "My Dear Readers of this autobiography, which I am the author of, I get leave to inform you that I was born in Edinburgh."

These are the stylings of William Topaz McGonagall, poet and tragedian, Knight of the White Elephant, Burmah, self-proclaimed Poet Laureate of Burmah, considered by many to be the author of the worst poem ever written, "The Tay Bridge Disaster." It is filled with forced rhymes and tortured syntax, the stuff that even a child thinks ridiculous:

> Had they been supported on each side with buttresses,
> At least many sensible men confesses,
> For the stronger we our houses do build,
> The less chance we have of being killed.

And you have never seen as many exclamation points in one poem.

> Beautiful silvery Tay!
> With your landscapes, so lovely and gay!
> And the beautiful ship Mars!

With her Juvenile Tars!
Both lovely and gay!
Beautiful, beautiful! Silvery Tay!

The exclamation point has been frowned upon, considered the tool of diarizing teenaged girls and small-town tourist information: "Some of the trains were thirty-six cars long!"

Overused? I say balderdash! I'm with McGonagall on this one!

There are so many exclamation points in life. In fact, they proclaim life! Ahoy! Hark! Westward Ho! Alas! OMG! Ach du lieber! I quit! Happy Birthday! The dog barks! The duck quacks! Rah rah ree! Kick him in the knee! Rah rah rass! Kick him in the other knee! The pilgrims trekking to Santiago de Compostela shout Ultreya! at each other far too often. There is a town in Quebec called St.-Louis-du Ha!Ha! If you have formal training in typing, you know that you must cross the most distance with the weak pinky in order to make an exclamation mark. It requires intention, planning, and a little extra oomph.

I myself am a trekking pilgrim. I have turned, in my old age, to long hikes—around the Ulster Way, across Corsica, across the spine of the Pyrenees, to Santiago twice (so double the Ultreya!s). This past winter break, I went wandering in the Cairngorms near Inverness, Scotland. When tromping about in northern Scotland in late December, you have to be deliberate, insistent, for the sun sets at 3:45 p.m. Despite the brevity of days, the landscape (which must have helped shape the mind of McGonagall) seems that much more crisp, insistent, emphatic: The weather! The mud! The sheep on the hill! The brief sun! The single malt! The snow! The badger! The fox! The pine marten! The song of the crested tit! Yes, you heard me, I said tit! The yuletide clementine oranges nestled in purple tissue papers in resinous wooden crates!

After a few days of hiking through snow and trees, we took a train down to Edinburgh, for I'm an indoor-outdoor sort of guy, like certain Sherwin-Williams paints. The conductor announced we were crossing the Tay, and I looked out the window as we rumbled across the trestles. Immediately I thought of McGonagall.

I have known his Tay Bridge Disaster poem since college, where it was recited each year in the humanities college "Frivolous Readings" event: faculty brought to students literary texts both major and minor, meant to make everyone laugh, though not always intentionally. E. B. White said that most humor has a shelf life of about twenty years before it goes stale—with a few exceptions. Intentional exceptions like Mark Twain, or accidental exceptions like William McGonagall. So many of my classmates memorized, wallowed, made hallowed his unsophisticated lines, but I believed that if you lay down with doggerel, you'd get up with fleas. I thought there was nothing to be discovered in the unpolished, unfinished, the abandoned, the unschooled, since I was in fact all of these things. I wanted a perfect world without compromise. Learning to love McGonagall has been a journey toward loving myself.

Flying over the water in our modern train, I discovered something a bit grim at the actual site of the disaster. By the pilings of our modern bridge, you can still see the abandoned pilings of the bridge that failed and cost the world seventy-five lives and spawned an absurd poem in which buttresses is rhymed with confesses. Don't say McGonagall didn't try to warn you. As with any chaotic event, it falls to artists to make sense of the stuff, and McGonagall knew his role.

McGonagall is the Charlie Brown Christmas tree of poets. It is fun and easy to laugh at his ill-advised metaphors and unimaginative diction. Apropos of nearly nothing, he also took to the stage and played Macbeth—but he had to pay the theater for the privilege; when he got to the end of the play, instead of enacting the death called for in the script, he feared the actor playing Macduff was trying to upstage him, so he refused to die.

Yet, dare I say it? I do!—He got a lot of it right in his poetry: tragic and celebratory subjects, the declamatory mode, and emotion, all the emotion an exclamation point can generate. He was never bombastic; he didn't go on for too long (one loves to read his poems even for their terrible choices and wishes they'd go on just a little longer in awfulness, the way a child wishes you to repeat nonsense poems by Edward Lear or Lewis Carroll); and his books are slim volumes that do not grandstand, like those bards full of their own song, books so thick the title can be printed horizontally on the spine.

And dare I say it? I do!—I am not that much different from McGonagall. He was the son of weavers, mostly uneducated, the first to leave that family trade, just as I was the first in my family to go to college. I loved poetry and chose it as an undergrad major. On the page of the first poem I wrote, my great mentor Alan Shapiro wrote, "Brian, this is a foolish piece of work. You have in this poem the attention span of a hyperkinetic three-year-old." I have spent my entire career and life compensating for my bad grammar, clumsy rhythm, and, most of all, my unbridled enthusiasm. I have never been afraid to make a fool of myself, just like McGonagall.

We were leaving Edinburgh in the morning, and the short day was closing with a cold rain and a sobering tour of the Children's Museum, where you can see a poor child's doll made out of a work boot, three hobnails describing its eyes and nose. That doll deserves its own exclamation point, if you ask me. My companion, otherwise curious and adventurous, had had enough of the raw weather, and I told her I would meet her at the hotel, for I needed to make a pilgrimage to the grave of William McGonagall. True pilgrimages, at any rate, are best conducted alone.

Walking briskly in wet boots, I passed many cheerful pubs and monuments to famous Scottish skinflints. There is a bank in Fountainbridge with a gloriously indulgent mosaic, full of decadent golds and blues, spelling out "Thrift is Blessing," the way somebody might spend a lifetime making a lace banner that read, "Reason over Passion." Both of these, I dare say, deserve an exclamation point.

Greyfriars Kirkyard, said to be haunted, has been taking permanent residents since the late sixteenth century. It is appropriately dark, and there are several graves with iron bars over them to discourage grave robbers. There is a famous terrier said to have stayed at his dead master's grave for fourteen years before finally dying himself. All of this, of course, draws the tourist to guided tours given by people in spooky rubber masks and attracts Harry Potter fans who wish to see the grave of Tom Riddle, believed to be the original Voldemort. The cemetery is not without its moss-covered tombstone and more than a few grisly skeletons. The ground is uneven from all those caskets settling among roots and rills. It's not a small place, and by the time I arrived, the sun had set and the rain had started to come down.

I thought there would be markers set for the more famous inmates of Greyfriars, but at dusk, in the rain, in an old cemetery, it was more and more difficult to read through the moss, the melting fade of acid rain on solid stone, and mud, always the mud! I dashed from stone to stone, leaned into the mausoleums. Desperation was running high as night came and hope waned. Where could I find McGonagall? It was a tragedy from one of his poems! Night would make the search impossible and also creepy.

And then I heard, in the distance, in the dark, near the back wall of the kirkyard, the sound of laughter. It was a tour group under black umbrellas, a chiaroscuro of wicked mirth, and I could just make out that their guide had told them something hilarious. Something hilarious dotted with an exclamation point and much emphatic laughter. The laughter kept coming. It could only mean one thing— they were standing near McGonagall's grave. I had to maneuver through a gauntlet of stones and markers, quick, before the tour group moved away!

Redmond O'Hanlon, in his travel narrative *No Mercy: A Journey into the Heart of the Congo*, describes adopting a baby gorilla orphaned by poachers, and because of the restless crying the gorilla made for its mother, he took the gorilla out for a walk in the thick dangerous jungle. He fell asleep and got lost, and as the sun set on his certain jungle doom, he heard the screams of a village woman being beaten by her husband, a man named Vicky who beat his wife each night, to O'Hanlon's great horror. This time, however, the beating and the screaming were a beacon. O'Hanlon followed the screams back to the safety of the village, gorilla on his shoulder, and all the time, he prayed the terrible prayer: "Vicky . . . please. Just this once. Keep at it. Keep beating her." I said a similar sort of prayer as I made my way, in the gloaming, toward the jeering mob. I knew they were laughing at McGonagall. I hated them for laughing at McGonagall. I needed them to laugh at McGonagall.

The little group of tourists had hardly shuffled to the next grave, that of somebody called "The Man of Feeling." I stood where they stood and used the flash on my phone's camera to illuminate the wall and the ground. I have a dozen photos saved that seem eerie, as I pointed toward places a stone might sit, or a bundle of flowers. All I got was lichen illuminated. I looked up at the twilit wall on which a plaque proclaimed McGonagall's body "near this spot,"

> I am your Gracious Majesty
> ever faithful to Thee,
> William McGonagall, The Poor Poet,
> That lives in Dundee.

Poor indeed! These were his words, but taken out of context, the double entendre regarding "Poor"—McGonagall's meaning of penniless, and our consideration of him as "the terriblest"—a fish shot in a barrel. I watched the laughing stock of tourists trundle away, and I felt protective of the Poor Poet.

There are many bad artists, and artists on their way from the depths to the heights. Great stuff does not just spring forth, like a child of Zeus out of his head. Sure, McGonagall had two flat feet and a tin ear ("Alas! I am very sorry to say / That ninety lives have been taken away / On the last Sabbath day of 1879, / Which will be remember'd for a very long time!"), but so did Susan Sontag when writing her brilliant prose, in my opinion. Have you never beat on your horn, stuck in traffic, shouting with any number of exclamation marks, trying desperately to get to the grade school in order to hear your daughter's choir concert and her wobbly adenoidal solo? You weep at the child's enthusiasm, at her ability to be game, to fearlessly try, to take off the cool-kid sunglasses and just sing out. "Desperado! Why don't you come to your senses!" There is nothing like a child singing a song about death to break your heart. So it is with McGonagall—in an age in which we are always looking for the flaw, can't we glean the wheat from the chaff, or must finding the flaw *be* our entertainment? Isn't enthusiasm crucial to the making of art?

The questions are as much for me as they are for you. My personal pilgrimage to McGonagall's grave was to meditate upon my own strengths and weaknesses. After touching the plaque, searching the dark mossy ground for any evidence of flowers left behind by anyone like me, I went down to the used bookstores below Greyfriars and found a couple of volumes of his work. I returned happy to my friend at the hotel, and we had a wee dram and toasted the terriblest poet. It was a moment of quiet joy—no exclamation points this time—yet still insistent and emphatic.

The Incompetent Pilgrim

Marta Maretich

Twenty thousand roads I went down, down, down
and they all lead me straight back home to you
Gram Parsons

*T*his pilgrimage is a funny one. I took its first steps without realizing I was starting out on a journey. It hasn't resembled the classic haversack-over-the-shoulder, robes-and-tonsure kind. Mine has been more subtle, almost secret, and it has lasted decades. It began when I wasn't looking, proving you can be an unwitting pilgrim. Only when I arrived did I realize I was a seeker.

The first step is a recognition.

Butt naked, with my hand in the lap of a river god, there I was, gazing down on the lobby of the Palace Hotel in Madrid. There were my ham-boned knees, my henna-red student hair, my grandmother's Sioux cheekbones, and my father's Slovene brows. There were the familiar, regretted contours of my own arm, chunky and powerful, thrown across the body of an older man. Bearded, with vine leaves around his head, this figure nestled into my shoulder and gazed up at me with lascivious eyes. Together he and I formed a sort of erotic hillock over the entry door to the Palace Hotel. Our bare legs dangled over the reception desk. The soles of our feet were dirty. It wasn't allegorical at all.

I turned and stared at the young man who had painted me into the picture, Michael. I'd met him only three days before in a bar. In the days since we'd met he hadn't spent his time sketching me, of that I was certain. I hadn't posed for this nymph portrait in any way. He hadn't taken my photograph or photoshopped me in. No. He'd painted me from body memory: that was the unsettling thing. He'd *felt* me into the painting, reproduced my likeness from touch and translated it to a figure first painted 237 years before by the Venetian artist Giambattista Tiepolo.

The result impressed and alarmed me. How little I'd suspected Michael was capable of such a thing. I thought back to the night I met him. It was February and freezing on the Castilian plateau, but the interior of the bar felt like Cuba, steamy and smoky with the lingering smell of a botched industrial revolution. A friend of mine was singing the blues on a tiny stage and my insane Scottish room-mates were getting rat-assed on a drink with blue flames shooting out of it. A Spanish boy was talking to me in a long stream of Madrileño—*theta theta theta*, the sound of a playing card clipped to the spokes of a bicycle—while looking longingly at himself in the mirror over the bar.

In the hot fug, Michael was the only person wearing a full-length tweed coat. We struck up a conversation. He was English, which explained the coat but not his presence there. When closing time came, he claimed to have no idea where he was. Fortunately, I had a map. I always carry maps of the cities I think belong to me.

In the bar Michael told me he was a painter. From the offhand way he said this, I took it he painted houses—I hadn't yet learned to interpret English understatement. I learned the truth when we stepped into the lobby of the Palace Hotel as dawn broke. The grand room was a building site complete with scaffolding and half-painted trompe l'oeil draperies. Along the walls were views of Mediterranean countryside framed by illusionary architecture and faux marble. On the ceiling, there were angels, cupids, swallows—all borrowed, no, stolen, from Tiepolo originals. Now, just days later, I'd been stolen too. Things were moving too fast for me.

My face must have gone pale. Michael had been so pleased with himself. Now he looked worried. "You don't like it," he said.

We were standing on the polished multicolored marble floor of the hotel lobby, a totally public place where people came and went at all hours. I was thinking about what my friends would say if they breezed in on their way to the Palm Court and clocked me up there with my hand in some demi-geezer's lap. Or, worse, my English students—I had scores of them in the city.

I opened my mouth to explain to Michael that, though I am from California, I am not an exhibitionist. I was going to ask him to make the nymph less obviously me, change her hair color, give her a slimmer arm, when Bruce Springsteen came sauntering down the stairs into the lobby.

Bruce Springsteen looked just like himself, which is to say like one of those small but powerful boys who distinguish themselves on the high school wrestling team. He had on a pair of jeans and a black T-shirt and was accompanied by two guys from his road crew dressed exactly the same, a kind of rock and roll crack squad. One of the crew guys peeled off when he spotted Michael and came over to where we were standing. He reached into his back pocket and produced a clutch of tickets. "There you go!" he said. The tickets were to that night's concert, a performance that had been sold out for over a year.

The crewman moved on out the door with Bruce, passing under my smutty feet. I came to my senses then. I remembered where I was.

Because that's what life was like in Madrid in those days. Just like that. Franco had been dead for more than a decade, but the party was still raging with no sign of letting up. That fun was *owed* us, a cosmic debt built up during forty years of a boring, cruel dictatorship. It was obligatory to go off the deep end in Madrid, to drown in fun, and we all did it: me, Michael, my English teacher friends, the team of young painters working with Michael in the palace. We all went in over our heads. Some of us never came up again. There just was too much fun on offer for mortals to bear.

At the same time Madrid was a generous Babylon where even the wildest, most raddled denizens were kind—Almodóvar films are full of characters I met while I was living there: gentle, debauched, out of their minds. They lent me money; they made sure I got home safe. They cooked me omelets at dawn on single gas rings so I could get to work on time. They told me they loved me and into my hands they placed concert tickets even the pope couldn't get, with dispensations.

It was those tickets that brought me up short. The tickets made me realize I was missing the point. My prudery was out of place. It was stingy and much, much too late. Rejecting such a gift—and by "gift" here I mean Michael's painting—is a very bad idea. Ask any nymph: it's the sort of thing that gets you turned into a tree.

I looked at Michael. What could I say? Erase me? Return me to my real self? Let me go back to America and attend law school, as I planned? None of these seemed appropriate. "Am I really that raunchy?" I asked him. I was clinging to the last scraps of my defenses. I had hoped it wasn't that obvious.

"Well, yes." Michael smiled. He said this like it was the best news he had ever delivered, like he was telling me we'd won a billion pesetas on the Once or inherited a Mediterranean island with its own freshwater spring where we could live together forever. He reached for my hand.

So that's what nymphs are! I remember thinking. All those years of reading Ovid fell suddenly into place. *They're us!*

And so my pilgrimage began. In the lobby of a chic hotel. Without a map or a walking stick. Without a known shrine to head for. Without my knowing it was beginning.

I am not always an oblivious pilgrim. On the contrary, I frequently set off with spiritual intentions. I love any excuse to travel. In fact I am so keen on pilgrimages that I will even go to places I know are the *wrong* place.

I once traveled from Berkeley to San Francisco to hear Frank O'Hara speak. I went with my friend Elke, who heard about the poet's appearance on the radio and very kindly thought of me. She knew I was writing my honors thesis on O'Hara and wouldn't want to miss this opportunity to meet him. She rounded up a couple of poetical friends and we set off. This was in 1987.

As the only person in the group who was actually writing her thesis on O'Hara, I was the only one who knew for sure that he was dead. He'd been dead since 1966, following an accident involving a dune buggy—it was stated in my thesis. I didn't mention this to my fellow pilgrims, however, and I think they may have blamed me after the fact. But I meant no harm. Hope simply got the better of knowledge. I was imagining that O'Hara might actually manifest in honor of our pilgrimage to see him. It would have been so wonderful to talk to him, or even to his shade. I was ready for him too: in my veins I carried fresh blood for his ghost—and I still do.

Of course, when we arrived at the windswept campus of San Francisco State, we found only a radio station and a lone technician running a reel-to-reel tape of O'Hara's reedy, fey voice. It had taken us so long to get there we'd missed most of the broadcast. It was a very sad moment; my companions were irked. I seem to remember buying everyone nachos by way of apology, but I wasn't really sorry. If that call came today, I'd do it again.

Jump cut to twenty years later.

I am traveling again, but I don't really know where I'm headed. I mean, I *think* I know: I'm on my way to Würzburg, a small city in Bavaria. I also think I know why I'm going there: it's the place where Giambattista Tiepolo and his two sons, Lorenzo and Domenico, painted their masterpiece, a series of frescoes in the palace of the Prince-Bishop von Greiffenklau. I need to see these frescoes because I'm writing a novel about Tiepolo and his family. Critical scenes are set in Würzburg.

You may never have heard of Tiepolo. His name isn't exactly a household word these days, like those of Vermeer or Da Vinci or even his contemporary, Canaletto. But Tiepolo was once, deservedly, the most famous and best-paid painter in Venice. He was a "history painter," which in the eighteenth century meant he painted massive, dramatic scenes based on stories from the Bible and the classics. He's best known for his frescoes, but his oil paintings were prized, too. You can still see examples of his work in Venice and the Veneto: the ceiling of the Scalzi, the Scuola Grande dei Carmini, the Villa Valmarana, the Archbishop's Palace in Udine.

By the time I'm on my way to Würzburg, I've been to see many of these deft, vibrant, imaginative works. All of them are good enough to merit their own pilgrimage, believe me. However, my trips so far have been businesslike, goal-oriented, and fact-driven—literally, impelled by the pursuit of fact, that fiction writer's dear commodity. I've loved them, and they've brought me closer to understanding Tiepolo and his times. But pilgrimage is as much a mindset as anything and I haven't done these trips with the mind of a pilgrim. The jaunt to Munich starts the same way.

Getting there is nothing. I take a short flight from London on a decent airline. There's no hardship or privation at all, no foot-slogging. I buy myself a Swatch in the duty free. Michael is with me—in fact, he bought me this ticket as a birthday present—and so is our daughter, Rafaela, ten years old and thrilled to be going anywhere. All this makes the trip more a family vacation than a penance.

When we get to Munich we hop in our souped-up rental car and belt down the autobahn at hundreds of kilometers an hour. Again, this isn't hard. In fact, we feel that wonderful sense of release at being again able to drive in Germany, on sleek German roads, *as fast as we want*. Repentance doesn't come into it. Neither do blisters.

Eventually we leave the autobahn and turn onto the Roman-tische Strasse, the Romantic Road. As you'd expect, the journey becomes even more pleasant at this stage. The Romantic Road does for Bavaria what Highway 1 does for California, with fewer land-slides. It delivers the essence of what tourists, even German tourists, come for: chocolate-box towns, fairy castles, tracts of pretty farmland strung out along a well-surfaced thoroughfare. The word "pictur-esque" doesn't really capture the intensity of quaintness concentrated along the Romantic Road. Imagine driving through scenes from Chitty Chitty Bang Bang with a much better, German-engineered car. For the skeptical, it is suspect. You resist the quaintness. You recognize the route as a construct, just as Romanticism itself is a construct, just as any sanitized version of the past is one.

And yet at the same time, the Romantic Road demonstrates why once upon a time, before the two world wars, before Kaiser Wilhelm and Hitler and the trenches of Flanders and the smokestacks of Dachau broke our hearts, civilized people felt free to love Germany and to express that love proudly. Germany is beautiful. Its specific beauty feels like a return. Germany is the place we've been longing for without realizing it, the pilgrimage most of us will never think of taking.

The Romantic Road is decked along its length with a single species of climbing red rose. This rose grows in every little garden and smallholding. It climbs every cottage—you imagine neighbors trading cuttings over their fences. In this way, rose-bedecked, without declaring its intention, the Romantic Road brought me to the point of my pilgrimage. It brought me to her.

I am standing on another polished marble floor. My head is thrown back, my mouth is wide open in a rictus of wow. I am in the heart of the Prince-Bishop's Residence, planted in the center of an oval-shaped room of stupefying opulence, the Imperial Hall. The chamber is an eye-watering confection of colored stone and swirling fantasy stucco that soars upward to a groined dome fretted with gold and pierced with a series of round windows. The top of this dome looks as if it's been peeled back to reveal a bustling heaven where something astonishing is taking place. A blonde girl flies through the sky in a golden chariot pulled by rampant white horses. She's hurtling toward a young man seated calmly on a raised throne. There are fluttering angels, snapping banners, swirling clouds, deities holding objects aloft: eagle standards, torches, bows . . .

At a certain point, when trying to convey the impact of this fresco, you are forced to stop describing and start listing. It's a sign of surrender. But listing is all I am capable of because I'm discovering there is something wrong with my head.

Michael sidles up to me, tickled and happy. "So what do you think?" he asks. This trip is his gift to me—another one of his gifts—and he wants me to love it.

Instead of answering, I reach up to finger the crown of my head, looking for cracks. Ever since I set foot in this palace, my skull feels altered, buzzing, no—perforated. The sensation hit me as I walked up the Treppenhaus staircase and saw the largest unsupported vault in the world bloom over my head, swirling with the color of Tiepolo's frescoes. It got more intense as I passed into the Imperial Hall, an experience I'd compare to entering a slightly flattened Fabergé egg. Now I stand there, speechless. I've been trepanned by the high baroque.

This is not what I expected to happen here. I've prepared for this trip in every way possible. I've been looking at pictures of these Tiepolo frescoes for years. I've talked to experts. I can tell you how the frescoes were commissioned, how they were painted, using which pigments. I can draw a chart of the way the light caroms around these regal rooms, creating the environment where Tiepolo's paintings live—*really* live—in a way few works of art ever manage to do. I can even tell you how much Tiepolo was paid for them (a king's ransom). My head is *stuffed* with facts—or it was until the direct experience of the frescoes punched holes in my skull and sucked all that information out.

It's not just book learning I've lost under Tiepolo's heavens. I've been a painter's wife, Michael's wife, for twenty years now. In that time, I've developed insider knowledge about painting and some technical skill: painting is a family business for us just as it was for Tiepolo and his sons.

Though it's never been my main job, I have pounced and undercoated and varnished. I've mixed sky blue in industrial-scale buckets. I can deploy a chalk line and a laser level. Painting foliage is not beyond me; I am no slouch at drapery. I've scrambled up and down more scaffolding than I like to think about. And I have served on the other side of the canvas, modeled for dancing girls and mermaids and sometimes, yes, knowingly, nymphs. This is not because I am particularly beautiful or because Michael adores me. It's because I am handy, a female form of last resort, and I will pitch in. I will pitch in with my whole self.

All this should mean that by the time I stand under the dome of the Imperial Hall, I am immune to the power of these paintings. Michael certainly seems to be cool with it. So does Raf. I spot her on the other side of the rounded room. She has discreetly removed her shoes and is skidding around the purple-and-white checkerboard floor in her striped socks. She is a painter's daughter, blasé about grand pictorial effects. Her father used to gild her fingernails for playschool with real gold leaf: ormolu, even on this scale, holds no mysteries for her. Probably she would have preferred to stay in our comfortable hotel room, watching the uncanny German children's show in which the faces of actors were grafted onto the bodies of cartoon insects. Yet she seems to be enjoying herself in the Imperial Hall. The sliding is obviously good.

Michael's voice comes to me. "Are you all right?" Now he sounds worried. I am always worrying him. Am I really so difficult? I should reassure him but I find I still can't speak. I point silently upward to a figure that, suddenly, has to explain everything for me.

Michael spots her then and his worry melts away. He laughs out loud. "Thar she blows!" he says. There are certain signs he's been living with an American too long.

I don't say anything. I continue to stare as my hand returns numbly to palp the top of my skull. My first reaction to seeing her is simple human pleasure. It's like bumping into a friend in a foreign city—in fact, that's exactly what it is. The nymph is just the same as she was in Madrid, blank-faced, young, and without shame. She's been recently restored and the blue of her wrap, the ruddy bloom on her thigh, sing out. Offhandedly, she fondles whatever her elderly beau has in his lap—in context it's clear that he's a personification of the river that flows through Würzburg, the Main. But this doesn't really matter. He and the nymph are what they are, what they always have been: a dirty pagan couple. The two of them perch on the edge of the main scene—a depiction of Beatrice of Burgundy being delivered by Apollo to the Genius of Empire (seriously). Their rear ends are planted on its gold frame and their legs and cloaks, partly in 3D stucco, jut out into empty space. For the first time, I notice that her gaze is trained downward. It meets mine.

It is only at this moment—only now!—that I realize I have reached my destination.

I am a crap pilgrim, I begin to see that now. I just can't seem to get it right. First I go to places where there is nothing to visit, not even the ghost of a poet. Then I bump into the central mystery of my life where I didn't even expect to find it. I never seem to be able to pull off the normal pilgrim thing: to set off with humility, to endure hardship and suffering in a cleansing fashion, then arrive at my destination and find redemption. I have it all back-assed.

Here's another example of my incompetence: Ravenna.

It's years ago, before Raf. Michael and I are driving toward the city to see its Byzantine mosaics. Dante Alighieri is also buried there, but I'm not planning to visit his tomb. Oh no. I don't love Dante the way I love Frank O'Hara and Tiepolo. On the contrary, I pooh-pooh Dante. I have a grudge against him, and I spend the trip telling Michael all about it, blabbing on and on, as we shoot across the swampland of Emilia-Romagna.

My dislike of Dante is because of *The Inferno*. I have read *Purgatorio* and *Paradiso*, which I found tedious, but *The Inferno* is my real reason for dissing Dante. Other people find it awesome, its *terza rima*, its nifty nine-circle schema, etcetera. But I am a member of Amnesty International: I have a hard time with the torture. What I really can't get over, though, is Dante using the framework of a Christian hell to devise highly personalized punishments for his enemies and even for his friends, like his teacher Brunetto Latini. What kind of poet uses his gifts to do that? Even if they are great gifts?

I should have kept my mouth shut.

I sensed trouble as soon as we arrived in Ravenna. The town was full of Italian conventioneers; there wasn't an available hotel room in the place. We nearly crashed the car doing a three-point turn in the town square, then proceeded to have a massive domestic right there, in the Fiat, in full public view. As we beat a retreat from Ravenna, we came close to driving off the road and ending up in a ditch. Finally, we fetched up in a miserable modern motel out in the bayou. It had a view of the nuclear power plant and was mainly occupied by mosquitoes and the entire Bulgarian youth basketball league. The management squeezed us into a tiny, dirty room where we went to bed angry, backs to one another, listening to the Bulgarian youths dribble up and down the hallways until dawn. In Italy—in Emilia-Romagna!— we went to bed with no dinner.

I knew why. In the morning we got up and drove straight back to Ravenna. Before I even had a coffee, I went and bought a bouquet of flowers and a clutch of pears and took myself to Dante's tomb. There I humbled myself before his effigy and apologized. It was my own fault. Of course I knew he was a jealous, spiteful spirit—I'd read his poetry. For the same reason, I knew him to be powerful. Yet I ran my mouth, and I had to un-run it there, in his tomb. It was a sort of pilgrimage, I suppose. Again, it didn't follow the usual pattern. Yet it was effective: Dante forgave me. The rest of our visit to Ravenna went without a hitch.

Thar she blows.

Back in Würzburg, my mind begins to work again. Tiepolo is not the painter to lobotomize you permanently. He may cosh you with his flamboyance—he's a showoff—but he will also let you get up again and think for yourself. He is the opposite of Dante in that sense, a lot more like Frank O'Hara, a playful genius with a light touch. You can trust Tiepolo's humanity. His realm and his aim is always delight.

I look at the nymph. A lot of time has passed, and I find things have changed. I am staring up not at myself—the time for that sort of narcissism is over—but at my sister, my doppelgänger, and my original. *Nymphs are us.* Her plundered image was the starting point of a totally unexpected life for me. Being turned into her turned me into someone I never expected to be—on hard days I can still picture that other self, that lawyer, encased in a shiny corner office, dressed head to toe in Chloe neutrals, kicking corporate ass. Surely she is a partner by now, surely she has a pension, a houseboat in Sausalito . . . And yet here I am, with a hole in my head and a daughter with golden fingernails and a man who gifts me pilgrimages without even realizing he's doing it. Everything catches me unawares.

And maybe that is the real point of pilgrimages: you find what you are not looking for. You get to places that don't appear in guidebooks. And when you arrive, you don't see what you thought you'd see. The expected patterns are not in evidence. The payoff you looked for (Forgiveness? Wisdom? Spiritual guidance?) is not automatic, not delivered with a decorative stamp or a blessing or anything like finality.

I'm beginning to think it's better to forget about pilgrimages and travel without expectation. It doesn't seem to make any difference: you still arrive at the moment of transformation. Despite yourself, you arrive, and you become someone else.

Part II. Carrying the Bones

Man is a creature who walks in two worlds and traces upon the walls of his cave the wonders and the nightmare experiences of his spiritual pilgrimage.

Morris West

Driving the Fairy-Tale Road

Raphael Kadushin

*T*he first time I was introduced to the Brothers Grimm, at the age of four, I collapsed onto the floor of a movie theater. Bawling and clawing like some sloppy old drunk, I was peeled off the tiles—really just a scrim of chewing gum—and hauled out of the cinema by two puffing ushers. "He's scaring the other kids," one of them told my sister. And while my revisionist sister isn't the most reliable family historian, the incident does sound like the plausible start of my long and storied career as an alarmist, always the first to hit the ground.

In the end, though, the traumatic moment probably says more about the enduring power of the Grimms' fairy tales than any personal neuroses. What sent me into such a seizure was the mounting shock of two images, courtesy of a Disney cartoon retrospective that my sister and I were watching. The first was the face of Snow White's step-mother, and though Disney tended to soften the original, grimmer Grimms' tales, his stepmother is all arched, boomerang eyebrows, cutting cheekbones, and unhinged fury (ultimately of course she is much more beautiful than the moon-faced Snow White; angular lines, hugging tight to the looming skull, are always scarier than pillowy baby fat). The second cartoon, though, made the stepmother look benign. That's because the second cartoon was the Pied Piper and the only lesson I took from that, when I dropped and rolled, was the haunting lesson every kid fears most. Some curses can't be lifted and some villains succeed. Children, it turns out, can simply disappear, for good, in a moment; they can just walk out the door and never come back.

The fact that the sucker punch of the Grimms' stories could survive even Disney's prettified, neutered translation suggests the way the tales can still throw down their own kind of curse. Sure, there is usually a happy ending. But these are mostly very black comedies, and before the wedding comes the whole cavalcade of our fears, marching out like the seven pitiless dwarves: abandonment; infanticide; boiling cauldrons; chopped limbs; witches whittled down to one long bent bone, warped and creaking like old wood. And those missing children. Where did they go? It didn't really matter. They were already ghosts, proof the whole world can vanish in one awful second.

The fear was still just haunting enough to make me pause for a minute, a little nervously, when a travel magazine asked me to find the authentic backstory and drive the actual Fairy-Tale Road. The hook for the feature was the 2012 bicentennial of the original 1812 edition of *Children's and Household Tales*, the original, twee title for the Grimms' tales. If that cozy title was deceptive—unless you come from a household that spit roasts the kids for dinner—the road, judging from a sketchy map, seemed unreliable too, like it was curling in on itself and hiding an ugly surprise. And of course it was. I'd only been in Germany once before as a boy when we lived in Holland—where we must have watched the Disney retrospective because it would have been too prosaic back in America—and my parents decided they had to see what they were avoiding, because we were Jews. So we drove over the border into Germany, quickly, and my mother and father held hands, like orphans, and ducked into the camp, the gas chambers I suppose, leaving my sister and me behind in the car, safe from the photos of stacked bodies, whittled down to the bone too. When they came out they weren't talking and we drove off quickly, racing back toward Holland.

But the dusk swept in too fast. "You want to see the room?" the woman who owned the B&B asked my mom when we stopped for the night in some back-roads German village. The room looked like a crawl space and when my mother said, "No, we'll go back to Holland now," the woman—okay the old crone-like woman because that's what I see in my cobbled memory, just a dispirited witch losing faith in her own spells, tossing single-lady stir fries in her abandoned cauldron—seemed to puff up with purpose. "I put a curse on you," she said. "On you and your children," she added, and my mother just laughed, a long low laugh, a laugh that kept building until we bumped back into Holland, because the bent piece of angry wood couldn't touch us now with her puny threat. Too little too late.

In the end, though, after one long, ambivalent night debating, none of that was enough to stop me from returning. In fact, the route, too often dismissed as a tourist board brainstorm, and the gooey epicenter of Teutonic kitsch, seemed worth reconsidering for several reasons, and the first was a crucial one. Volume 1 of the *Tales* (volume 2 was actually first published in 1814) is the collection that includes Cinderella, Hansel and Gretel, Snow White, and Rapunzel, and that helped launch Jacob and Wilhelm Grimm's lifework. That makes the circuit, which follows both the trail of the brothers' own evolving careers and the tales themselves, a key to understanding the fairy godmother of all storybooks. But the drive also seemed to offer something more. Twisting approximately 380 pastoral miles north of Frankfurt, mostly through the backroads of Hesse and Lower Saxony, before petering out in Bremen, it promised a German dreamscape. If the villages and castles, judging from photos, looked ethereal enough to inspire fairy tales—the hectoring pitch made by every European pit stop boasting a shaggy thatched cottage or two—this time, at least, the claim seemed justified. That added its own kind of gravitas. The backdrop of our earliest shared stories and nightmares was a pure example of that thing so many people travel to find: the place as bona fide muse.

So I set out, on a mid-July day, nerves steady. Behind me was Frankfurt, the shiny, largely rebuilt city, as anodyne and familiar as a strip mall, and ahead of me was the same scary trip all the lost boys and girls made—the proof you shouldn't leave home—into the bramble, the forest, the strange place. The path didn't look so sinister though. I was well seasoned enough to know that every journey features its own bogeyman or two—even if it's just the stranger in the window seat next to you unwrapping the really big sub sandwich— and it was a cloudless afternoon. And my first stop, in Steinau, was an easy, apt start to the route, because it began with the storytellers themselves.

Fittingly, Steinau was picture-book ready; it's mostly a one-cobbled-street town framed by the half-timbered houses that make the state of Hesse look like an austere study in stippled black and white, all chopped wood, so you wonder why any German forest is still standing. While the brothers were born just south, in Hanau (Jacob in 1785, Wilhelm in 1786), this is the town they settled in as young boys and that they would remember most lovingly. It was easy to see why. Their childhood home—now the recently renovated museum Brüder Grimm Haus—turned out to be a sprawling manor sprouting one small, aspirational tower, a starter castle, though it would come to symbolize, for the boys, their first pin prick too.

"The brothers were unfortunate," Burkhard Kling, the museum's director, told me as we took a quick tour of the house. "Their father had a high court position as a magistrate, but when he died, in 1796, their childhood was finished."

In fact the quick plummet sounds familiar. Maybe they were trying to reclaim their own boyhood when they started their collection, or maybe they were trying to relive it. But the brothers, it turns out, didn't need to go hunting for fairy tales because their own story was informed by all the classic tropes. Exiled from their happy castle, booted straight out of the magic kingdom, they ended up next door, literally in the town poor house, which still stands, like some kind of threat, right beside their abandoned manor.

Yet the museum wasn't a study in gloom. True, downstairs the restored kitchen featured an open oven big enough to barbecue babies in, but otherwise the house was a cabinet of curiosities that read like a homage to the brothers' coming success. There was a gallery of foreign translations of the tales, the obligatory Hockney edition, and a collection of storybook toys that included one modern Little Red Riding Hood doll kitted out like a Goth vamp in scarlet miniskirt. And there was a room hung with the etchings of a third Grimm brother, Ludwig, one of the museum's most evocative revelations. Sort of the Branwell Brontë to his literary brothers (if Branwell was talented), Ludwig would complement their work; a cultural ethnographer too, he was sketching a vernacular German landscape just as it was disappearing, capturing women in folk costumes and a Jewish salesman wearing a drooping beret. "Ludwig," Kling said, "kept coins in his pockets to give to people he wanted to sketch. People with interesting faces."

If the interesting Jewish face (the deflated droop of that beret indicating what? Torpor? Impotence?) maybe suggested more than genial empathy—and set off some distant alarm, a nasty little kick— I didn't want to recognize it, because it was too soon to get sidetracked. What about the Jews? My sister had asked me, before I left. What about all the fairy-tale Jews? But that I had decided would be a different conversation, left way back there with my own childhood crone, with my own fearless parents, who came to Germany together one other time, before we were born, as postwar volunteers to help resettle refugees, those bony Jews that Ludwig could have sketched, if he held on. It was a conversation I'd leave with all the Jews whose shell-shocked memoirs I edited, in my other job in book publishing, all the grasping ghosts waiting for their own personal witness. Sometimes history has to leave the Jews behind; I couldn't juggle twin fears. And Ludwig, I guessed, didn't meet those Jews on the Road, which I wanted to see as harmless, enchanted by its more universal curses. Maybe he sketched them when he was passing through bigger cities, Hamburg or Bremen.

Certainly I figured he didn't see any Jews an hour north of Steinau, in Kassel, where the brothers pop up again and stayed, working partly as court librarians for thirty years, making periodic pit stops at the Brauhaus Knallhütte tavern, which was easy enough to find. It was hard to tell if the pub—now an all-purpose restaurant and event space—had been repurposed, or if the air of almost manic authenticity was a phony thing. Inside, everything was a veritable lumberyard of beams—ceiling beams, wall beams, beams apparently supporting nothing but other beams—and maybe the only men's room featuring framed fairy-tale illustrations hanging above the urinal. The food, like most of the food along the route, was a fittingly traditional roll call of all the schnitzels, wiener to apple, and brats (clearly I could have stayed home in the Midwest), plus some flourishes. There was a special beer-infused menu (start with beer goulash, end with beer tiramisu) and on weekends there was a Cinderella meal, including a baked potato carved into the shape of a buttered slipper.

But you don't come here just for the delicate spud sling-backs. Most people stop at the Brauhaus Knallhütte at least partly for the sense of history, because the inn is where one of the Grimms' top fairy-tale suppliers, Dorothea Viehmann, was born, in 1755. Serving mugs of beer in the family pub, she grew up listening to the fables of the tradesmen, soldiers, and peasants that she would ultimately bring to the brothers, adding a proudly colloquial accent to the second volume of *Children's and Household Tales*. This made for a sometimes rawer version of already familiar stories like Cinderella, which is fairly genteel in the Gallic, Perrault rendition but takes a macabre turn in the German telling. Forget dainty French girls. The Grimm stepsisters, who slice off a toe and then a chunk of heel to squeeze into their bloodbath of a slipper, are the kind of muscular Hessians who get the job done, with the kind of can-do spirit that can plant a field fast. And there they are still standing at Cinderella's wedding stoically hemorrhaging, like the world's worst bridesmaids, even after pigeons pluck out their eyes.

I knew about Dorothea, the collection's peasant figurehead (despite that she was actually a savvy businesswoman). But when I sat down with Grimm scholar Bernhard Lauer, back in Kassel after lunch, he revealed a corkscrew twist to the story that I didn't expect. Junk that image of the brothers hacking through primordial forests, knocking on cottage doors, and chasing after every village crone. It was a loose sisterhood of women, not the pair of brothers, who in fact collected the vast majority of the tales, led by a coterie of the Grimms' literate, upper-class friends and relatives—more Virginia Woolf than Mother Hubbard—who were steeped in both local lore and fancier French and Italian folktales. Ultimately, by most counts, the brothers themselves only contributed a sum total of two stories, that would be one each, though the puny haul doesn't diminish their pioneering concept, or the fact that this was much more than child's play.

"The brothers were serious academics—they initiated the first definitive dictionary of the German language—and their story collection was the original scientific collection of folktales from all sources, really the starting point for German studies and folklore studies," said Lauer, who serves as the secretary general of the International

Association of the Brothers Grimm, overseeing the voluminous archives. "It is also part of a larger nineteenth-century German Romantic movement. For Germans, especially at a time when France threatened to overtake European culture, the emphasis on a return to national roots and traditions, to the beauty of the past, and to stories full of castles, princesses, symbolism, repetition, is essentially Romantic."

Again the sense of little foreboding. National roots and Teutonic traditions spell trouble; German Romanticism can go very wrong. But it can just be a pretty thing too, and the brothers were only conduits, middlemen. What I was really looking for were the settings of the stories themselves and increasingly I felt a sense of disappointment. In the southeastern Schwalm region of the road you can still see village girls dressed for folk festivals in a variation on Little Red Riding Hood's red cap, like a baptismal drop of menstrual blood. But too many of the other landmarks and villages posing as storybook backdrops could only claim some very loose, and occasionally bogus, associations. In a way, though, it didn't matter, as something else became increasingly clear. If the fairy tales reflect a fairly recent vernacular culture, they also encode strands of history, saints' lives, legends, and pagan myths, half remembered and twigged together like the nests Disney's singing birds are always building. And the result is a more allusive fairy-tale trail. What you mostly find, in the road's towns and villages, are subtle echoes and roots of the stories that still resonate in haunting ways.

In my next stop, Marburg—a typically ethereal Hessian town, dropping in tiers down a hillside, where the brothers studied at the local university—there was a version of a genuine Sleeping Beauty. She was Saint Elizabeth, a thirteenth-century Hungarian princess who married King Ludwig IV of Thuringia, donated her wealth to the poor, and wound up living in a pigsty, before dying of exhaustion at the age of twenty-four. The sleeping beauty template—the chronic fatigue version of suspended animation; the tumble from castle to stinking barnyard—were all clearly commemorated in the town's early Gothic Elisabethkirche, where the saint's life is memorialized. Among the treasures: the pedestal of Elizabeth's very democratic mausoleum decorated with the bas-relief of a barking madman, his bug-eyed head looking ready to pop off above a big neck chain. Call it foreshadowing. Elizabeth's own hapless skull went missing for a while, seized as booty by the invading Swedish army and tossed around Europe like a basketball.

It's Hannoversch-Münden, better known as just Münden, though, that maybe ranks as the route's finest beauty spot and the essence of the brothers' lush Romanticism. There aren't any specific fairy-tale landmarks here, but in a way that's for the best; instead you get a whiff of every story because the whole town is poetic enough to compel you to suspend disbelief, so you can impose whatever tale you want. On the day I arrived, the fourth morning of my trip, when I was already growing jaded from quaint overload, the sun was out and the town, sitting beside the Fulda River, looked like one big pop-up picture book. This was a visual feast, a rush of storytelling inscribed on the half-timbered houses and ornately gabled Weser Renaissance buildings, in a riot of statues, door plaques, allegorical figures, and bas-reliefs, like so much gorgeous medieval graffiti (just ignore the town tattoo parlor, the official proof that every backwater in the world now will feature at least one heavily inked body-art maestro). The figure of justice holding a sword, and wisdom reading a book, were perched on the town hall. And everywhere, on the buckling, stooped townhouses that seemed ready to keel over into the cobbled streets, the half-timbering had broken free and was crawling across façades in painted pinwheels and sunrises, palmettos, talismans, hexagrams, pentagrams, as if the whole town were fortifying itself against any passing curse.

But the doom still came sweeping in. What had preserved all this beauty, a sustained artwork itself, was a big fall, and in that sense the town mirrored the braiding of beauty and terror that drives the stories. Hansel and Gretel and their abandoned fairy-tale siblings, the feral orphans and dethroned princesses—all sick, exiled, and ravenous enough to eat a house—are partly a collective memory. Crop failure, the Great Famine, and the Black Death reduced Germany's population by about 40 percent in the fourteenth century. "Bremen and Hamburg seem to have lost up to two-thirds of their inhabitants," according to Simon Winder's *Germania: In Wayward Pursuit of the Germans and Their History*. "Whole villages ceased to exist," and people "were driven to eat the seed corn needed for the following year's crop," knowingly devouring their own future.

And then it resurfaced, the thing I was hoping to avoid, that I had almost neatly sidestepped all this way far north along the road until I got to the most photogenic, twisty corner of Münden, lined with wooden houses so old they seemed ready to pitch forward, onto the hooked side street, all their brittle bones just crumbling. "This," my local tour guide told me, looking a little puzzled, like someone who misplaced something, "this is sad." I was ready though; I knew what she was going to say, with a certainty seasoned psychics must know, when they feel the buzz of a premonition, when they hear the voice of grandma Yetta break through, hungry for gossip after wandering aimlessly through the infinitely boring ether. "This is what was originally the Jewish quarter, the ghetto, though now it's only for the rich." But where, my sister would have asked for me, were those Jews? All the hexagrams and charms, it turns out, didn't work. "Gone," said my tour guide, a woman who knew how to keep things simple.

Some local purges, I read that night, in an abbreviated town history, trimmed the ghetto, so it dwindled to a street or two, and then of course the big curse prevailed, the Nazis marched through, and all the Jews vanished, the town wiped clean, the pentagrams dangling useless on all those door fronts.

And once revealed, of course, it couldn't be contained; all the curses seemed to come spilling out and gather, furiously, in Hameln, an hour and a half north. That was fitting. Hameln was the town I was itchiest to get to, because the place—actually the name alone— brought me back to my first shaky encounter with the Brothers Grimm. The city, an oddly dour, cranky mix of elaborate Weser Renaissance gabling and some bad sixties bunker architecture, felt slightly harsh and gritty. Blame it on the busloads of tourists or a sense of collective trauma, and maybe guilt. Clearly Hameln itself was trying its best to turn a sinister pedigree into comic relief. The official Pied Piper who greeted me, a man named Brian Boyer working as a tourist board guide, was all dressed up in yellow curly- toed shoes, a multicolored tunic and tights, and feathered cap.

Following him through Hameln was a little like following Papa Smurf through Williamsburg—count on lots of eye-rolling from the local hipsters, under their straw boaters—but enthusiastic Asian tour groups made up for the disdain with their Sure Shot cameras. Twenty years from now, an entire Beijing suburb will be puzzling over a photo of me and the piper taking turns on a green plastic flute. How do you top the piper himself? Consider the haul of local kitsch that makes Hameln the road's one-stop shopping for bad souvenirs. It's hard to top the rat-killer herbal liquor, the deodorant soap rats on a rope, and the Pied Piper hoodies. You can snap up the worst of the lot before you dine on rat-tail flambé at the Rattenfängerhaus (Rat Catcher's House) and catch the weekly performance of "RATS: Das Musical."

All this was almost enough to recast the single-minded town as more goofy than scary, until the Pied Piper said something that made me freeze. "You know the story is part of the Grimm Brothers' collection of German legends, not the fairy tales," he observed, quietly dropping the bomb, "and legends are based on historic fact."

The proof, it turns out, is scrawled all over town, if you know where to look, and it is the cold, concrete evidence of a real mystery. The original clue was contained in a glass window of the town's Market Church, mounted around 1300, which pictured the piper towering above a mob of smaller figures. The window, now itself missing, was framed by an inscription dating to 1384 that is also entered, slightly altered, in the Hameln Church book, and now copied on a plaque of the Rat-Catcher's House. It reads: "In the year of 1284, on the 26th of June, the Day of St. John and St. Paul, 130 children, born in Hameln, were led out of town by a piper wearing all kinds of colors. After passing the Calvary near the Koppenberg they disappeared forever."

What is chilling is the specificity of all this, after the wispy vagaries of the other fairy-tale backdrops. Everything, based supposedly on eyewitness accounts, is recorded here like a crime log: the date, the number of children, their destination. And the event resonated in seismic ways. "After 1284," Boyer told me, "the town seemed paralyzed. Nothing was built for more than a century after the disappearance." In 1352, the Hameln book of statutes, the Donat, is still registering the collective sense of shock, lamenting all those "years after our children left."

What happened? The theories ticked off by my piper really reflect the way different eras can project their own obsessions on every spongy fairy tale and legend; each culture sees what it fears, or desires, the most. Among the more prevalent explanations for the children's disappearance: they were consumed by the Black Plague and exiled from town; they joined the Children's Crusade; they were afflicted with dancing disease; they emigrated to new colonies variously situated in eastern Europe or northern Germany; their ship sank in the Baltic Sea; or they died in a bridge collapse. Among the dicier suggestions: they were abducted inevitably by aliens or—why not?—beheaded by Dracula.

The emigration theory wins the most votes from traditional scholars, and it comes backed by some proof; still-existing family names in parts of eastern Europe seem to have roots in Hameln. But as I walked through town the argument felt shaky. Emigrations tend to happen slowly, people are prepared for them, and families stay in touch. Hameln's children disappeared suddenly, leaving behind a reeling sense of dislocation. The only reading that seemed to mirror the local sense of horror is a less-accepted notion proposed by another, quirkier wing of local historians, though it dovetails neatly with the evidence. Hameln was known to be a region slow to convert to Christianity, and underground pockets of pagan worship persisted all over medieval Hesse and Saxony in the Middle Ages. Midsummer ("the 26th of June") would have been the time of the most lavish pagan rituals, and those celebrations were traditionally held in the surrounding *koppen*, the old German word for hills ("after passing . . . near the Koppenberg they disappeared forever"). "Some theorists, though not many, now believe," Boyer told me, as I listened to a rising rush of drumming in my ears, "that the city council or the local monastery approved a massacre of the pagan worshippers as they headed off to their rituals, to convert the town for good." Playing wild, druggy, hypnotic music—the phallic flute no less—and decked out in shamanistic colors, the piper would have been the very image of the bacchant. The children in the end were part of another Grimms tale; they were chopped up, boiled down, left for dead, buried under the pagan stomping grounds of their midsummer mountain.

I wanted to stop there of course and leave but the trail wouldn't let me. The trail in the end had to tell its own nastiest tale and make sure it all came crashing down. Münden wasn't enough. So it was inevitable that my last day in Hameln, just when I had almost escaped, I found two sad books. The first was proof of what I already knew but didn't want to, an unexpurgated Brothers Grimm that presented all their tales and proved of course that the brothers weren't the sweet orphaned boys, aging into sweeter, avuncular, big-hipped bachelors, that I had started to picture hopefully, like an easy convert. No, they were bogeymen too; they weren't just collecting curses but casting them too. In the back of the uncensored volume, in the adult section, like a bad peep show, the scariest porn, is the usually excised tale "The Jew in the Bramble." It's not a particularly poetic tale, but its almost celebratory sadism is striking—even Disney couldn't have softened it, though he would have probably licked up its message if he ever saw it—and it is true to its title. A Jewish merchant is forced to twirl in a hair-shirt thicket of very thorny brambles, whirling to the strains of a demonic violin played by an honest servant who delivers the punch line with a deadpan growl. "You've skinned plenty of times. Now the brambles can give you a scraping." The skinned Jew, reeling off sheets of flesh, perfect for a lampshade, wasn't quite sacrifice enough. The tale, not through with its thrumping, ends with a literal hanging of the Jew, swinging from a noose, because you can't leave behind a breathing corpse.

The brothers' own blithe contempt seemed just as predictable, and I knew it would come; you always work hard to avoid the inevitable. What you will not see. Because of course they were collecting a whole braided series of hoary stories that usually started and ended with the Jews, the original witches, the tribe that boils Christian children down and sucks out their marrow, driven by bloodlust, the nosey, humpbacked moneylenders bleeding everyone dry.

Hameln though had one other surprise waiting for me, before it was finished. Because sitting beside the unexpurgated Brothers Grimm in the town's used bookshop (a store devoted, apparently, to collecting all the saddest volumes) was one final book. This was the *Life of Gluckel of Hameln*, lying face out, its spine broken, waiting patiently, and staring out at me on the frontispiece was Gluckel herself, the only other Jew left in Hameln now, aside from me. Gluckel, a name that catches in the throat, was a hard woman to refuse. In fact, it turns out she was a far better collector of tales than those lazy brothers (just the two stories each!) and their original soul sister, though they'd disown even a literary bloodline. But then she had a lot more to choose from. Because Gluckel didn't need to go hunting for stories. They came pounding on her door, one after another, like a Yiddisha horror show.

Starting to write her long life story in the late seventeenth century, after having escaped from Hameln to Hamburg, where she became a successful businesswoman, and then the only known medieval Jewess diarist, she never developed the facility to soften things or sentimentalize what she saw. Skimming through the memoir, I was confronted by a litany bordering on crime log; her memories have the graceful arc of a tale and none end well. After a while you just have to read the first few lines of each withering entry and that's enough.

"My daughter Mattie . . . was in her third year, and a more beautiful and clever child was nowhere to be found. . . . But the dear Lord loved her more . . . and in the third year her hands and feet suddenly swelled."

"The house which Samuel has inherited from his father was plundered and burnt."

"The baby had brown spots over his head . . . he lay like a lump of clay."

"In my seventh month I fell into an unnatural fever."

"The fear and anxiety that fell on the poor Jews can be imagined! All fled in fear. . . . The mob had decided."

"I cannot refrain from mentioning what happened on the Sabbath of the Feast of Weeks . . . when we were in synagogue. . . . Within half an hour six women were killed and thirty injured . . . while others had to be attended by the barber-surgeons."

On her last page Gluckel is spent ("I would that everyone, man, woman, youth and girl . . . take this to heart and pray to god that . . . he redeem us from this long exile"), but she musters one last mysterious vision that she manages, with a final leap of intrepid faith, to read as hopeful. "In Nissan 5479 (March 1719) a woman was on the bank of the Moselle, scouring dishes. About 10 o'clock at night it began to grow light as day and she looked into the sky . . . and sparks leaped from it and afterwards the heavens came together as though a curtain had been drawn across and it was again dark. May God grant that this is a sign for good. Amen!"

Of course that vision—a teasing sliver of light before the celestial curtain slams shut and the bright skylight cedes to darkness again—can be read as more ominous than hopeful, and all Gluckel's prayers, though you sense she knew it, were useless in the end. The Jews of Hameln were expelled from town several times from the fourteenth through the sixteenth centuries. By the start of World War II there were only 153 left in town. On the night of Kristallnacht their synagogue was torched. Of the 153 survivors, 101 were gassed. None of the remaining fifty-two refugees returned to Hameln, a town that can't seem to hold onto anything: its children, its pagans, its Jews, its pipers. It's the end of the road because everything vanishes here. And the town, full of far too many stories, just keeps telling the same one. Everything in the end gets devoured: the starving babies eat the crops; the witches eat the babies; the missionaries eat the children; and the Grimm brothers spit out the bones of the parents. The Jews.

These aren't cushioned stories of some distant primal fear but a road-map of real crimes, a spree that justifies all our childhood fears, and of course the truest message of the route, once you reach its sorry end, can't be tucked away. You can avoid the forest, but it doesn't really matter; the forest will still find you.

Though at least Gluckel got one prayer met, I thought the next day, leaving Hameln, and the route, and Germany, for good this time. When there is no one left to exile, the long exile really does come to an end. "Just keep heading north," the Pied Piper told me, when he waved me off. It was a warm morning and for a moment I thought of inviting him along. They'd just find his curled up slippers and his feathered hat lying by the side of the road, like a broken spell. But the Pied Piper is an official appointment that lasts at least a year and I knew he was stuck in Hameln. Yet I was free and for a moment I felt exuberant, heading out of town, though the feeling only lasted a few minutes, as I raced toward Bremen, trying to reach some safe border that I knew now had vanished for good.

Buen Camino

Sharman Apt Russell

*I*t feels like the screws are coming loose," my friend April said. She and I were on the Camino de Santiago in northwestern Spain, walking a pleasant ten miles a day for the last twelve days, with fifty miles more to go before reaching the tomb of Saint James in Santiago de Compostela. Behind us, my husband, Peter, murmured with April's husband, Merritt, about Carlos V of the Holy Roman Empire, reputed in 1520 to have visited the church we had just visited. We were passing thickets of yellow gorse and purple heather, passing fields of white-flowering broom, accompanied by the high-pitched click-click-click of a bird—a stonechat, the sound of stones clicking together. We were following the sign of a scallop shell posted and painted and imprinted in cement to mark the road, *the way* of Saint James, the shell the apostle used in his posthumous miracles (saving princes from drowning, removing goiters from knights), the shape of an open hand from which good works flow, a symbol that pilgrims on this route have worn or followed for over a thousand years. We were walking through eucalyptus, oak, fern, cities, vineyards, in rain and sun. "*Buen camino*," we said to other pilgrims. A ritual greeting. "*Buen camino*," they answered back.

Nine months earlier, a surgeon had made two small cuts in April's thigh, removed arthritic bone and cartilage from her sixty-two-year-old hip joint, and replaced the head of the femur and socket with new parts made of titanium and polyethylene. These artificial parts had a porous surface that allowed remaining bone to grow into them. Only one screw was actually used.

"Maybe I should take a bus," April said, "just to Palas de Rei."

But taking a bus just to Palas de Rei would mean that in the climactic moment of reaching the end of the pilgrim's route, after pausing to stare at the great Cathedral of Santiago de Compostela, after waiting in line up the winding staircase in the Pilgrims' Office, when ceremonially questioned by some official of the scallop, *the way*, the open hand, "Did you ever take a taxi? Did you ever take a bus?" she would have to say yes. And so would not be eligible to receive the *compostela*, a certificate of completion issued only to pilgrims who had walked at least the last sixty-two miles (one hundred kilometers).

Taking a bus might also suggest that the metal and plastic in April's new hip were loosening, which causes pain, and which might mean that she needed "a revision," a replacement for the replacement. This surgery would be more complicated than the original with the outcome generally not as good.

"Look!" My husband spoke with some reverence as we turned a corner and saw yet another small café. The plastic chairs and colored umbrellas over outside tables were another sign of the *camino*: the promise of food and drink, *la limonada* or *una cerveza*, every few miles. We were not, after all, in a hurry. We had pledged to be more interested in exploration than distance, in small cafés and Romanesque churches, in a second evening stroll before dinner (lighthearted, light-shouldered without a backpack, having secured our place in the pilgrims' hostel)—and after that walk, of course, we were interested in a rather nice dinner. We were, as you might have guessed, middle-aged and not so middle-aged, with me the youngest at fifty-six and Merritt the oldest at seventy-four.

A limonada, a rest, and April's hip stopped feeling unglued and we walked on to Palas de Rei, her achiness just achiness, something to be expected like the occasional blister and the man snoring next to you all night long, all night long, all night long, in the pilgrim hostel's room of twenty bunk beds.

By now, in these last sixty-two miles, the camino was crowded, and all those bunk beds likely to be full. As early as the ninth century, pilgrims have walked part or all of this five-hundred-mile route for penance, in the hope of a cure or miracle, and as an expression of religious devotion to God. Practicing Catholics who walk the last required miles and who make their confession in the Cathedral at Santiago de Compostela, attend the Pilgrims' Mass, pray for the Holy Father, and perform some charitable work (for example, give a donation) also receive a remission of time spent in purgatory for themselves or their deceased loved ones.

Today most of the more than one hundred thousand pilgrims on the camino every year might pause at the idea of religious devotion. They might speak instead of a reflective journey or spiritual quest. They might say they want to take certain intangibles—love, hope, forgiveness—and shape them into something they can believe in. Something they can depend on. They might say they want to be better people. Calmer people. They want to move more gracefully through life.

The authorities at the Pilgrims' Office seem to be in touch with this modern sensibility. In addition to "Did you walk all the way?" you will also be asked "Did you walk for a religious or spiritual reason?" with "spiritual" good enough to receive the compostela. Any other motive, such as recreational, earns a *certificado* rather less glamorous—in Spanish, not Latin, and without an embossed seal.

In the last few days of our trip, April and Merritt and Peter and I talked often about what we would say at the Pilgrims' Office. Was this a three-week vacation from our jobs and obligations? Or were we here, as well, on a spiritual quest? Merritt comes from five generations of German Reformed ministers, and he set himself a high standard: he would ask for the recreational *certificado*. The rest of us felt equally sure; we would ask for the *compostela*.

We were walking, after all, through yellow gorse and purple heather. We were following a scallop shell through eucalyptus, oak, fern, vineyards of delicate curling green. We stood in buildings nearly animate with age and use. The breathtaking beauty of the world. Beauty beating at us from all sides. Beauty and culture and history and privilege and conquest and suffering and loss. Beating at us. And the monkey mind running back and forth. The monkey mind jerking at its chain, the sacred music and the monkey-grinder music. Arguing with your husband, irritable with your friends, doubtful of your worth. Tired of yourself. And worried about those hips too. The frailty of flesh, the loosening of fleshy parts.

Wasn't this like every day of my life? "Isn't every day a spiritual quest?" I asked Merritt. And every day open to transcendence? How that golden light illumines a field of grass? How the furred hills lie down, gentle as sleeping animals, and the rain brushes your face in a moment of requited love? The ritual greeting: buen camino. Could these weeks of walking be anything less?

In the end, we came into the city of Santiago like mendicants, dehydrated and limping from shin splints. The Pilgrims' Office was even stranger than I had imagined, a satire of bureaucracy but weirdly *meaningful*, like being in a play by Sartre. And the famous Pilgrims' Mass had an unexpected adrenaline kick, the heavy swinging canister of incense clanking back and forth over the crowd, a sense of danger and suspense, gilt and gold, like being in a James Bond movie. Peter and I took pictures. April and Merritt held hands.

The orthopedic surgeon stares at Peter's X-ray, the pattern of bone touching bone, and just can't help himself. "By god, but you need a knee replacement!" Then he backtracks because protocol dictates a series of steps before that kind of surgery. First a steroid shot to reduce inflammation. If that doesn't work, there is arthroscopy to remove torn cartilage, a tiny camera and tiny surgical instruments inserted through small cuts in the knee. Next, if Peter still has pain, the surgeon could inject a series of gels to lubricate the joint. Finally, if all that fails, he will replace the lower end of Peter's thighbone with a metal shell and the upper end of the shinbone with plastic and metal. More plastic will be fitted under the kneecap. Again, screws will be required to keep things in place.

Peter wonders how long this will take. We have plans with April and Merritt to return to Camino de Santiago in a year, this time walking the first two hundred miles of the route from the border of Spain and France in the Pyrenees Mountains. Can he get that new knee and be fully recovered by next spring?

The orthopedic surgeon looks prim: you don't schedule surgery around a *trip*.

But three years after walking the camino, all four of us yearn to go back. We have forgotten all the unpleasant moments and remember only the good times. Meanwhile, Merritt has had quadruple bypass heart surgery, blood veins taken from his leg and grafted onto four blocked blood vessels in his heart. April's replaced hip is still fine, but she badly injured her knee in a bicycle accident. Peter began limping about four months ago.

Arthroscopy is an out-patient procedure with a 1 percent chance of complications. A camera in your knee, a bit of snip, nothing to worry about. Two days after the operation, however, we are in the emergency room. A blood clot in Peter's leg has broken off and traveled into his lungs. Pulmonary embolism. Okay, yes, sometimes that does happen after knee surgery. Suffocation from the inside. Your husband could have died, the nurse explains, could still die. Someone will come in every hour to take his vitals.

His vitals. I had never fully considered what that means. How we are composed of vitals. You could hardly get bored measuring those every hour, although we are in the ER for many hours, and later in the hospital, for many more hours. In truth, we never feel in danger, surrounded by good people and expensive technology. This is such a comforting, sweet illusion.

Months later, the physical therapist is more optimistic than the surgeon and says that Peter's knee is making great progress and he should put off a knee replacement for as long as possible. These days, over a million hips and knees are replaced in the United States every year, and the techniques just get better and better. In Europe, doctors now successfully use stem cell injections from the patient's own body to repair damaged cartilage. Interestingly, a number of European countries have a higher proportion of hip replacements than the United States, although Americans rank only second to Germans when it comes to knees. Yes, she enthuses, certainly Peter will be able to walk the camino! Just keep doing those exercises!

Meanwhile I continue my regular walking, sometimes with April and other friends, sometimes alone, having been a walker for a long time here where I live in southern New Mexico. Walking through grama grass and invasive tumbleweed, through fields of yellow sunflower and purple bull thistle—and the song of a mourning dove, a high-pitched, plaintive *coo-whoo-hoo, coo-hoo*. Walking through sycamore, juniper, hackberry, yucca. Through the town of Silver City where I teach and write. Through working-class neighborhoods, the houses small, sometimes disheveled, sometimes gentrified, an arty sculpture in the yard, nicely painted trim. Sometimes I feel that I am walking toward the camino, an ocean away, and of course we are making our plans now. We will be there next spring, along with thousands of other pilgrims on their replaced hips and replaced knees and repaired hearts, walking not in the hope of a cure, not looking for a miracle but grateful for the one that has already happened.

The breathtaking beauty of the world beats at me from all sides. The gorgeous blue New Mexican sky. White-flowering yucca. Me worrying about me, worrying about loss, about privilege, about climate change. My sins, my guilt. Sometimes I feel so strongly that I am walking toward the camino that I think I'll turn a corner and see la limonada. Here's a scallop shell showing the way and a note in the guidebook that Carlos V slept here, the head of the Holy Roman Empire and the Spanish Empire too, the man who oversaw the Spanish conquest of the New World and whose self-proclaimed rule in the sixteenth century extended to the very ground I am standing on today.

"Buen camino," I say to the woman coming out of the Silver City Food Co-op. She looks confused. But then, I smile back, aren't we all?

<hr>

It is the second day of our first time on the camino and snow is falling on the pass of Foncebadón, snow dusting our backpacks, edging the trail, snow on the summit's Cross of Iron with its pile of rock that pilgrims over centuries have built up, bringing and leaving a stone from their homeland. Shoes are also left and messages and marbles and other mementoes. It is mid-May, and although we are exhilarated by the snow, we have to wonder—do we need to buy warmer clothes?

We don't know that by tomorrow afternoon we will have descended 2,500 feet, breathing now the perfume of wild lavender and thyme as the sun breaks through the gold-rimmed clouds. We don't know much and we admit that easily, despite having lived so many years, but we have hope—that April's hip will stay in its socket, that our knees will take the strain of the next climb, that in three weeks we will dance into Santiago de Compostela, dance and sing and clap our hands like happy fools. We have hope for the world and for ourselves too.

In Soft Panic

Jonathan Monroe Geltner

Somewhere there is a picture of me standing with my brother on one side and my friend on the other, each of us proudly holding a loaded touring bike by the handlebars. The chevrons on our panniers blaze igneous white. We are in a gravelly turnoff from a country highway outside West Lafayette, Indiana, and we are trying to smile. If we are not quite succeeding, it may be because it is half past ten in the morning and already ninety degrees in the shade, or would be if there was any shade. Invisible in the photograph are three small plastic figurines of characters from the original *Star Wars* films: Chewbacca, Han Solo, and Boba Fett the bounty hunter. Each of us carries one of these secured to our gear. The photograph was taken by the beautiful friend who deposited us there. She gave us the little icons unexpectedly at the last minute by way of good luck and we carried them faithfully. Let us be known by them, my friend Chewie and my brother Boba.

In those days my moral and poetic imagination was being fired and shaped by the agrarian writer Wendell Berry. I had written to him, foisting mediocre poems on the man and telling him of my plan to write a dissertation in some way to do with the sense of place such as he had conceived it so artfully in all his varied work, both in writing and in the land itself. The sense of place was so important to me, I declared, that I would like to visit him in his home. What's more, I insisted that the most fitting way for me to make that visit was by bike. If the relationship to one place is important, then so is the way of moving over a great stretch of country, though it might never be our home, or even anywhere we should like to remain very long. He accepted all this—I think impressed more (if at all) by the physical feat involved in reaching him without the use of an internal combustion engine than by the vainglorious symbolism of my plan—and we agreed upon a Sunday afternoon to meet.

So I was instigator and architect of this doomed expedition. My intention was to descend the valley of the Wabash River and then ascend the valley of the Ohio River. We would not begin in Chicago, where Chewie and I were living, because it would have added two days we could not afford, and because it would not accord with my quaint idea of determining our course by the lay of the land, not going in a straight line, but sticking to the great river valleys. Berry's farm lies between Louisville and Cincinnati, on the Kentucky River not far from where it empties into the Ohio. I would have my rendez-vous, but then we would go a little farther, finishing in Cincinnati, which is my hometown, if not quite my native town.

I doubt I would have so desired to visit Berry, whether by bike or any other means, if I had not decided that his home was basically my home, in what I considered to be Cincinnati's hinterland. But what of my companions, what visions were theirs? Chewie's native clime is in the rich vineyards and golden hills of the California coast, and that is where his heart lies. As for Boba, by a quirk of family history Cincinnati is just a place where he happened to spend some years of his childhood. The seven-hilled city by the banks of the Ohio (once upon a time it too was a place of prized vineyards) is not for either of them, as it is for me, an image of the celestial city.

Why, then, did Chewie and Boba accompany me? It could be far otherwise, but the great valley of the Ohio, with all its tribu-taries whether Yankee or Rebel, is not a country renowned for its splendor—and this despite Thomas Jefferson declaring the Ohio the most beautiful river on earth, and the French calling her La Belle Rivière. Nor did either of my companions hold the causes of agrarianism in especially high esteem. No, they came for the sake of friendship, perhaps for the sake of prowess, but above all to share in a purposeful excursion—even if the purpose was not their own.

The ride from West Lafayette to Rockville, Indiana, where we camped the first night, can be made on reasonably comfortable roads in a distance of not more than sixty miles. My notes tell me that according to our odometers we accomplished that leg in eighty-five miles. Our specific course is lost now, as it seems we ourselves were for most of that day. We were attempting to follow some sort of plan. The record is clear on that. But what that plan was and how we contrived it and whether it was intended to meander so much—we cannot know the answers to such questions. It should be noted that I speak of a time just before smartphones. This inefficient routing continued for each of the three days of the Wabash catabasis, the journey down country: the ride from Rockville to the little campground just north of Vincennes where we stayed the second night could have been made in eighty-five miles, but we did it in one hundred and three; Vincennes to the John James Audubon State Park in Henderson, Kentucky, feasible in about sixty-three miles, we did in eighty-one. Let all the extra miles be taken for our sins, though at the time they were nothing but the toil of incompetence.

That first day we suffered. Within an hour I was covered in a greasy slime of sweat and sunscreen. Fumbling with a water bottle, I dropped the thing and it somehow got caught between the front wheel and the fork. I went over the bars. I was not badly hurt, but my left shoulder and left knee, on which I landed, grew sorer as the day progressed. The brake on my front wheel was damaged and had to be disconnected.

We were carrying far too little water and developed fierce headaches that copious dosing with ibuprofen could not extinguish.
There is little shade in the land of soybean and corn. There are few
settlements, at least it feels that way if one is traveling by bicycle.
Several times we knocked on doors to plead for water, but none
opened to us, there was no one around. Often it was as if we rode
through no earthly country. Signs dotted the edges of the fields, pro-
claiming the science-fictional names of the crops growing there. In
one tiny town we passed through the temperature flashed from an
electric marquee: 102°. Whenever we stopped, even for a minute, our
entire bodies became coated instantly in a slick of sweat. When cycling
in extreme heat without breeze or shade it is best to keep moving, for
the resistance wind is your only relief.

We arrived at the campground in deep dusk. Tents were pitched
by flashlight. There was no question of showers. We discovered that
Boba could not stomach the vile pseudo-Mexican carryout we got
in town for our dinner. He would begin the next day's ride under-
nourished. While Chewie snored peacefully in his one-man tent,
Boba and I shared the new, supposedly two-man tent I had brought
for both of us. But the tent, we discovered, was not even large enough
to share with a passionately loved woman. The cramping was pitiful,
and the next day my brother woke hungry, I woke sore, and both of
us stiff and poorly rested.

Nevertheless, it was a better day. No one crashed, for one thing.
But to begin with, there was the beginning. I mean waking out of
doors before sunrise. It is a precious thing, among the chief treasures
inevitably won in any tour, no matter how ill-conceived or ill-fated.
There is nothing timid about the open world's reveille. At the time
of year we were riding, the dawn chorus is mostly gone. But at any
time of year, especially in the warm seasons, there is something as
potent as any song: the redolence of the earth when it smells only of

itself, cleansed by night. You clamber out of your tent, and—even badly slept as I was—the scent stirs you, and you can dwell in the ephemeral moment and say in Berry's words:

> In this time
> I could stay forever. In my wish
> to stay forever, it stays forever.
> But I must go. Mortal and obliged,
> I shake off stillness . . .

In Terre Haute (pronounced *Tara Hote*) we found a shop and I was able to fix the brake. The roads were peaceable and our winding route took us through more places where we could hydrate. When we gained our campsite that evening, just outside Vincennes, we were able to order pizza from the town, which was good, since we had once again finished late after failing to lay in supplies. A solitary wizened fellow, picking desultorily at a banjo in the shadow of his camper, was our nearest neighbor. Upon discovering we had no beer, this man, whose name does not appear in the chronicle, drove Chewie to a liquor store. He had little to say, wise and minimal as saints often are. I believe he had been there from eternity and remains there still. We fell asleep to the accompaniment of his random picking.

The third and final day of the journey down country began well enough. For a brief while the morning was almost cool. Eventually the blistering heat built up, but this time we found succor. In the middle of the shadeless nowhere, in a town the chronicle identifies as Haubstadt, we stopped at an old but air-conditioned restaurant. Here we feasted on the best fare so far: fried chicken, mashed potatoes, green beans, salad, and cornbread. Most importantly there was cheap beer in great round frosty glass chalices they called fishbowls. A little down the road, outside of Darmstadt, we paused at a melon farm. A daughter of the farm, sweet as her family's produce, brought us great slices of explosively juicy watermelon and refused to take money. We talked with the girl while we ate and were sorry to part from her.

But after Darmstadt we descended into the valley of the great Ohio. Our way was a shoulderless, curving road loud with rush-hour traffic. We survived into the center of town, where for the only time we were able to buy food to cook in camp. We remember nothing else of Evansville. It was an island of brimstone in a lake of fire, heat from above and heat again from below, radiating from the pavement and buffeting us in clouds of car exhaust.

There is only one bridge across the Ohio in Evansville. There, US 41 is a multilane, limited-access highway. That particular summer it was under construction. Coming south out of town there is a good shoulder, but the bridge itself is another matter. As the road lofts over the broad floodplain of the curvaceous Ohio, the shoulder shrinks to about eighteen inches. On your right is an apparently pointless concrete curb about a foot high, and a totally useless, low railing that a toddler could climb. Beyond that: empty air between you and the muddy fields and muddy river below, a good two thousand feet wide in that place.

The road's slim littoral was cumbered with orange cones, for the so-called shoulder was closed. The pavement was littered with rusted bits of metal and glass. Ideally, we would have asserted ourselves in a lane, riding three abreast, and the traffic behind us be damned. But semitrailers were barreling down the road and there was no way to interpolate ourselves in that torrent. So we held the bikes on our left and began walking them, our feet lopsided on the rounded curb. We had to weave the bikes awkwardly between the cones. One of Chewie's panniers fell off and he had to rescue it from the traffic and sling it over his shoulder, further disrupting his balance. Had one of the bikes been struck, the jolt would have sent its owner over the side.

Just as we were coming over the river itself, which seemed vertiginous miles below, a pickup truck pulled over—or rather, stopped in the right lane, since there was nowhere to pull over—ahead of a gap in traffic. An arm gestured to us urgently from the open window. We knew what to do. We hurled the bikes into the bed, Boba hopping in with them to keep them secure, and Chewie and I jumped in the cab and we took off. The driver was an old man, Joe, a postal worker on his way home from work. He drove us all the way to the state park and dropped us off with a friendly wave. Like the nameless saint in the previous night's camp, he said barely a word.

We fixed the flat Boba's bike suffered on the bridge. We showered. We bought firewood from the park and cooked franks and beans over the fire and drank the beer we had bought in the brimstone city. In the last light each read in silence what he had seen fit to bring with him. That night we no longer minded the heat and slept soundly.

Two good rides lay ahead. Our route the next day, the first of the anabasis or journey up country, wended eighty-seven miles through the fertile bottomlands of the Ohio. We went among fields of tobacco and past sheds where the harvested leaves were curing. In Owensboro we ate perhaps the best meal of the tour, pork chops with some kind of sweet, saucy stewed apples, in a place called Colby's. The record declares that Colby's had its own beer and that the beer was good. The thermometer at the Lewisport library that afternoon proclaimed 105°. We were getting used to it, but by the later afternoon we were slacking and hurting.

Paused in shade on the shore of the Ohio, in the yard of an abandoned plantation house, we watched a coal barge silently glide downstream. An old lady drove up in a sedan, told us the name of the place—Emmick's Landing—and that her name was Phyllis Emmick. She said we were looking rough and was surprised we were not picnicking, so she insisted we come back to the farm house for dinner.

The house was very modest. Phyllis and her husband, Bill, shared the Pizza Hut they had ordered with us, apologizing it was not the usual fare from their own garden. We stayed as long as we could. I talked a bit about Wendell Berry, whom of course they knew of. We heard stories of their five children and eighteen grandchildren and the six hundred acres the family farmed, though Bill and Phyllis now considered themselves retired. The Emmicks had been in that part of the world two hundred years. My friend asked them if they had ever thought of going elsewhere and Bill laughed, saying the only place farmers go is in the ground.

We had to get going, already fearing we would arrive after hours at the campground, a place that the chronicle gives the very excellent name of Vastwood, outside of Hawesville. Phyllis insisted on calling a person she referred to only as the Judge and seeing to it that we be charged nothing to camp. And indeed we slept free that night. Some hours later, after we had stuffed ourselves with a supper of burgers and root beer floats at the little restaurant by the park, Bill and Phyllis pulled right up to our tents. They were on their way to evening Mass and wanted to make sure we had got in all right. It was the Feast of the Assumption.

Just looking at them, these two could almost have been my own grandparents. But the chronicle notes that here I began to realize it was at least three generations since anyone in my family had farmed, that I was not from the Ohio Valley in the way that some people are, and that when I finally met Wendell Berry I might be at a loss for words of substance. Berry writes in a poem,

> Our names will flutter
> on these hills like little fires.

The words came to my mind that evening as I thought of the Emmicks and their kind everywhere in the world. But in my heart I pondered the hills I love well, the hills that were our destination, and how neither I nor my name flutter among them like fire.

But as usual the freshness of waking with the day quelled evening's malaise. The fifth day was glorious hilly riding and there was even something like a breeze. We ate towers of pancakes in the morning in a restaurant perched high over the river in Hawesville. My notes mention a cruel ascent I must never forget near a place called Wolf Creek. In Battletown we drank more root beer floats while a terrible storm passed. But as we pulled into Brandenburg, packs of lightning flashed and cackled all around us and black skies were outraging the Indiana side of the river, our intended destination that night in Corydon. Considering the hills, it would have been a very long day if we had made it. We stopped short in Brandenburg, having ranged eighty-three miles, and rented a cabin upon the recommendation of the man in the store where we bought beer.

In the morning we sped over the foggy Ohio on the empty Brandenburg bridge. Our aim was Louisville (pronounced *Loo-uh-vull* or simply *Loo-vull*), but we would be traveling through Indiana. It is curious. The chronicle sheds little light on the reason behind our route. The point of crossing into Indiana may have been to avoid the Dixie Highway, the only way through Fort Knox.

The attack came midmorning on the Lickford Bridge Road—a place where, lost once more, we had no business being. I was in front by about a hundred yards, Boba behind me and Chewie in the rear, another hundred yards back. To my left was a cow pasture. To my right a massive rottweiler erupted from a house. I gauged my rate of acceleration and his, and the vector of his course, and I foresaw the place where we must collide.

Yet I cannot now remember the collision. Boba and Chewie had only imperfect views. We may assume the ungainliness of a fully loaded touring bike piloted by a panicking man played some role in the crash. I built up decent speed before I went over the bars. The bike may have swung out from under me at a crucial point and given the dog a solid blow. The first lucid memory I have is of myself wielding my pump at the dog, which was backing off as Chewie and Boba beared down on it, shouting madly. Blood poured down the right side of my face, but as yet I felt no pain.

We hobbled down the road a little ways. No one ever came from the house to retrieve the beast. The chronicle tells me that the name of the woman who pulled up in a minivan as my brother was bandaging my head was Carol. She was a nurse at the hospital in Corydon, where she promptly took me and my bike while Boba and Chewie rode there. Carol was on her way to a wedding.

They sewed up my head and my arm and told me there was nothing to be done about my cracked rib. But they did give me some powerful pain medication. Boba and Chewie arrived and cooled their heels while I recuperated. I was told where to go to file a police report, but I saw no sense in bogging down in paperwork. Full of drugs, I rejoined my comrades and we rode the twenty miles or so to Louisville. When we arrived at the hotel, I knew I was finished.

It was a very fancy hotel, so fancy it was partly an art museum. Chewie is a mastermind of dubious Internet deals. He had secured, for sixty or seventy dollars, a room that must normally have cost two or three hundred. For that reason they were suspicious of us. Also, I suspect, we were greeted with something less than enthusiasm because of the condition in which we arrived. The staff did not want us to take our bikes inside the hotel. Such flagrant disregard for the security of a machine with which one has an intimate and interdependent relationship is an insult to the serious cyclist. So Chewie brought me in to the front desk where he was arguing with them, and from my patched head and arm I bled and oozed puss in front of the other, more respectable clientele until our hosts relented and even pitied us to the point of supplying a separate storage room for our bikes.

We cleaned ourselves and wandered into the hazy evening. We found a place to drink bourbon and then another place, a brewpub, to drink beer. It was only then that I called the Berrys to tell them of my debacle. I made the call from a pay phone, difficult as that may now be to believe. My primitive cell phone had been killed in the crash when a bottle inside one of my bags exploded and drenched it. (This spill also rendered illegible much of the record I had been keeping.) I did not talk to Wendell Berry but to his wife, Tanya, who spoke with as charming a Kentucky twang as you can imagine, though I believe she is originally from California.

Our budget in tatters anyway, we dined at the hotel's gourmet restaurant. We could only make ourselves so presentable. The other patrons watched us with a mixture of curiosity and mild disgust. Then we walked out upon the city once more. It was a Friday night. It was good to see young people in the streets, for we had seen almost none for six days. The backcountries of America are sadly empty of them. Finally we found the Ohio and sat by it, watching the city lights play in the water. She is broader there than at any other point in her course. We laid plans to go back to Chicago the next day, our goals unachieved. On the last blurred page of the chronicle I can make out only one word distinctly, and the word is *failure*. But chroniclers are known to make mistakes. It could be the story ends with three tipsy fools who for once knew what Wendell Berry knows:

> Gravity is grace.
> All that has come to us
> has come as the river comes,
> given in passing away.

An Accidental Pilgrimage

Russell Scott Valentino

Seeing me genuflect for the first time in his life in Angra do Heroísmo's Sé Cathedral on the island of Terceira, my nine-year-old son, Dante, asked, "So, we're basically Catholic then?"

I could have just said yes—basically. But it wasn't that simple. First, neither he nor his elder brother had been baptized, as Catholics or anything for that matter, though not for lack of trying. I really had tried when Peter was born, even took him as an infant to Saint Mary's in Iowa City and sat through a baptismal orientation of sorts. But something about Sister Isabel's description of the Church's claim, Jesus's claim, upon him and upon me, had filled me with evangelical dread. My brother-in-law Joe, who would have been the godfather, was disappointed when I called to tell him I had backed out. "What if he's in a foxhole one day," he asked, "like the guys I was with in Korea? He'll be thanking you then." My sister must have been looking at him to ease up because he softened, a little like her, and said, "But I guess if you just couldn't do it."

Dante had been following me closely, doing what I did, kneeling where I knelt, sitting, standing, dipping his fingers in the holy water. I thought I was doing all this for the same reasons that I weed and put down saplings and little packages of food and burn incense and pour water over the graves of my Japanese ancestors-in-law during Obon each summer. Dante had done this many times, putting his little hands together from a very young age to murmur *naminaminaminami*. He was also used to Shinto shrines, where he knew to wash his hands and cleanse the inside of his mouth with the well water before entering. I was smiling when I answered no he could not wash his face with the holy water.

He went with me into the pew, asking with his eyes what to do next, so I showed him what I remembered, told him to think of the bad things he had done, just remember them and try not to do them anymore. A picture of my aged *avó*, kneeling uncomfortably on her brittle knees, her rosary dangling, settled before me, and I heard her incessant unintelligible murmuring with all those sibilants that her thoroughly American grandchildren, me among them, used to make fun of, not so much *naminaminaminami* as *shbthshbshthshbthsh*. Dante was good with rules. Rules were something he knew from games, and this could be something like a game for him. I remembered the passage in *The Brothers Karamazov* where Father Zosima is visited by a woman who has lost her faith. He tells her to try this and that, and she says she's tried everything and nothing has worked, so he finally says to go through the motions as if she has faith, pretend, act as if, and eventually she will stop acting as if and merely be acting as. It occurred to me that this would be good advice for a child who was thinking of it as something like a game. Had my avó prayed in this church, I wondered? I was surprised to feel tears in my eyes as I left it.

He repeated his question as we made our way down the painted cobblestones outside, and I decided to make it something light. "Sure, you're Catholic," I said, "except for the Buddhist and Shinto parts."

To which his elder brother responded, "Papa, I think you mean in addition to."

Yasuko, walking ahead of us a few paces, turned back to nod her approval. Well, of course. When you've already got eight hundred gods in your corner, adding one more is not a particularly big deal. I somehow doubted that Sister Isabel would have approved of this way of making sense of our hybrid home, but Peter's correction seemed a good one to me.

Pilgrimage, like parody, I think, should require intention. An unintentional parody, that is, one whose creator was unaware of its existence, would be something forced on it from outside, likely a very clever interpretation that was mostly about itself. In the same way, I have trouble imagining someone convincing me that I went on a pilgrimage without my knowing it, without my intending to do so. Pilgrimage doesn't happen by accident. An accidental pilgrimage might look like a pilgrimage from the outside, but if you didn't set out on it, knowing from the start, even before the start, where you were going and, especially, why, then it wouldn't be a real pilgrimage. Nor would it be a parody of a pilgrimage, though it might look like that too.

The why sets the mood. When my father died a few years ago, I knew I wanted to be away, traveling in some slow mode, by foot, or boat, or train. It felt like I needed a pilgrimage though I had only a direction, from east to west, and no shrine or holy or historic site that would help me put things in place, make sense, once I arrived. But I felt the why of it from the start as I set out, even before, and understood that it was a pilgrimage in effect if not in fact. Near the end I met up with my friend Ksenia Golubovich, a writer and editor in Moscow, and told her about my wanderings that didn't seem to have a clear purpose, and she immediately cut to the chase, reminding me that "travel for its own sake is always a search for God." Don't you just love Russians?

But there are varieties of intention—I know this. Sometimes you don't know what you want. Sometimes you say you want something but inside that want is another want you were only dimly aware of or not at all. Sometimes when you find that little lump or get the pathology report back, all your wants change at once and you realize you wanted something else all along. The sort of devout person who might set out on an unaccidental pilgrimage would say that all accidents are purposeful. That sort of person would not see anything contradictory in the notion of an accidental one, as I did just a minute ago. Please don't make any assumptions about me based on the title I've chosen. It could have a question mark as easily as not. All these words have a way of confounding one at times, the punctuation too.

My mother's parents, Martin and Rosa, emigrated from the island of Terceira in Portugal's Azores Islands in the early twentieth century. I had never visited the island before and was looking forward to meeting the few living relatives who remained there. My ninety-year-old Aunt Lydia had put us in touch. It would be a pleasant family outing, ten days of business cum pleasure in a subtropical setting.

The faces in the gate area were recognizable from family photos, especially the common expression, that hint of resignation to the weather, fate, the available in-flight food. I passed, but Yasuko and our two half-Japanese boys stood out, even immersed in their books, and I noticed people once in a while noticing us. Yasuko and I had grown used to this behavior in Europe, the failed surreptitious glance from the diners at the corner table, the snickers from the boys along the scenic walk. It was benign mostly; here it felt merely curious, and only mildly so.

Almost a thousand miles from Lisbon, the Azores are not the sort of place you visit on your way somewhere else, unless you're traveling by boat. They call it an autonomous region, and indeed it seems to be its own place altogether. The Azorian poet and social activist Natália Correia once noted that she had to travel to America to discover that she was from Europe. The largest town on the eastern side of Terceira, Angra do Heroísmo, is a quaint port of some thirty thousand people, with cobblestone streets painted with white and pink curlicues. This must have been where Martin and Rosa set out on their initial journey to the United States—separately, for they didn't know each other then—and where they returned to visit—together, after their marriage and the birth of their five children.

Officially, I was here for the annual conference of the Mediterranean Studies Association (several participants pointed out that the Azores are not part of the Mediterranean either), but from the start it was hard to keep my personal connection to the island separate. At the conference's opening reception, I mentioned to the mayor that my mother's parents were from this island. He asked which villages, and within five minutes of our shaking hands good-bye, a small, portly, smiling man had come up to me through the crowded room and said that he was from the same village as my grandfather, he was interested in genealogy, and maybe he could tell me something about my family.

The next day Father Mendes—he turned out to be a priest practicing canon law, with responsibility for record keeping for several of the parishes on Terceira—showed me the extensive trees he had compiled, partly through interviews with people like me, partly with the help of a multi-tome family history archive in the local library. He was quickly able to tell me that my grandfather's was an old Terceira family, with ancestors reaching back to the 1600s in Altares, and later Cinco Ribeiras. He knew the names of the living descendants, where they lived, where they had lived for many generations. He was even related to one by marriage. My grandmother's family was more obscure, less distinguished, poorer. She was from a parish he didn't have responsibility for, in the other direction from Angra, in the old Vila de São Sebastião, one of the original Azores settlements from the mid-1400s. To learn more, we would need to go there.

And so one sunny Sunday afternoon, our rental car wove the winding roads along the coast, through the villages of Ribeirinha, Feteira, and Porto Judeu, as we made our way toward the little parish church where my grandmother and her siblings were once provided with the sort of foxhole cover my brother-in-law thought my sons would have appreciated. Across the street from the church we met my cousin Marília, "the schoolteacher," as everyone referred to her because she taught school. She spotted us immediately—how could she miss us? In fact, she had posted a lookout just in case, her elderly neighbor Mrs. Romero from down the street, to let her know if anyone who looked like they might be American showed up.

The house where my grandmother and her siblings were born sits at the top of a sharp slope some fifty meters from the sea. The slope itself is green, like most of Terceira, with low stone walls separating small fields, where cows and goats graze, often right up to the water's edge. The man who lives there now, a cigarette between his tense lips, came out to see why we were standing so close to his pickup, pointing at his home. Maria Nelia, Marília's mother, talked for a long time, explaining. Afterward, it occurred to me that he must be used to this, though not because of my grandmother. He gave a dismissive sort of wave eventually, not satisfied, just resigned, as if to say what could he do about it anyway.

The family relations were murky in my mind. The strings of names and nicknames all jumbled together. It took me twenty minutes to figure out that Tia Rosinha was actually the way they referred to Rosa, something like Auntie Rosie, though of course she'd never been anything but Avó to me. Tia Rosinha had been hardworking, they said. Tia Rosinha had been kind. The boxes Tia Rosinha sent back were so big they had to open them outside the house because they wouldn't fit through the door. Tia Rosinha had loved to talk. I said I didn't remember my avó talking much, but quickly realized she had jabbered pretty much all the time, though to me it had registered as *shbthshbbthshbshthshthsh*. I asked Marília to go through the names of the siblings once more so I could jot them down. There was the eldest girl who married first and left for America; there were the twins, including Tia Rosinha; there was Tia Isabel, who went to Angola, married, lost everything, and returned; there was Manuel; there was Erita; there was Maria Vieira—Marília pointed to a sign on the street above her head—and there was the youngest, her grandmother, Jesuina, who stayed.

The litany of departures, which Marília recited as she went through the names, made me wonder what it must have been like to stay behind when so many of your friends and family had gone, more by far than those who stayed with you. The sense of loss, it seemed to me, was still palpable. But I hadn't understood the gesture, the sign. Why, I asked, was my *titia*, my grandmother's sister, on a sign on the street with an arrow pointing? What was it pointing to?

And this is where, I suppose, the idea of accidental pilgrimage might enter, if I am the sort of person who believes there is nothing contradictory in the phrase. For pilgrimage is something one sets out on not just in order to take stock after a loss. It is something one does in preparation for an ordeal as well, in the midst of difficulty, when you need help, when you are experiencing crisis, illness, doubt.

One June day in 1940, thirteen-year-old Maria Vieira was on her way out to the fields with her four-year-old sister when a man from her village, José Quintero, forced himself on her. She told her sister to run, and she fought back. In the struggle she was killed. When the villagers found her, they brought her home, laid her out on the bed, and sent for the priest. When he came into the room, she opened her eyes, identified her attacker, and said she forgave him. Then she closed her eyes again and passed away. Another version of the story has it that she made her way home, covered in blood, identified Quintero, and said that they should not harm him. Later the villagers started to notice things about her, and people from there and elsewhere began to come to São Sebastião to ask for the young girl's help and blessing. A small shrine was built, then a larger one, then a chapel on a hill, with a niche for people to place pictures, articles of clothing, jewelry. Before long, her name was known throughout the island, as it is today. In 2006 a petition to canonize Maria Vieira as a martyr *in defensum castitatis*, "in defense of chastity," was presented to the Vatican. A diocesan inquiry has yet to be conducted.

This was what the arrow pointed to, the figure of a relative, unknown to me, whose healing powers were holy to the people of the island and beyond. Were this a work of fiction, I might have myself place some object at her shrine in a moment of fancy, something of my wife's, I don't know, an earring, a picture from my wallet. It would function as a subtle clue whose importance could be revealed later in the story, in a doctor's office, or a hospital room. After the little lump. The pathology report. Readers would piece things together then, reading backward, finding all the pieces perfectly placed such that one revelation would lead to another and that to a third and that to the fulfilling climax. But I didn't place anything of Yasuko's at Maria Vieira's shrine, though later I wished that I had. Perhaps I really do believe in accidental pilgrimage.

There was some graffiti along the side of the stairs leading to the main chapel, and several plants had been vandalized. I picked up one of the broken saplings and tossed it into the flower bed behind the votive candles in the lower shrine, where others had left pictures. Then Dante, standing beside me, picked up another, and the two of us put our hands together and bowed our heads.

At the Grave of Sadie Thorpe

Miles Harvey

> Time forks, perpetually, into countless futures. . . . In
> most of these times, we do not exist; in some, you exist
> but I do not; in others, I do and you do not; in others
> still, we both do.
>
> Jorge Luis Borges, "The Garden of Forking Paths"

Was she a relative of yours?" the old man asks, leading me toward your grave.

"Well, not exactly," I begin to reply. "She—" But then I pause. In the middle of my sentence, in the middle of my life, in the middle of some small-town cemetery in the middle of the Midwest, I pause, unable to explain who you are or why I'm here. What I would tell the man, if it didn't sound so absurd, is that although I am not your descendant, although I only recently learned of your existence, although you barely left a mark on the world, and although your corpse was buried here more than forty years before I was born, I can't get you out of my mind. What I would recount, if I could figure out a simple way to do it, is the history of happenstance that connects me to you across the years, a bond that at this moment feels almost as strong as the ties of blood. What I would confess, if I wasn't worried he'd laugh in my face, is that I woke up this morning, a couple months shy of my fiftieth birthday, certain I had to drive more than one hundred miles from Chicago to visit a total stranger's grave in this tiny hamlet of Dana, Illinois.

A dog barks in the heat of this August afternoon. A killdeer swoops in on slender wings, offering its distinctive call: *kill-dee, dee-dee-dee, kill-dee, dee-dee-dee.* And still I pause.

"It's a long story," I say at last.

The old man doesn't press me for details. Having taken care of this graveyard for more than two decades, he must know that the place is full of long stories—tales that haunt the living for decades after their protagonists have vanished beneath the soil. And perhaps he also realizes that people don't come here to recite those stories but to reckon with them. So I follow him through the tombstones, searching for the one marked *Sadie Thorpe.*

The first time I saw that name was in the pages of a court document from 1932. I had visited the regional office of the National Archives in Chicago to hunt down information about my maternal grandfather, who was convicted of bank embezzlement during the Great Depression. My goal was to figure out whether he was guilty, as the judge who sentenced him to the Leavenworth Federal Penitentiary apparently believed, or a fall guy, as my mother has always insisted. I never solved that mystery, but I did stumble upon another one, a story that would jostle my notions of self.

Like a lot of Americans who grew up in the late twentieth century, with its TV culture and its massive migration from small towns and cities into suburbs such as mine, I had never learned much about my roots. I knew that my grandfather was of German descent (though I did not know when his family emigrated); that he grew up in Iowa (though I did not know what town); that he worked for a railroad (though I did not know which one); that he settled in my future home of Downers Grove, Illinois (though I did not know when); that he took a job at a bank and wound up in prison (though I did not know for how long); and that he died years before I was born (though I did not know how many). I was also aware he had been married once before my grandmother came along, but I didn't know who the woman was or what happened to her. Not even my mother knew her name.

But at the National Archives, I discovered that when it comes to genealogical research, having a felon for a grandfather can be a godsend. Among the court documents was a twelve-page biography, prepared by attorneys for the accused, full of rich details about his life. I learned, for example, that in 1901 at age fourteen, having just graduated from grade school in the eastern Iowa town of New Vienna, he "sought and obtained employment" with a certain F. X. Gerken, "in whose business he worked at the cooper trade for two years," and that after laboring as a farmhand for a couple of years, he "decided to improve his ability," landing a job with the Chicago, Burlington and Quincy Railroad for twenty-five dollars a month.

And then, on page 3, I met you.

My grandfather, according to the document, "was united in marriage on the 10th day of June, 1910, to Sadie Thorpe, of Dana, Illinois." I skimmed forward through that dense text, rushing past the details of your married life to learn what became of you in the end. In the fall of 1918, during the height of an epidemic that killed more Americans than all the wars of the twentieth century combined, you fell ill with what was then known as the Spanish flu. Although many of its victims expired soon after infection, the virus seems to have worked more slowly on you. Nonetheless, your "illness continued from day to day developing into a serious case." You died on Christmas day, two weeks shy of your fortieth birthday.

The implications of all this did not hit me right away. But then one afternoon, as I read back over that document, the back of my neck suddenly went cold. I had been aware of my own good fortune—loving parents, a moderately happy childhood, a supportive brother, a wife and two children who offered constant proof of why life was worth living, friends who were in it for the long haul, a writing and teaching career that I could describe without irony as a calling. When people said I was a lucky man, which happened with some regularity, I would knock on wood and nod in agreement, never giving it too much thought. But now I saw that my luck did not just appear from the blue. It grew straight out of someone else's suffering and misfortune. Between twenty million and one hundred million people died in the Great Influenza Epidemic of 1918, and if you had not been among them I would never have been born.

My mother came into the world a little over five years after you left it. By her own estimate, she has lived a "long, long time," her days more than doubling yours. But now, at age eighty-six, she too is reaching the final chapter, her body shriveled by osteoporosis and arthritis, her mind fogged by dementia, her ability to communicate hampered by severe hearing loss, her horizons narrowed to her own four walls.

Until she was almost eighty she led an energetic existence, socializing with friends and maintaining her career as a travel agent while working what amounted to a second job as a political activist and Democratic Party functionary. Now, however, she requires twenty-four-hour care. When I visit her in the Chicago suburb of Downers Grove, we sit on the front porch of the rickety Victorian where she's lived for almost fifty years, building a life with my father, who died in 1986, and raising two sons. As squirrels chase each other around the yard, she complains about the strangers who now feed her and bathe her and follow her from room to room to make sure she doesn't fall. "It's like rotting in a prison," she says in a conspiratorial whisper so her attendant doesn't hear. "It's like being locked up."

I spend hours with her on that porch. She took care of me when I couldn't take care of myself, and now it's my turn to return the favor. This, I believe, is a privilege as much as an obligation, a hard kind of good luck. Still, it can feel overwhelming, all the shuttling back and forth between doctors, all the time spent arranging her affairs and handling her finances, all the worry about her happiness and health, both of which, I know, are beyond recovery. I never feel like an adequate son anymore, much less a good husband to my wife or father to my children or teacher to my students. And lately I've begun to doubt myself as a writer, my opportunities to sit quietly at the keyboard far less frequent than in the past. With mounting debts and diminishing sleep, I've never worked harder to accomplish less.

And today I'm accomplishing nothing at all. After putting off plans to get some writing done and asking my wife, once again, to take care of the kids on a beautiful day, I feel furious with myself for allowing you to take over my imagination, to bore under my skin in ways I still can't quite pin down.

The man leading me to your headstone is Carl Klendworth, a robust seventy-four-year-old with a compact build, animated blue-gray eyes, and the boot-leather skin of someone who has spent decades outdoors. He lives on the far end of the village, which in a place this size also means that he lives only a few blocks from the center of town. Beyond his property, on which cows wander slowly through the shade, is the cemetery, and beyond that sits a field of soybeans and then a seemingly endless vista of corn, bisected by high-tension power lines, which fade into a vanishing point on the horizon.

As we weave our way through the headstones, Klendworth stops and gestures to a grave. "This is my grandmother," he says. "Her maiden name was Thorpe too."

Addie Marshall, 1875–1950. That first name sounds strangely familiar, so I stop and check my notes. For some time now, I've been trolling libraries, archives, and databases in an effort to piece together the fragments of your past. Sure enough, according to the 1880 federal census, this same Addie Marshall was your older sister.

I had expected that finding information about an obscure person, dead for nearly a century, would be tough going. But my research has been full of lucky breaks, clues that keep popping up as if someone is leaving them in my path. And now it's happening again. The first person I speak to in Dana—a man I greeted in passing as he mowed his grass—turns out to be one of your close relatives.

"Is that so?" Carl Klendworth says with a surprised chuckle when I inform him the woman I am looking for is his great-aunt. He's clearly never heard of you. I ask him if he remembers any stories about some relative who died in the flu epidemic. He grew up in his grandmother's house, he tells me, so he's listened to plenty of family lore. "But no, I can't recall anyone ever mentioning anything like that."

It occurs to me that I may be the last person alive who knows your story. And then it occurs to me that by writing it down, I can offer some sort of cosmic recompense—a payback, however overdue and inadequate, for the great gift I have received at your expense.

Your life ran its course along train tracks. This very town owes its name to a certain Thomas Dana, superintendent of the Chicago,

Pekin and Southwestern Railroad, which laid a roadbed through the prairies of central Illinois in 1873. Before the arrival of those rails, your village didn't even exist—but by the time you were born just six years later, Dana could boast two grain elevators, six stores, a church, a mill, and a population of 250.

The boom would end almost as soon as it began. Beset by a series of financial troubles, the railroad struggled to stay in business from the start. Even so, investors and local boosters clung to their dream of extending the line to St. Louis and beyond. The first transcontinental railroad had been completed only a few years earlier, and everyone now knew of the astronomical fortunes being made by moving people and goods west and raw materials east. Unfortunately, the line through Dana had been "laid with inferior rails, which together with a defective roadbed, made it wholly inadequate for the traffic of a transcontinental system," according to one chronicler. When the Atchison, Topeka and Santa Fe Railway purchased the railroad in the late 1880s, linking Chicago with the Pacific Coast, it laid new tracks north of town, bypassing Dana by less than five miles. Cut from the umbilical cord of national commerce and relegated to a quiet stop along a rural branch line, the town lost its only reason to exist.

By the time you were a teenager, a mood of despair must have already started to drift through the village, as it dawned on residents that history had passed them by along with the Santa Fe. Perhaps like countless other kids who grew up in dead-end towns, you dreamed of a different future, a different place to call home. But you were stuck. Your mother was ill, so you remained in Dana to take care of her "with unfailing love and tenderness," as your obituary would later put it. You were twenty-seven—still a young woman, but barely so by the standards of the day—before she died and you could start your own life.

Across the road from the cemetery looms the ruin of what was once the Dana Township High School, a three-story, red-brick building with smashed windows, a boarded door, and a collapsed roof. At one time, it must have embodied the town's hopes for the future; now it's a crumbling reminder of the lost past.

"The death of family farming," explains Carl Klendworth, "has drained this place of young people."

Only 159 souls live here now, down by almost half from when you were growing up over a century ago. The trains no longer run to Dana. Even the tracks are gone. The interstate highway system never arrived. Other nearby towns landed universities and prisons; Dana's main industries are a bar ("The Best Little Place in the Middle of Nowhere," according to its sign) and a sleepy establishment called the Gold Dust Diner, its very name a memento of the failed dreams and missed chances that make up the story of the town that time forgot.

Your escape was made possible by the railroads. In your late twenties, you moved to Valparaiso, Indiana, home of Dodge's Institute of Telegraphy, one of the largest and best-known telegraph and railway instruction schools in the country. The telegraph was at that time vital to the communication system of the nation's railroads. And as one historian observed, "telegraphy was one of the first white-collar jobs where women could compete on a more or less equal basis with men."

By April 29, 1910—the date when a census taker came to your door—you were describing yourself as a "telegraph operator" and living on Main Street in the western Chicago suburb Downers Grove, my future hometown. In an issue of the *Chicago Tribune* from the following month, your name appeared in a story about women who worked in signal boxes—those little buildings along the tracks making possible the safe passage of trains. The work—until then performed by men—was, as the article put it, "the most lonely, the most arduous, and, to a woman at least, the most dangerous job known."

Often, you would have to stand a few feet from speeding loco- motives in order to pass documents to the men inside with a specially designed, hoop-shaped device, your face prickling with the rush of air, your nose filling with the smell of steam and oil, your long skirt lapping at the maelstrom of wheels. You worked the four-to-midnight shift at the box in nearby Western Springs, which the *Tribune* article described as "one of the most difficult posts" along the Chicago, Burlington and Quincy Railroad. Running the signal box all alone, you monitored traffic up and down the line and operated a series of mechanical semaphore signals that told trains whether to proceed, slow down, or stop.

I try to picture you in that box, rain rippling against the low- hanging roof, wind rattling the window, some lonely dog howling in the distance. You were thirty-one now, and you spent your nights in restless isolation, the stretches of dead silence shattered by the sudden pandemonium of passing trains, their roaring engines engulfing the tiny house in a cloud of white smoke. It must have been exhausting work, but if you or one of the other women "should become drowsy enough to drop her head down on the table in front of her a little too long some night . . . there might be a disaster," explained the *Tribune*.

That same issue of the paper—May 15, 1910—contained an article about how suffragists were planning a car tour through the state to drum up support for women's access to the ballot box. ("We want the men to be good to us just the same as ever and there isn't one of us who will pretend that she isn't afraid of a mouse," explained one organizer, "but we want to vote anyway.") I can't say whether you embraced the idea of gender equality, of course, but I do know that, intentionally or not, you were helping to bring about a radical change in the role of women—and that you must have had plenty of courage and pluck. Perhaps you agreed with the unnamed "signal girl" who told the *Tribune*: "The love of the trains gets into your blood. We feel like railroad men in that way. You know they will get disgusted and go away and think they are going to give up the job, but they always come back to it."

True, some of those railroad men "resent[ed] the invasion of women" into their ranks, as the paper explained. But at least one of them seems to have delighted in your company. Eight years your junior, he was a skinny, twenty-three-year-old farm boy from New Vienna, Iowa, with an outgoing spirit, gentle blue eyes, and a slightly misshapen nose, the result of being smacked in the face with a clarinet during some childhood horseplay. He lived just a block away from you in Downers Grove and, like you, was a telegrapher for the Chicago, Burlington and Quincy, a job that had already left him with a mangled right wrist, grazed by a speeding train as he stepped carelessly out of the signal box one day. By the time the *Tribune* article came out, he was in the habit of wrapping that maimed forearm around your waist and pulling you close. The following month, he would become your husband, and a few years later your widower, and long after that his picture would hang above the stairs of my home and my mother would point to it and say, "That's your grandfather." His name was Henry M. Kaut.

A railroad man always carried a pocket watch. Henry Kaut's timepiece—an elegant model with a double-sunk porcelain dial, stylish numbering, glimmering blue hands, and a gold-filled case— now hangs in a little glass-dome display case at my mother's house. It was manufactured by the Hampden Watch Company of Canton, Ohio, in 1913. Perhaps your husband bought it to mark the birth that year of Rankin Thomas "Tommy" Kaut, who, like his mother, would be doomed to die within months of his fortieth birthday.

The experience of time changed radically during your short life— a revolution driven by the telegraph and railroads. For much of the nineteenth century, Americans had kept time by the sun. Most towns and cities relied on a central clock tower, where a jeweler or amateur astronomer would fix the hour when the sun appeared directly overhead. This meant that when it was noon in Chicago, it was 12:19 in Columbus, 12:13 in Atlanta, 11:50 in St. Louis and 11:27 in Houston. By one estimate, the United States used some eight thousand of these local time conventions in the 1870s. Before the arrival of the telegraph and railroads, this "mess of hours," as one expert described it, hadn't mattered much. But now, with information and people shooting across vast distances at previously unimagined speeds, the lack of a coordinated time system was proving to be a logistical nightmare. In Pittsburgh, for instance, railway passengers, engineers, and employees had to contend with six different time standards for the arrival and departure of trains.

In the face of such chaos, the railroads took it upon themselves to rationalize time. Meeting in Chicago in 1883, representatives of the train companies agreed to divide the United States and Canada into four different time zones. This decision, wrote one expert, marked the moment "when the modern meaning of 'now' was legislated into existence." Another author called it "the most momentous development in the history of uniform, public time since the mechanical clock in the fourteenth century."

Although these zones did not yet have the force of law—Congress, in fact, would not enact a standardized-time bill until 1918—major U.S. cities quickly decided to get in sync with the railroads. From now on, everybody would be on the same clock. Time would be legalized, synchronized, metered, and global. In 1913, the year my grandfather's pocket watch was manufactured, the Eiffel Tower used a wireless telegraph to send out the first time signal to be transmitted around the world—a universal clock tower to replace the old local ones. That same year, the automobile magnate Henry Ford initiated his system of mass production, slashing the time it took to make a car from fourteen hours to just two.

The world was getting smaller, moving faster. Did you feel it picking up speed? The telephone was already replacing the telegraph, even at your own job on the Chicago, Burlington and Quincy Railroad. The experimental technology of radio was becoming a reality, thanks to the first wireless audio transmissions of music and the human voice. The airplane, invented only a few years earlier, had already "come to stay," in the words of a 1909 *Chicago Tribune* article, which predicted this new form of transportation would unleash "the most far-reaching revolution that has ever transformed the world."

Many more revolutions would follow, technological breakthroughs you could not have begun to imagine during your life, each one adding to the collective sense that there's no escape from the clock, that fast and faster and fastest are never fast enough. The TV, the PC, the Internet, cell phones, smartphones, social networks, tablets, tweets—life just keeps rushing ahead like a train shooting past some boarded-up old signal box as it races onto the plains, on and on until everything outside the windows becomes a blur, on and on until a passenger can begin to feel dizzy, disoriented, suddenly unsure of where he's headed or how the trip began.

This much I know: you had a big heart. In 1911, just a year after you married Henry Kaut, one of your three sisters came to you "in ill health, out of funds and in need of assistance," according to that biography in the court documents. She had a lung condition— tuberculosis, by all indications. You and your husband not only took her in and "accepted her as one of the family," but in 1914 you picked up and moved with her to Colorado on the advice of doctors, who in those days believed that mountain air helped treat lung diseases. Now the mother of an infant, you no longer worked as a telegrapher, but your husband still was with the Chicago, Burlington and Quincy, which agreed to transfer him to Denver.

Despite the change of climate, your sister's health continued to decline, and doctors advised that desert air might offer the cure that mountain air had failed to provide. So the whole family moved again—this time to Phoenix, where your husband found a position with the Atchison, Topeka and Santa Fe. But not even this new setting could help poor Minerva Thorpe, who passed away on October 6, 1918, at the age of thirty-eight. Henry Kaut boarded a train and accompanied your sister's body back to Illinois for the funeral, but you did not go with him. By that time, you, too, had fallen dangerously ill.

Dr. W. R. Harvey, 1849–1918; Jennie Harvey, 1855–1953; Wilber R. Harvey, 1886–1917; Benjamin Harvey, 1846–1933; Mary Jane Harvey, 1853–1934; Dorothy G. Harvey, 1906–1971; John E. Harvey, 1904–1969; Glen B. Harvey, 1907–1937; John Pierce Harvey, 1858–1914; Elizabeth, his wife, 1868–1938. As Carl Klendworth leads me to your grave, I see my own surname over and over on the tombstones. There's even the mysterious Mary J. Harvey, whose tombstone has no year of death (*1892–19___*) and whose grave apparently has no corpse. ("She's dead, all right, but she was never buried," Klendworth explains. "I don't know why.") Later I will learn that Mary J. and the other dead Harveys of Dana are not my direct relations. Still, the coincidence feels disconcerting. Or maybe it's not a coincidence at all. From that first day in the National Archives, this journey into your past has had a vague air of inevitability, as if I'm being swept along by some force beyond my control. For an agnostic like me, it's both unsettling and thrilling to feel myself under the spell of fate, everything around me pulsing with omens. My father died at sixty-one; if I follow in his path, I only have a decade left. And just in case I need another reminder that the end can swoop in at any time, here at my feet is the grave of little Newton S. Harvey, 1876–1877.

One-fifth of the world's population became sick during the great influenza epidemic of 1918, with an even higher percentage in the United States. The plague came in two waves. In the spring, a mild strain swept across much of the globe, causing fever, aches, and pains but relatively few deaths. The epidemic appeared to die out during the summer, only to return in autumn with a vengeance, the virus mutating into a killer. Many victims experienced high fever, chills, coughing fits, earaches, headaches, and agonizing pain in the joints. In some cases, they vomited blood; in others, it would suddenly spurt from their noses, ears, even eye sockets. Pockets of air would often accumulate beneath their skin, sometimes spreading over the whole body, as oxygen leaked from ruptured lungs. And as those lungs filled with a bloody froth, many patients turned blue as they drowned from inside—a horrifying final image for loved ones.

This second wave began on the east coast in early September 1918 and quickly shot west. It reached Arizona the same way you did: "along the silvered rails of the Santa Fe Railroad," as one writer put it. With their cramped and closed-off quarters, trains had become lethal vectors of disease. That same autumn, for example, the future novelist and literary critic Mary McCarthy, then six years old, boarded the Northern Pacific's North Coast Limited with her family, bound from Seattle to Minneapolis. Eight days later, both of her parents were dead.

Your sickness coincided with first reports of outbreaks in Arizona. Often the virus would kill its victims within days, or even hours. But for other patients, the infection would begin as an ordinary flu until the fourth or fifth day, when a sudden onset of pneumonia would leave them in a battle for survival. You hung on for weeks, long enough to hear church bells ring in the end of World War I, the Armistice having been signed at eleven o'clock on the eleventh day of the eleventh month of 1918.

Perhaps you were also aware of the panic that the flu unleashed in Phoenix, where a vigilante Citizens' Committee deputized a special police force to arrest those who spit or coughed without covering their mouths, as well as those who ventured out in public without a gauze mask. Soon Phoenix was "a city of masked faces, a city as grotesque as a masked carnival," observed the *Arizona Republican*. The situation only got more surreal as the weeks wore on. Spurred on by rumors that dogs spread the flu, police began killing all strays they found on the street. Soon normal citizens were taking guns to their own beloved pets. "At this death rate . . . Phoenix will soon be dogless," observed the *Arizona Gazette*.

The dogs, of course, had nothing to do with the disease—and unbeknownst to scientific experts at the time, the influenza virus was small enough to pass through a gauze mask. So the epidemic raged on, killing with its own confounding logic. "Ten people sit in the same draught, are exposed to the same microbes," one local physician observed. "Some will suffer and perhaps die, while others go scot free."

The confounded flu is on the loose again," Albert Einstein reported in October 1918. "It's uncannily rampant here." As you lay dying in Phoenix, the famous physicist was in Berlin, where thousands were succumbing to the disease.

Unlike most pandemics, which inflict their worst ravages on the very young and very old, the Great Influenza of 1918 attacked the healthiest part of the population. Young adults, ages twenty to forty,

were the most likely to die. Born the same year as you—1879—
Einstein too was in real danger of being struck down. But while people
close to him contracted the virus, he was, as he put it, "spared."

The great scientist would not have attributed his winning ticket
in this cataclysmic lottery to God's will. He did not, he once wrote,
believe in a deity who "concerns himself with the fate and doings of
mankind." Nonetheless, he refused to describe himself as an atheist,
insisting on the "lawful harmony" of the universe. "I see a clock," he
wrote, "but I cannot envision the clockmaker."

He had devoted his life to discovering the inner workings of that
clock. In 1905 he published a paper that would change our understanding of the nature of the universe. Prior to the theory of special
relativity, scientists and average people alike viewed time as absolute,
flowing on and on in an orderly and measurable way. But Einstein
argued that neither time nor space is absolute; how we perceive them
depends on where we are and how we move. To illustrate this idea,
the physicist Kip S. Thorne, author of *Black Holes and Time Warps:
Einstein's Outrageous Legacy*, employs the analogy of a speeding train:

> One can measure the Earth's velocity only *relative to other physical
> objects* such as the Sun or the Moon, just as one can measure a train's
> velocity only relative to physical objects such as the ground and the
> air. For neither Earth nor train nor anything else is there any standard
> of absolute motion; motion is purely "relative." . . .
>
> By rejecting absolute time, Einstein rejected the notion that
> everyone, regardless of his or her motion, must experience the flow
> of time in the same manner. *Time is relative*, Einstein asserted. Each
> person traveling in his or her own way must experience a different
> time flow than others, traveling differently.

Sometimes this idea staggers my brain, but today even the most
counterintuitive conclusion of Einstein's theory—that time runs

more slowly for fast-moving objects than for stationary observers—
seems simple and self-evident. I've only been on the road for a few
hours, and already I feel less frantic, lighter, as if I've managed to
outdistance some of my worries. As I was speeding through a huge
wind farm a while back, the giant blades spinning steadily, the road
stretching on and on, I could feel my body relaxing, my brain making
space for contemplation.

I once mentioned you to a Christian friend, a poet who writes
and speaks about God so beautifully I often feel envious of his
faith. When I asked him what he made of my fascination with your
story, he just laughed. "Do you hear the words you're using?" he
said. "You keep telling me this person died so that you could live.
That's the language of the cross. That's God's way of bringing you to
Christ."

If so, I'm still waiting to hear the call. Despite the unsettling
sense of fate that's haunted me since I stumbled upon you, my views
on religion remain close to those of Einstein: "I cannot conceive of a
personal God who would directly influence the actions of individuals,
or would directly sit in judgment on creatures of his own creation."
And yet for all that, this trip reminds me that the idea of rebirth has a
powerful hold on my imagination. It's been a long time since I got
out on my own like this, and I had almost forgotten the freedom that
comes with wandering country lanes, every fork in the road offering
a new adventure, a different chance at the future. It makes me nostalgic for bygone days—before I had a mortgage to cover and kids to
take to school and office hours to keep for my students and prescrip-
tions to pick up for my mother—when I could just climb in the car
and speed off, intoxicated with the idea, however illusory and fleeting,
that if I drove far and fast enough anything was possible.

Mr. Kaut arrived with the body from Arizona on Sunday night,"
reported the local paper on January 10, 1919. No doubt he brought

you home on the Santa Fe Railroad, just as he had done with your sister's corpse a few months earlier. The funeral took place at the house of your sister, Addie—the future grandmother of my guide. A quartet performed music, and the Reverend W. H. Love delivered a eulogy. Then the mourners made their way to the cemetery where I now stand, pallbearers lowering you into the ground.

The widowed man did not stay in town for long. Explaining that he had to return to his job as a telegrapher and chief clerk in the Phoenix office of the Santa Fe, he headed back across the country, likely aboard another train—leaving your motherless five-year-old in the care of the boy's Aunt Addie.

I sometimes picture him on that train, staring out the window at night, the car rocking grimly, the lights from some town splashing across his face before shadows overtake him again. And the train rushes on, deeper and deeper into the great dark void of the American West and his own grief.

"Now there would be time for everything." When I try to imagine what he must have been thinking then, I remember that haunting final line of *Pale Horse, Pale Rider*, Katherine Anne Porter's novella about the 1918 epidemic, in which the protagonist recovers from a serious case of the flu only to learn that it has taken the life of her lover. All her plans, her dreams, her obligations have suddenly vanished. What awaits her is only an awful emptiness, "the dead cold light of tomorrow."

Perhaps my grandfather believed that westbound train could outrace his anguish. Perhaps he planned to start over, leave every reminder of you behind, even his own son. But it didn't work. In Phoenix, as his biography would later note, he was haunted by "unpleasant memories." So after eight months he came back to Illinois, reclaimed his boy, and set about the business of living life. A couple of years later, he returned to Downers Grove, where he fell in love again, married, and had another child (an accident, it appears: the girl was born six months after the wedding). In this new version of his future, the one that did not include you, he experienced many heartbreaks and hardships—not least, fourteen months in federal prison, after which he struggled to find work during the worst days of the Great Depression. But he was welcomed home by the members of his community, hundreds of whom—including the mayor, four members of the city council, and six directors of the bank from which he was convicted of embezzling—had petitioned the judge not to send him to jail. His new wife, Lucille, never wavered in her love or support for him, and the years that followed were filled with countless quiet moments of happiness—long drives in the country with his family in a used Model A Ford; Sunday afternoons with his daughter at Comiskey Park, watching the great Ted Lyons pitch for the White Sox; lazy summer evenings on the front porch with the woman he loved and a pipe full of tobacco, the song of cicadas, and the rumble of passing trains. I'm told that when he died in 1947 he counted himself a very lucky man.

His daughter would mourn his passing and then mourn again when her half brother Tommy died of heart failure in 1953. But she too would get on with life, falling in love with a baby-faced World War II vet named Robert Harvey, whom she married in 1955. Like her father, she would move west, where she would have one son, then come home to Downers Grove, where she would have another (an accident, as well: failed birth control). And one day, half a lifetime later, that second child, now with children of his own, would happen upon your name in a yellowed and forgotten document and suddenly wonder about his place in the world. And then he would visit your grave in search of answers.

But of course there are no answers, no epiphanies, no ghosts—just a silent hunk of red granite.

It's late afternoon when I take my leave from Carl Klendworth.

We usually think of time "as if it were a straight railway line on which one could only go one way or the other," wrote the physicist Stephen Hawking in *A Brief History of Time*. "But what if the railway line had loops and branches so that a train could keep going forward but come back to a station it had already passed? In other words, might it be possible for someone to travel into the future or the past?"

If I could board such a train, I would purchase a ticket to Dana, Illinois, circa 1905.

I've never even seen a picture of you, but in a town of no more than three hundred people, you wouldn't be hard to find. Perhaps someone would point you out to me as you sat on a bench in front of the general store, a young woman in a shirtwaist blouse and trumpet skirt taking a rest from the August heat. You would still be living at home, caring for your dying mother. Your dreams would still be in front of you.

Maybe it would be enough simply to lay eyes on you. Maybe my urge to seek you out across the ages finally would be satisfied. Maybe I'd turn around and catch the next train back to the twenty-first century.

Or maybe I'd stroll over to the general store.

In physics, there's something called the grandfather paradox. Einstein's theory of general relativity—the second of his landmark papers that redefined the universe, published in 1916—makes backward time travel at least hypothetically possible. But what would end up happening if we could actually journey into the past? As the grandfather paradox illustrates, that's a confounding question.

Suppose a man builds a time machine. He travels back to the day before his biological grandfather and biological grandmother slept with each other for the first time. The two men get into a fight, and the grandson kills the grandfather. That means one of the time traveler's parents would never have been conceived, which means the traveler and his time machine would not exist.

Now consider a different version of the grandfather paradox. Suppose a man travels back to a time before his grandfather's first wife fell ill, before they met, before she even left her hometown. He finds her sitting on a bench in front of the general store. Suppose she is bored enough on a slow, sweltering afternoon to share some small talk with a stranger wearing a straw boater hat.

Suppose they start to gossip about the headlines—President Theodore Roosevelt's latest efforts to end the Russo-Japanese war, or the crackdown on gambling houses in Chicago, or the deadly outbreak of yellow fever in Louisiana, or the scandalous cream-colored bathing costumes that women have been spotted wearing in Atlantic City, outfits the *Chicago Tribune* describes as "practically . . . transparent." Suppose the conversation slowly turns to personal matters, as sometimes happens between strangers with time on their hands. Suppose the man jokes about his eight-year-old boy's obsession with baseball, a passion passed down, generation to generation, from the maternal grandfather whom the man never met. Suppose he brags about his twelve-year-old daughter, who gets her middle name, along with her sharp mind, gentle spirit, and big ears, from her great-grandmother Lucille.

Suppose the man finds that he can't stop talking, that he needs the woman to know all about himself. Suppose he's not sure why. Does he want her approval? Her advice? Her forgiveness? Suppose he tells her the story of how he met his wife, a long and convoluted tale that all his friends have heard a hundred times, about how he loved Rengin Altay from the minute he saw her at a party in Bloomington, Illinois; how her black eyes haunted him for years though he rarely crossed her path; and how a series of unlikely coincidences and chance meetings at a laundry in Chicago finally brought them together.

Suppose the woman says, Sounds like destiny.

And the man says, I wish I could believe in destiny. The thing is that if you change a couple of random and tiny events, my life would be completely different.

And the woman says, But if you're happy, why does it matter?

And the man says, Because, among other things, it bothers me to think that my life is something that has *happened* to me rather than a narrative of my own making.

And the woman says, Do you have a penny?

Suppose the man reaches into his pocket and to his surprise pulls out a freshly minted 1905 Indian-head cent piece. Suppose he's admiring the face of Lady Liberty in her feathered headdress when the woman rises quietly and takes the coin from him, her fingertips sliding softly across his open palm.

Suppose the woman says, I am not very lucky in life so far. I have neither a husband to love nor children, and I am stuck in this suffocating town. Since you seem to be so bothered by your own good fortune, let's make a wager. Heads, you'll keep your luck; tails, you'll get mine and I'll take yours.

Suppose that before the man can say a word, she flips the coin high into the air. Suppose that it rises slowly, then seems to hang there, the spinning copper glimmering in the fierce sunlight.

"God does not play dice," Albert Einstein famously declared. In his view, everything in the cosmos came down to cause and effect. There was no room for chance. That's why Einstein had trouble accepting the discoveries of quantum mechanics—a field of science he helped to create—which describes the behavior of atoms and their constituents. He could never quite trust evidence that the world of subatomic particles is chaotic and unpredictable, a place where events in the present and future are not entirely determined by the past.

But it turns out that, for once, Einstein was apparently wrong. In this case, God does play dice. And it's precisely the capriciousness of those dice that may offer an answer to the grandfather paradox. Quantum mechanics opens the possibility that although human beings are only ever aware of one world, the particles that make up that world may exist in multiple universes at once. According to one interpretation of quantum theory, when two subatomic particles collide, slamming off each other like a pair of rolled dice, one of those particles does not simply go left or right. It goes left into one universe or right into a *completely different universe*. This means "it may be possible to go back in time and change the past," writes the noted physicist Michio Kaku.

> However, at that point another quantum universe opens up, and time "forks" into two rivers, each one leading to a new universe. For example, if we go back in time to save Abraham Lincoln at the Ford Theater, then in one universe Lincoln is saved and the direction of time is altered. However, the universe you came from is unchanged. Your past cannot be altered. You have merely saved the life of a quantum double of Lincoln in a quantum parallel universe.

So suppose we are standing there, you and I, shielding our eyes as an Indian-head penny slices through the thick August air. We keep watching, but it does not come down.

And I say, That's inexplicable.

And you say, So many things are like that.

And for a long while we stare silently at that tiny copper star.

And then you sigh and shrug and say, It has been pleasant to meet you, but I'm afraid I can't remain here all day. My mother is ill and I need to get back to her.

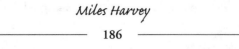
And we linger for a few moments more, talking about the limbo of watching a loved one leave the world, the way time eddies around the sick person, death moving slow while life rushes on.

And you say, Now I really must go. Perhaps we can settle our bet on some other afternoon.

And far above us, the penny spins, heads, tails, heads, tails, glimmering with possibility.

That night, on the drive back to Chicago, I find myself stuck at a rural railway crossing. A freight train rolls slowly past, lumbering on and on until the final car rolls into view. Then, still stretched through the crossing, it stops and sits, as if catching its breath. After a long wait, the train begins to crawl the opposite way, boxcar after boxcar after boxcar rattling through until the locomotive reappears. Then it stops again. From the dark, railroad workers emerge with flashlights and examine something along the tracks—a malfunctioning switch, perhaps—their shouts drowned out by the incessant ring of the crossing bell.

Ten minutes pass, then fifteen, then twenty. On the lonely two-lane road, a long line of cars forms. Some peel away and speed off in the direction from which they came, but I'm in no rush. After leaving your grave, I hung around Dana, stopping at the Gold Dust Diner to sample the catfish plate before returning to the cemetery so that I could kiss the tips of my fingers and press them to the polished granite that bears your name. By the time I left town, the sun had started to set, hanging over the ruins of Dana Township High School like a giant red wrecking ball.

Now a clear night sky looms overhead, planets spinning, stars forming and imploding, the universe feverishly expanding. And beyond all that, perhaps, other universes come and go as well; every-thing that exists and can possibly exist swirls around out there in the dark. But here, in the middle of nowhere, nothing moves. The crossing bell drones on and the White Sox game plays softly, hypnotically on the radio. Then, as if awakening from a trance, the locomotive groans into motion. The switch, it seems, has been fixed; the journey can proceed. I watch that train rumble off into the night—then the gate lifts, the road opens, and once again I'm carried away by time, racing toward home.

The Place Between

Jivin Misra

We hit a bump. I lose a dream to the road, or at least what the locals refer to as a road but I know to be a strip of dirt. The driver, pressing his weight against the squeaking brakes, curses as beggars crowd the windows—hordes of them, shoving and yelling, drawn by the promise painted on the side of the van (a garish, gold label that reads TOURIST VEHICLE).

My eyes meet those of a woman who is cradling an emaciated baby. She wipes tears, real or performed, and then touches her hands to her lips, signing for food. I shrug, the timid gesture meant to articulate that we cannot really help her, as there would not be enough money in my mother's fanny pack, let alone in her bank account, to save all these beggars of bone. We give her rupees anyway, if not to assuage guilt or falsely relieve pity, then to rid ourselves of the nuisance. It doesn't work. The woman snags the money and runs as other beggars fill her absence, this time a charming young child, next time, assuming they stick to the line (which they won't), a leper. I see the woman in the distance now being heckled too.

A man pushes her, she falls, the baby cries, and, in the haven of the van, I turn away, forcing my mind to lesser anxieties such as the condition of our engine that clicks as if it has been borrowed from a lawn mower. What if it failed? Would we really have to walk among these people? There are so many of them, and so many dogs and cows and monkeys roaming about—hungry, hairy, and diseased—as if they too could be citizens of Varanasi.

Raghao, our guide of twenty-four, swings the sliding door of the van, the sound of cheap plastic brushing against its horizontal counterpart becoming less and less audible as it opens further, sinking beneath the racket and the dust. He motions me out of the car, yelling over the squabbling beggars, "We walk. Here, no vehicles beyond."

"Oh. Why is that?" I ask.

"No." He nods in the affirmative.

Helpless, I convince myself that his response is sufficient before my family and I follow him blindly into the depths of the congested city. Motorbikes—like fish darting through anemones—each driven by a man with another man's hands at his hips, part the crowd, and whenever he gets the chance, Raghao leads us behind them so that they can do the aggressive clearing work for us (a trick that the others in the crowd don't seem to catch, although perhaps this is because they lack our impulse to escape).

"Wallet out of back pocket, yes?" Raghao asks (or instructs?). It is not, and although I'm afraid of having it stolen in the time it will take to switch pockets, I do as he says, only to learn that extraneous movement is best left to those in familiar surroundings: distracted by the fumbling of my wallet, I step in a pile of shit. I can tell that, luckily, it's not from a human, judging by its towering height and the ashamed expression on a nearby bull.

"This is bullshit! Where is our driver? Mom! Did we not pay for a driver?!" I exclaim, scuffing my shoe in the dirt and hoping that Raghao's ears, despite their low capacity for comprehension, are out of reach. My mother grabs my arm and pulls me aside.

"We cannot bring a car into the holy city. It's a rule. Don't ask why. Whatever answer you're looking for won't satisfy you. Stop complaining, focus, and walk."

And then, not so much from her uncharacteristically stern tone or the military officers who shove us aside or the decapitated dog in the middle of the road, but either from the totality of Varanasi's severity or, more likely, some stimulus unplaceable as a ghost, I finally feel it, the gravity of our task: we each have a role to play as we venture closer to the Ganges River. With Raghao leading us through the labyrinthine alleys, Drisana, my older sister, keeps us close to the streetwise guide so we don't lose him when playing children cut across us or a camel kicks up the dust; Hans, my younger brother, surveys the ground for the spatterings of bile and animal dung, which are everywhere; I fend off the beggars, who are also everywhere, prodding us for attention and cash; and my mother—my mother carries, in her steady hands, the package that contains the ashes of my father.

❖

My father was the kind of traveler who was always behind a camera. As a result, we have very few photos of him. He would tell me that his own father treasured photographs and would scold him for wasting film (this continued, for some reason, even after entering the digital age). But my father was not like his own; when he came to America and his withheld photographic aspirations were finally released, he quickly matured into a proper amateur photographer, shooting shoddy pictures at every turn. It was always such a bother when I was a boy and all he wanted to do was take pictures of the places to which we traveled and all I wanted to do was get off the boring, historic streets, return to the hotel room, and sleep.

In selecting the objects he would attempt to capture, my father was particular. When he was mindful enough to remove the cap, it was only monuments and natural scenes that blurred through his half-focused lens, only the accomplishments of humanity and the casualties of those accomplishments—never humanity itself. Once when I was fifteen, my family traveled to Paris but, with good reason, never returned to the city. On the first day, my siblings and mother yielded to their jet-lagged bodies while my father and I went out alone to appreciate the bleak and austere Eiffel Tower. When we arrived, my father whipped out his camera, took more than a few pictures, and, after growing unsatisfied with the backdrop of Parisian gloom, handed the machine to me. Minutes passed, and both of us became so engrossed in the picture-taking process—in trying to capture that postcard moment—that by the time we realized we had ventured into the bike lane, it was too late. The rider crashed into my father and, to the amusement of his cruel countrymen, tumbled across the pavement. He jolted up, marched over, yelling a furious string of words in French, and raised his fist at his equally uninjured victim. He meant to hurt us, it appeared to me, though my father knew it to be a show, laughing at the angry biker until he pedaled off. I wish I had taken a picture to mark this occasion. Instead I took thousands of that glorified cell tower, all alike, replicable, existing in the memory cards of almost every camera that has ever been lugged abroad.

We are halted in the crowd because a street vendor has spilled a crate of cabbages, rousing the nearby cows. While my mother and Raghao help the man salvage his goods, my sister tells me that I should use this opportunity and take pictures. Uninterested in the muddled cabbage scene, I look through the viewfinder at a sore-ridden boy who is tossing stones at a wall. He stops and attends my lens with clouded red eyes, and my sister mentions that he looks like I did when I was a child. Unfazed, he continues throwing the stones. My finger twitches over the button. I try. I sigh. I turn off the camera and put it in a bag, which I hand to Raghao for safekeeping. As we resume walking, I imagine the untaken photograph. It could have been so striking, with proper cropping to remove less meaningful objects from the frame. But what meaning could it even designate, this wall and its battering? The boy's sickly eyes revise themselves in my mind for the sake of sympathy, and I wonder if my father would have taken that picture, if a childhood in India had left him sufficiently numb to such objectification.

✦

Created by Lord Shiva, the Destroyer, Varanasi is the oldest city in the world, locals insist, a plane between this world and the next. It is the place where the living come to die and the dead await their coming lives. Some souls, they believe, when laid to rest in Varanasi, can break from the relentless cycle of reincarnation and achieve salvation (*moksha*). And so, in keeping with the tradition of his people, we bring my father's ashes to the Ganges to give him a chance at transcendence.

Having left the chaos of the city center, we walk with less caution in our steps. Hans, who suffers from obsessive-compulsive disorder, grabs his ankles to survey the soles of his shoes.

They're not as soiled as he expected. Still he decides that, upon returning to the hotel, all of us should dispose of our shoes, for we cannot know what substances, or what apparitions of previous substances, we have trampled.

As he rambles, the river comes into view—Mother Ganga, they call it, in a tone that holds more affection than reverence. Tourists, bathers, and quiet mourners from all corners of the world stroll along the holy, fetid bank. I see priests, boys studying to become priests, and skeletal old men with painted faces (*sadhu*) who Raghao says sit around all day, just waiting for death. My sister points out a laundry servant (*dhobi wallah*) whipping soaked bedsheets against the dock, as if to straighten them, or spank out the parasites; the water, which apparently contains enough fecal matter to blind crocodiles, flings into her eyes. She doesn't blink.

Raghao sends a text message to the priest who will lead our ceremony (*puja*), informing him that we will be waiting at Vijayanagaram ghat. Hans notices this name on the banner hanging over the steps and, though denouncing it as awkwardly long, he finds, embedded within it, one name that we can actually pronounce—our father's: Vijay, meaning Victory. Raghao translates another sign for us: "Knees and elbows must be covered for all religious sites." He laughs and, in what I assume to be an attempt to lighten our spirits, jokes that we could technically run around wearing nothing but knee and elbow patches. Hans says that would be less than sanitary . . . Silence. As if only to pass the time, Raghao finally asks our names; he boasts that he can guess the meaning of them all.

"Jivin," I say.

The silence resumes.

"Oh, Jeevan!—Life! Means life!" Yes. Life. Like many Hindi words, my first name means life, my middle, the same. Life Life Misra. It seems a name fit for anything that is born in this world, life does, and apparently so fit for me that I am called it twice. The name game continues for a while, and, despite being in the country of their origin, the exchanges are surprisingly awkward: "Drisana" is misheard as "Drishna," "Kristina," "Douche-ana," and so on. Ironically, my mother's name is the only one he recognizes immediately: "Mary! Jesus's mother from Bible story! If you is Jesus's mother and Jeevan is

Mary's son—is you Jesus, Jeevan?" Raghao jokes, unaware that, perhaps more so than other men who were raised Catholic, I have often entertained fantasies about being Jesus, fueled by the possibility of resurrection that my name, Lifelife, connotes.

It was my Catholic mother, Mary, who named me Jivin Josh, my sister Drisana Ruchi (daughter of the sun), and my brother Hans Kirtan (swan wearing a crown)—Indian names, all of them . . . Two spelled incorrectly. She didn't know any better, nor did my father, who, despite being a Brahmin, never learned Sanskrit, and who, according to his family, forgot how to speak Hindi after his years in America. Often it even seemed that he had forgotten the gods (although who could blame him, given that there are thirty-three million of them), telling my inquisitive sister to go to his siblings with her questions about Hinduism. But because we rarely spoke to his siblings, it was our mother who told us the stories of Brahma and Saraswati, Vishnu and Lakshmi, Shiva and Parvati, Krishna and Radha, Surya and Saranyu. Ganesha. Hanuman. It was from her that we learned of the gods, at least these primary ones, and their various emblems—Shiva's trident, Brahma's swan, Vishnu's conch shell—which serve both as tools for distinction and gateways to allegory . . .

❖

In the braids of Lord Shiva, the immortal Ganga flows. There are many stories about how she got there, most of them too convoluted for me to understand. My favorite explains that, on Ganga's descent from the Himalayas, she became entangled in Shiva's matted hair and stayed there, situated above his third eye, because she loved him. She was there when he used this eye to burn Desire and smear its ashes all over his body. And because she was there, she could see that, despite his efforts, the lord still desired—not her, since no god, save one of tautology, desires immortality. In her place, Shiva desired the goddess Parvati, so much so that through his desire he found love and, through his love, he and Parvati fused into one (the lord who is half woman).

Hans chuckles at the lone breast that Shiva, rendered in graffiti, bares on the city wall for all who row to see. But Ganga will not be stirred; when Shiva joined with Parvati, Ganga married Shantanu, a great king, and drowned seven of their sons at birth. The Immortal was freeing them, freeing them from her unmoving waves, from the inertia of the world . . .

❖

A black sedan stalled amid the commotion of the Hyderabad airport, awaiting the arrival of my parents, who, within six months of meeting, despite the hopes of my father's family to arrange a marriage between him and a nice Indian woman from a nice Indian family, had eloped. Now it was time for my mother to face the consequences of that decision. As the family excitedly greeted my father, my mother, who didn't understand their language, realized that for the remainder of her stay, or perhaps even longer, the distance between her and her in-laws would persist. But she didn't expect the distance between her and her new husband to grow.

After a series of reluctant handshakes and half-acknowledging nods, the moment came to get on the road. My father and his siblings piled in the backseats and their parents occupied the front, leaving my mother nowhere to sit. Upon noticing his wife, abandoned outside the vehicle, my father reemerged. His mother soon followed and directed her new daughter-in-law to the trunk, where she was to be stuffed with the luggage.

"Try not to worry, love . . . You'll be fine . . . The roads may look rough but they're safe enough," my father said. "My brothers and I would ride to school each day—all three of us on one motorcycle . . .

You'll be fine!" He shut the rear door. The exhaust rose over his fearful face, forming a veneer of reassurance that my mother and Shiva and Parvati, and anyone with willing eyes, could see as false. But how could he object to his family? He had already gone against their will by marrying a Puerto Rican Catholic. One more defiance and who knows if they would ever even talk to him again. He had no choice, he reasoned as the crowded car bumped along the ever-shifting rickshaw jigsaw, the jumping baggage bruising my mother's pale, white arms.

I was amused upon hearing this story and assumed that my mother was being histrionic in her depiction of the horrors of India. Across the dining table, the shame on my father's face seemed undeserved. But then I saw the alleged highway where children walk and oxen dwell and rackety eighteen-wheelers propel their weight ahead. I saw the chaotic frolic, the dance to some rhythm that only the locals appear to know—the influx of modernism, the cars and trucks lugging resources to some anonymous factory, never bothering the barber under the bridge or the monkey juggling apples, never bothering the camel in the teashop or the roadside robber, never taming them as they can never tame that river by which they wilt and thrive.

❖

After waiting by the ghat for half an hour, ignoring stares from European travelers, Muslim women, and passing beggar boys who can't quite figure out if we are mourners or tourists, we finally notice a man in a red silk robe approaching from the riverside huts. This, I figure, is the priest.

Accompanying him is another man whom I assume to be an assistant of sorts. Judging by the enviable thickness of his mustache, the assistant is much older than me. He wears casual clothes and a black beanie that reads, in a decidedly overstated font, "COOL." Slung over his shoulder, he is lugging a plastic bag that contains, I will come to learn, the objects that the priest plans to use in our ceremony: metal bowls, jars of spices, flour, and oxidized utensils, all clanging along with the casual pace of their bearer.

The priest greets us with a smile as the assistant wipes his nose on his sleeve, oblivious to the fact that the bag is tearing. Watching him, Hans wonders where the fabled graceful women are. "You know," he asks, "the ones who balance fruit baskets on their heads?"

With a clunky immediacy, the priest points to the box of ashes in my mother's arms. "Who this?" he asks. There is a pause. The question is uncomfortable. This is not anybody. This is a box. It had been tucked away on a closet shelf for a year and a half. At this point, it would require too much imaginative work to consider that its gray, particulate contents were once my father, or the body that contained him.

The priest looks over our group, does some mental arithmetic, and arrives at the solution:

"Oh—father," he realizes, "so sorry for loss." He takes the bag from the assistant and begins assembling the bowls on a rug by the ghats. "Sorry," the assistant chimes in, a soggy cigarette now dangling from his lips, "so, so sorry."

The lack of sincerity in their voices doesn't bother me. In the time since my father has passed, I have heard many kinds of condolences, enough to become numb to them all. And the people of Varanasi have witnessed many kinds of torments, grief being only one of them, and one that they believe to be detrimental to the parting soul when prolonged beyond the customary thirteen-day allotment for mourning.

When the bowls, candles, and spices are all in their proper places, we begin chanting together, the priest and I, the eldest son and thus the so-called chief mourner (my mother and sister and brother watch, silent next to our guide). My fingertips coated with turmeric and flour and my forehead decorated with saffron and sweat, I attempt to mimic the man's foreign cadence and, while reciting the name of my father and his father and his father's father, I stumble on all the ancient words whose foreign music blisters my tongue in a way that is both painful and exciting, awkward and beautiful; the exercise possesses me to the point of having almost forgotten the two young boys in front of me, playing cricket over the rotting carcass of a man . . .

"Be wary of the priests," said the cab driver who took us from the airport to the hotel in Delhi, "they're going to try to take advantage of you." I'll be okay, I thought. What power can a priest have over a nonbeliever? "The citizens of Varanasi survive on death," he continued. "Death is their business. They may call themselves holy men, but truly—they are bottom-feeders." The driver chewed his bubble-gum, and he and his Ganesha bobblehead, in unison, bobbed along to the static-laden radio song.

I remember this warning as the ceremony continues, for although he is speaking a different language, I can tell that this priest, who markets himself as the most renowned in all of India, is improvising. He stumbles, repeats phrases, and pauses, struggling to remember what comes next. Suddenly, he yells something at his assistant, who is smoking with a friend by the river. Then, a lighter comes flying our way. It smacks into my nose. The priest points to it (now resting in the mud between my folded legs), hands me a stick of incense, and demands, "Light it." I can't. He rolls his eyes and does it for me.

"Now, spin this," he says, pointing to the incense stick, "'round this." He directs me to an old dry lear onto which I had previously sprinkled an array of spices. I do as he says, or so I think. "No, no! Other direction!"

Watching from afar, the assistant puts out his cigarette, runs over, grabs my hands, and moves them in a way that I apparently could not—not without his hands, covered in abscesses, ghosting mine.

"Is there a point to this?" Hans interrupts. "Does it mean anything? What does it all mean?"

The assistant hushes him while the priest begins humming the holy syllable "*om*," which, like much else in Hindu theology, has so many meanings that it seems to mean everything and nothing at once. Hans would later ask me, in private, how much of our encounter with the priest was ritual and how much of it was scam, and I would later tell him to consider that the two evolved simultaneously and thus prove difficult to parse. What he means to ask is how much of this scam was institutionalized. That's the kind we both prefer, the kind we're used to, the kind we know how to mistrust.

About an hour into the frenzied whiplash of a ritual, a girl, no older than three or four, jiggles her little legs over to the assistant, pulls down her burlap diaper, squats, and, next to his neon flip-flops, releases her bowels. I try not to laugh, but I reason that if she didn't have to hold in her excrement, then I don't have to hold in my laughter, and so I don't. I laugh—not at the strained look on her face, but at the situation: this is the place where I am about to lay to rest my father's ashes. I might as well be flushing them down a toilet. My mother gives me a scolding look, and I immediately regret my outburst. I imagine my father walking by the murky river among the wearied people, and I realize that my view of Varanasi is reductive. There is something more here, an importance so undeniable that even I can feel it, despite my inability to fully register it. It permeates the temples, which were erected at a time so long ago that only a god could fathom the distance, and I see it in the people too, who continue eluding me as I try, again and again, to unfold those stubborn first layers of their being.

✦

One night as a child, I wanted to ask my mother a question. What this question was, I no longer recall. It must have been important though, since it pressed me to seek her out, despite my bedtime having passed. Her room was empty, and the lights were off. The red glow of the heat lamp crept out from under the bathroom door. That's where she was, I assumed, so I opened the door. Suddenly, everything felt unfamiliar. Thick mist wafted into my face, and the rhythm of the shower water washed over my mind as I followed the exhaust's monk-like drone to a figure, kneeling on a rug, illuminated in red, reflecting endlessly in opposing mirrors. As I neared, the encircling haze cleared, revealing my father, who was wearing nothing but a white string (*janeo*) around his torso while he chanted:

> asato mā sadgamaya
> tamasomā jyotir gamaya
> mrityormāamritam gamaya
> Oṁ śhānti śhānti śhāntiḥ

> [From ignorance, lead me to truth
> From darkness, lead me to light
> From death, lead me to immortality
> Om peace, peace, peace]

"What does it mean?" I interrupted.

Startled, he sprung for his towel and growled, "I don't know—I just say it—Don't worry about it—Why are you up this late?—Go to sleep!"

In bed, I tried to understand why he refused to tell me about this ritual. Surely he should have, if it were important, if it concerned life and death and whatever comes next . . . Could it really be that he didn't know the meaning of the chant? Why would he chant something he didn't understand? What would be the point? I fell asleep on the assumption that ritual was just a compulsion to him, a licking of some incessantly festering wound.

After he died, I returned to that bedroom, searching once again for an answer, this time to a vague and unanswerable question. Rummaging through his closet, I found, in one of his jacket pockets, a small booklet, the cover of which depicted Hanuman, the god of strength.

As I opened it, a picture slipped out. It was my Baptism portrait.

Confused, I brought it to my mother. Why didn't he ever teach me about his beliefs? He was trying to protect me, she explained. But from what? I loved him, and I knew that he loved me, but he always felt so distant, so emotionally absent that I couldn't understand why I was in so much pain now that he was gone . . .

Somehow, despite its wavelessness, the river rocks the boat. Many blame the oars, fewer, the wavelessness.

✦

We watch the sun descending as the pyres, the thousands of pyres lit like incense sticks, pullulate a blanket of smoke. We inhale the miasma, the holy decay. In the midst of that scent, the excrement, the coals, synthetic silks, and chai, we approach the river that flows from heaven into earth and from earth into hell. Carefully, we enter one of the many wooden boats along the banks and are taken.

My mind drifting between formless dreams, I look over the city, mostly obscured under fog, and smoke from the cremation ghat (Manikarnika ghat) where, amid stacks of lumber, beside the mourners who amble through scorched land like dispirited ghosts, our priest and his assistant wait. One of them, now a mere silhouette, grabs a handful of ash and releases it into the wind. Raghao says that, at the cremation ghat, bodies burn all day and night. One flame, he says, has been burning since Shiva founded Varanasi, and is kept burning by generations of dutiful priests.

As we pass the ghat, I notice a stained stone wall. This is from the tide, I learn, which swells unpredictably, at any time. When Ganga's waters rise, it is said they eclipse everything known—first the ghats, of which there are nearly a hundred, followed by the markets (and the rumpled strays that wander there, awaiting rotting spoils), until finally they reach over the rooftops of temples—Hindu, Buddhist, Baha'i, and Jain (and mosques and churches too).

Although she sits for days, drowning her worshipers and destroying their homes, eventually Ganga's waters drain. Though damaged, the ancient walls and prayer halls remain.

Mother Ganga conceals this violence well. Her placid expanse is only interrupted by external forces—the diving of fowls and the cutting of oars and the washing of clothes and the bathing of pilgrims and the tossing of corpses unfit for cremation (lepers, children, pregnant women). She appears to move by no volition of her own. But Raghao reveals otherwise, disclosing that beneath her tempered surface, she blinds the creatures she houses, dolphins and crocodiles alike, with a poison that Raghao believes the goddess brews to protect them. Ganga always protects, he says. This poison, of course, is waste from the four hundred million people who live at Ganga's banks.

To prevent Hans from making any obvious objections, I kick his leg, causing the water to bleed into the boat. He shrieks as it collects beneath my feet, the only feet required to be bare.

"Boy, no scream! Mother's water is good, is purify," the boatman says.

"Not for the dolphins," Hans mumbles.

"I prove to you, boy," Raghao says. "Jeevan, will you bathe in Mother Ganga?"

Bathe in it—like the woman I see, nude, next to the floating cow body?

"Later perhaps, when it isn't so windy," I reply.

To relax, Raghao removes his shoes and dips his feet in the river. I ask him about his suppurated soles and he explains that, for his gods, he participates in an annual race through the city, barefooted in the manure and the ash and the cold dry dirt. Usually, the race leaves him "hurting and paining," he says. I ask him what the purpose of this ritual is. He says he cannot explain it in English. I struggle to maintain a nonjudgmental expression. There is a pause. Looking at my bare, unblistered feet, he observes, "Western life—good life."

"It is a city of many names," Raghao continues, his words trailing off into the disjointed Wikipedia facts that he had memorized to repeat, word for word, to each of his unknowing customers. It is a city of many names, as are many cities that have seen so much. But most others are not still called by their prior titles by foreigners and locals alike. Raghao doesn't know why that is or from where the names (Varanasi, Banares, Banaras, Kashi, Anandavana) came.

It is a city of many names where many names go when they cease to be—only the so-called worthiest of them to the part of Ganga that flows through Varanasi. Unlike this river of names, which carries, to eternity, the ashes of all, my veins are flooded with the blood of one name, my father's. It is apparent in the way that I quiver on this boat, not from the frigid winds or the rotting lumber nearly splintering my sole but from nervousness, the way he did but always tried to hide. Physicians say these nerves, which clustered in his blood and flowed into mine, might kill me too.

From across the boat, my sister grabs my ankle. She has, in her hands, a packet of antibacterial wipes which she uses, against my will (or, rather, my desire to be considerate), to clean my feet. Raghao and the boatman stare.

"You're offending them," my mother whispers; this is their god that graces my toes.

"So let them be offended," my sister replies. I would pull away, but I know she would just grab me again.

These are the habits my father instilled. He too was excessively hygienic, I remember as I pan the miscellaneous trash that mars the banks. How he could have survived in India with that trait, I have no idea. That must be why he came to the United States. His siblings explain it differently; for all his rationality, my father was fascinated by myth, perhaps more so by cowboys than Pandavas. Cowboys are what brought him to the west, they say, and he brought the Misras with him . . . Those cowboys must have carried him on the mightiest of stallions, the kind that misrepresent what it is to be a horse. My father wasn't naive. He must have known that he was better off with the pandavas; he must have known that an immigrant has no place in an American cowboy myth. It was fear that brought him to cross the world and leave this place—fear of filth, fear of sickness, fear of death.

The other side of Ganga is a grayed and level plain. No one seems to live there. From afar, it appears obscurely tranquil, foreign in a way that is unhuman—so unlike the foreignness of the opposing cityscape, whose jagged buildings mimic the flour-filled ridges of my fingers and palm. And in the face of all the city's clatter, the plain somehow abides, and in its withstanding evokes God or gods or something (maybe nothing). The land appears cold, as if on the verge of ice, and the waters there fade away, elusive like air, insistent like stone. I see the fog flowing over and the boats in the distance fading too, into another world, I almost want to believe.

Keep rowing, Charon,
slowly, to the rhythm of sorrow,
but do not let us cry,
for tears can encumber the parting soul
halting his swim to salvation,
anchoring him into another body,
only to suffer and love again.
Keep rowing, Charon,
and we will be rowed.

Suddenly, the rowing stops. "Now put the ashes in the river," the guide instructs, *and pay Charon's toll.* First I take in hand the flowers, orange and red and pink. Those that are not in the form of a necklace, those that are separate from the chain, are enlightened by a flame. I place these floating flower candles into the water. They linger to the right, which I assume to be east but could be west (my father never taught me what these flower things are [*diyas*], let alone the proper direction in which to toss them), and I continue with the necklaces, setting them afloat as well, one by one. They drift between the city and the plain, swayed by the faintest breeze; it is the sort of sight that allows a man to make too much of it: *and then, while the white bird soars over the sunset—over the burning wood, the soot, the vapors—the ashes, slowly seeping between my fingers, spiral to the river bottom, carried by the current into a mother's embrace.*

But that's not how it happens. Balancing on the boat's uneven surface, I fumble the heap of ash, as if unaware of its significance. The wind disintegrates the finer particles, the final clumps plop to murky liquid whose current is too weak, or possibly too strong in absence, and thus, their passage—lost.

It was a heart attack that killed him, my father, the heart doctor.

He was on a treadmill at the time, as was his normal routine, to be on a treadmill. It was irrational, a cruel irony, this crime of genetics.

I remember this as we are rowed back to shore. I remember that if these patterns carry over, as patterns are wont to do, from this world to the next (the side untouched, which is now lost behind the fog), moksha cannot be. If the morals of man are nothing more than, as it seems, river-dreams to help the wearied oarsmen endure, moksha cannot be.

The morning after his death, we performed a different Hindu ceremony. Under orders from a priest, Hans and I bumbled around our father's coffin, staring at his corpse, turning clockwise then counterclockwise, circling exactly thrice each time while throwing rice in his hair. Why we were doing this exactly, we lacked the energy to find out. We did it to get it over with. We did it so we could go home, which may have been emptier now, but at least it was quiet.

While the priest shook his bell and shoved us around, Drisana stood still, a couple feet away from the coffin, and watched. Meanwhile, my mother, unable to bear the sight of her husband's body, sat in the audience with the other mourners.

As Hans and I continued, I began to feel our gestures were meaningless—offensive, even: we sprinkled water on his eyelids, smearing the makeup that covered the bruises from his fall.

We placed petals on his suit jacket, tucked coins in his stiff hands, and strung leis from his neck, whose flowers were a shade too tropical, making it look as though we were sending him off for an extended vacation in Hawai'i. I remember wanting to say this to Hans, but I withheld. People were watching; I remember wishing that they weren't because this was embarrassing, sick. If I threw rice in my father's face while he was alive, he would have been furious, or at least mildly upset. I imagine him yelling at me, or even threatening to send me to military school, and that would have been okay, if it meant he would have stood up, brushed the assorted objects off his favorite suit, and driven the family home.

Eventually, Hans and I were made to carry his coffin to the crematorium. We placed it in the furnace, shut the door, and, together, we pressed the button that activated the machine. By our hands, any recognizable trace of our father was destroyed. In that moment, when I realized I would eventually forget how he looked, I felt a schism rip between me and my heritage, me and my father—one I felt I would never be able to close.

On the drive home, this sentiment manifested in an embarrassing whine. "I can't believe I just threw rice at my father's corpse . . . I can't believe I just burned his body . . . I can't believe they made Hans join me! This religion is for savages."

My mother tried to calm me. "You and Hans were very brave today," she said. "I'm proud of you both. Your father, watching from above, is proud of you too."

"Watching from above? How can he be watching when I just combusted his eyes!"

She went silent, so my sister spoke up. "If you were in India," she said, "you would have had to burn him with a torch. That's what he did for his mom, you know, and I doubt he complained at all."

"Well I'm not in India, and if he had a say, he wouldn't have made me do any of that . . . It's not like he really believed in it anyway."

"He did believe in it, Jivin," my mother said.

"Well, I don't."

My sister groaned. "I should be the eldest son."

Beside me, Hans had fallen asleep, his face pressed against the car door window.

Months passed. My father's clothes had cleared of his smell, and so my sister stopped wearing them to sleep. My brother picked up his video games again (although, because he was so quiet, it was hard to tell if this was a sign of having moved on or a method of escape).

My mother, who had barely been eating, started digging into the baskets of unripe fruit that my father's colleagues still were bringing to our house, apparently aware that my mother, in her pain, blamed them.

"They took him from me," she wept one night. "He worked at that hospital from before dawn to after dusk, wearing that heavy lead apron . . . That week he died, he had only slept a few hours . . . It was their fault. They took him from me." But my mother knew inside that his work was his choice; it was always his choice. That night, she conjured an image: a cardiologist, operating, catheters hooked to his veins, exchanging his good blood for that of the sickly . . . The surreal was the only comfort she could find at the time. God was nothing.

Her tears seeping, I tried to sing her sorrows to sleep. Words were nothing.

⁂

We are anchored at the main ghat, Dashashwamedh, where once, Lord Brahma the Creator destroyed ten horses for ceremony's sake. Wobbling off the boat, I believe the rites to be complete. But then the priest rushes over, demanding that I drink the filthy river water — for ceremony's sake, and for my father's sake, who had done the same for his mother's sake.

"Hands together," the priest demonstrates before submerging his hands in the river, "and drink." He swallows and then pats me on the back, wetting my shirt.

"Can't he just touch the water to his lips?" my mother asks.

The priest jolts back, offended. "No, woman," he replies, "boy must drink."

My traitor siblings don't say a word, afraid that if they do, the priest will make them join me.

Just as I'm about to resign to the river, the COOL assistant returns and whispers something in the priest's ear. The words inspire a pair of menacing, sharp-toothed smiles. Shoving the assistant aside, the priest informs me that, before I drink, there are other matters to which I must attend: three rituals included in their special deluxe package (for Brahmin mourners only). I look at the two men skeptically. I know what they're up to, trying to wring the final coins out of my mother's fanny pack; they know that I know, but they also know that I would do anything to defer my fate.

And so, while the priest chants once again, I am allowed, for only a couple extra rupees, to hold onto the tail of an anxious cow; it flings dried shit in my face for free. This cow, apparently, will accompany my father in his journey through Ganga, nourishing him with all the resources that a cow provides. Hans had several questions: How does the cow not drown? How do you milk a cow underwater or make cheese? And isn't this a bull? He continues to question and, like the horns on the head of the cow, he is ignored.

Inside the priest's riverside hut, I perform my second task, rolling dough into balls that represent, or maybe contain, the spirits of my ancestors. Supposedly, these dough-ball ancestors will help my father cross safely into the next world (what their policy is regarding the security of his cow, I am unsure). When I'm finished rolling, the assistant positions the balls in accordance to family relations on yet another giant, dry leaf with yet more candles and spices strewn about it and, while the priest asks my mother about her preferred method of payment, I carry the leaf, now laden with the ceremonial items, back to the river.

Still barefoot, I miraculously manage to evade the torments of the dirt path, descend the steps, and set the leaf afloat upon the river. That actually went pretty well, I think. And then I hear the chorus of furious spectators. I turn around and, much to my despair, I find that my ancestors had tumbled off the leaf during my distracted walk to the river. Many had landed into piles of excrement. Others were flattened by shoes or covered in dirt. This must be a metaphysical misdemeanor of some sort, judging by how the locals, pointing and shouting, are beginning to resemble a mob. More afraid of my earthly consequences than my father's spiritual ones, I hastily clean up the trail of doughy bodies leading back to the hut and then run back to the river, where I find that the leaf has drifted several yards away from the banks, captained by the wind and the mutinous ancestors who remain on board. I hurry as far into the water as I can convince myself to go (halfway up to my knees) and, without thinking, give an underhanded toss: the ancestors go into the air, gently tracing a parabola, and land perfectly onto their vessel. The berating of the onlookers abates. Then, after a calm second, the leaf cracks in half, plummeting to the river-bed . . . An adjacent bottle of Mountain Dew, bobbing from the ripple, floats west to meet the sun.

Back in the hut, no one asks about my blunder. My leg hairs decorated with droplets of water, my hands caked with dough and dirt, I continue with my final task: I am to feed the lepers. In anticipation of this event, a mob of people has already gathered around the hut.

They must have seen the cauldron boiling over a fire. The assistant hands me a box that reads Amazon.com, which contains hundreds of plastic plates (most of which appear to be used). Then he gives me a ladle with which to serve the starving people. As their ulcer-ridden hands pluck at mine, I try to distribute the food in a manner that is fair, but this proves nearly impossible. While timid people fade into the background, their servings are stolen by their more forceful counterparts. I withhold a plate from a man who is coming for a third serving, when I wonder why I'm trying to be so ethical about it. My actions don't matter to them. They don't even acknowledge me. They are not grateful; they don't resent me; for me, they seem to feel nothing at all. And how could I expect anything more?

Once he begins running out of food, the priest interrupts me. "Enough, enough, stop feeding them," he says. "It is time now. Now you will drink." The assistant carries my mother's money back to the hut, and suddenly I remember the object inside against which I had been sitting—a clear, plastic safe, brimming with rupees.

As we walk over to the river, I am ashamed that I am not more horrified at the suffering around me—the child fighting a stray dog for a piece of meat; the old man curled up in a blanket, convulsing; the paraplegic beggar who is shunned by all who pass—but I cannot seem to focus on anything else except what I am about to inflict upon myself (and for what?). It is either that I am too self-involved or that I have assumed the desensitized position that is required to endure the painful sights. When we arrive at the ghat, my mind finds a new focus: a woman's voice in the distance. Her embellished melody captivates me, so I ask Raghao to translate the lyrics:

> I come to you as a child to his mother.
> I come as an orphan to you, moist with love.
> I come without refuge to you, giver of sacred rest.
> I come a fallen man to you, uplifter of all.
> I come undone by disease to you, the perfect physician.
> I come, my heart dry with thirst, to you, ocean of sweet wine.
> Do with me whatever you will.

"By Jagannatha, Brahmin poet who fell in love with Muslim girl," Raghao explains. "We hear many days. He exiled for this love and sang ode to Mother Ganga. Very popular, very famous. You like?"

The echoes of my father in this poet, Jagannatha, are undeniable. My father was also a Brahmin; to much disapproval, my father also married outside of his religion, resisting the privileges of the world he was given, longing for a posture that his body could not fully accommodate. And so he was caught, between cowboys and Pandavas, between myth and science, between tradition and love—always between two places, it seemed, and never fully satisfied by either. With a heart dry with thirst, my father must have been in desperate need of uplifting. Lost, wavering, he submitted to the firmness of faith—a faith unhaunted by contradiction, a faith in which simplicity is a truth one can only reach through entangling complexity.

"Drink," the pointing priest repeats.

Do with me whatever you will. I am abstracted, lost in these words, troubled by this relinquishing of self, this acquiescing to clouded waters. I reach for the water tentatively, anticipate the taste of malady, and withdraw. Instead, I look around. Although the sun has set, the colors are brighter now that it is dark; the city of lights, some call it. The evening festival begins, the sartorial hues saturating the gray palette of mourning. Street food is cooked and served, the emerging spices masking the stench of day. The people chew and laugh and talk so loudly that I can no longer hear the coughing of the diseased.

Distraction is key, and the enhancement of the beauty that dimly exists. I see a boy putting his sweater on a shivering goat (he might have been an adult). I see our guide playfully kiss a pauper's feet (he might have only threatened to kiss them). I see women with bedazzled faces and painted babies smiling to celebrate Mother, the Immortal (or perhaps they smiled at something else, something less). From this I gather that the truest victory of the human spirit, for the people here in this city of extremes, is fabrication—the power to extract reality so thoroughly from existence that they are able to graft their own design in its place.

I look back to the river and do not see a river into which citizens release two hundred million liters of human waste each day. I do not see cholera, dysentery, hepatitis, and typhoid proliferating, making new diseases with one another. I close my eyes and, into the water, cast a dream . . . *The bull softens into a cow. The lepers, by the food I give them, are cured. And, despite the heavy balls of dough, the drowning leaf rises again, candles still aflame, and all the ancestors in their proper place* . . . By my resolve, the river is made pure. I inhale and cup my hands and, not looking at the color of the water or what floats in its midst, thinking only of my father above me, watching, I bring them to my lips and drink from the Ganga.

What Means Go?

Lucy Jane Bledsoe

P at thinks she should be the one at the wheel, the one who interacts with the armed guard when we drive across the Slovenian border. She's afraid of my mouth. I'm not particularly hotheaded, and I don't think I have a problem, in general, with authority. But I do occasionally have a little trouble with impulse control, especially when it comes to speaking my mind.

Nevertheless, I silently think I'm the better candidate for speaking with people who hold power over us. Pat's Irish gift of gab is delightful at dinner parties and makes her my favorite traveling companion but can be ineffective when efficiency is in order, such as at border crossings.

I keep driving and don't respond to her suggestion. Undoubtedly she's thinking of the incident with the ship captain. A few years ago my good friend Deborah died, on my watch, of lymphoma. The experience was profound, and I bonded with Deborah's sister, who'd also been there at the time of her death, and her brother, who'd arrived a few hours later. The brother, let's call him Dan, worked as a sailboat captain for various wealthy yacht owners, and at Deborah's memorial service, he and Pat talked at length about their shared love of sailing. When Dan invited us to join him on a job he had sailing a ship from the Dominican Republic to the Virgin Islands, as his guests, we immediately said yes. It seemed like the perfect way to celebrate Deborah's life. We learned, not long after the ship set sail, that Dan had needed crew. We worked like dogs: scrubbing the deck, cleaning the head, keeping watch at the bow of the boat at three o'clock in the morning during a storm. Unlike Pat, I don't have a particular love of sailing, and worse, I get horribly seasick. Nor did I understand the sailing culture, or more specifically, the captain thing. The line of command. How, when at sea, there is no room for discussion. Dan, who I had difficulty seeing as anyone other than my good friend's baby brother, was a tyrant, and he was using us. So I eventually spoke an emphatic No to one of his orders, which happened to be staying awake all night to check the bilges, which were filling with water due to leaks in the hull. Everyone on board was shocked when I talked back, and Pat was mortified. We jumped ship in St. Thomas.

There have been other times when I've decided that my voice is more important than protocol. But I'm not an idiot. While men with guns do trigger my sense of the absurd—really, you think I'm supposed to respond to that piece of hardware at your hip?—I'm not about to jeopardize our trip by arguing with a border patrol guard about anything. I would behave.

Besides, what would there be to argue about? Both Slovenia and Croatia are now members of the EU and eager for international acceptance, not to mention tourist cash. Pat has done an inordinate amount of research, which has been paying off beautifully; everything is going smoothly. As for the border, she'd learned that to drive through Slovenia, a traveler needs a sticker called a vignette. Without it, we would be subject to a three-hundred-euro fine. One woman had blogged that her husband had been detained and questioned for hours at the border, while she sat alone in the car, because they hadn't obtained the vignette. Nowhere along the roads leading to the Slovenian border is the requirement of getting this little sticker shared with travelers. You have to have found out on your own, pretty much by chance.

But we have the vignette! It's stuck neatly and visibly on the upper corner of the driver-side windshield: our badge of goodwill and rule following.

So I don't pull over and relinquish the steering wheel to Pat. Everything is in order, including my attitude. I drive blithely toward the Slovenian border.

By now we've been seduced by luscious swims in the crystal clear and azure waters of the Adriatic; by the octopus salads and heaping plates of grilled shrimps, whiskers and all; by the deeply satisfying house wines, red and white; by the artists we've met, and their fresh and urgent paintings and sculpture. One painting in the Lauba Gallery in Zagreb especially moved me: it depicts a ragtag group of twenty-first-century young people standing around a table in a café where a document—perhaps a peace agreement or maybe the new constitution—is being signed. The painting is enormous, wall-sized, and meant to mock American and European historical document-signing paintings. It captures perfectly the rub in Croatia between the conflicts of the past and the young people's hopes for the future.

The Croatian Homeland War ended just twenty years ago, having devastated the region and the economy. Landmines still menace the countryside and travelers are advised to watch their step—their literal physical footsteps. It's impossible not to think about some of the brutal details of that recent war while visiting the region. When some nice man is going far out of his way to help us find an address or inviting us to share a drink with his family, I can't help but wonder where he had been during those years, what he had done to his neighbors. We are finding the people to be exceptionally kind and generous and open.

But then that's the very nature of war, the complete mindfuck of it: how do good people become ruthless killers of their neighbors? War is something that can never be understood, even with every political, economic, and even biological explanation, not truly. Anyway, I'm more interested in studying and writing about how people connect, how they heal, how they make art, than in figuring out dysfunction and hatred.

So I resist dwelling on what sometimes feels like a sinister underbelly, the recent history of the Croatian and Serbian conflict, and instead enjoy the abundance of kindness and creativity we're experiencing in so many of our encounters. We visit art galleries and studios and talk to artists about how they are using photography and paint and collage to shape the new Croatian narrative. We go to local fairs where beekeepers are selling honey, bakers their tarts and cupcakes, and vintners their wine. We focus, every chance we get, on finding out how people in twenty-first-century Croatia want to live now.

I'm in this expansive and happy state of mind as we approach Slovenia. I'm not even ruffled by Pat's announcement, just moments before reaching the border, that she's somehow "lost" my passport. Since I'd handed it to her while driving, and we haven't stopped, it has to be with us in the car, but it takes pulling to the side of the road and digging around under the car seats to locate it.

Moments later, we pull up to the overbearing border structure, made of blue-painted steel beams. My hands are at ten o'clock and two o'clock on the steering wheel. I arrange a pleasantly neutral expression on my face. I come to a complete stop at the kiosk where the first border patrol *policija* awaits. As at most borders, there are a couple more guards milling just beyond the kiosk. I hand over our passports and the guard barely glances at them. He hands them back, waves his hand, and says, I think, "Go."

I don't roar out of there. I inch forward slowly, glancing at the next guard standing with hands on hips, the right one just over the big gun. I'm not two feet past him when he shouts, very, very loudly, "What you think you doing?"

Of course I stop. I look over at him. I'm not exaggerating when I say I've never seen a more hateful glower in my life. He looks livid.

"I'm sorry," I say. I gesture back at the guard in front of the kiosk. "I thought he said 'go.'"

He doesn't speak for what feels like minutes, holds my gaze, makes me feel as if that gun at his hip is in fact against my temple.

Finally, he shouts, "What means go?"

Later I'll joke with friends about how I might have answered the question, beginning perhaps with a Kantian definition of "go," moving on to a Socratic explanation, wondering what Wittgenstein might have said, exploring several historical implications of "go." I will come to realize that I am most interested in a feminist interpretation of "What means go?"

At the moment, though, in the presence of the armed border patrol policija, I am stunned to silence.

"Are you blind?" he shouts. "Is it dark?"

How, he wants to know, could I have not seen *him*. Of course I had seen him; I just didn't know I was supposed to stop again.

"I'm sorry," I stammer. "I misunderstood."

My speaking seems to further enrage him. I'm not thinking particularly clearly, but I sense that he will get off on my fear, that more apologies will excite rather than appease him. I decide to keep quiet. I break eye contact and hand him our passports.

He glances at mine and notes my birthplace. "You think 'go' means you can just go all the way to Oregon? That means go?"

I stare out the front of the car windshield. Later I'll learn that this is the moment when Pat's fear spikes. She's sure I'm about to share my feelings, or put another way, about to blow. But I'm far from that. My heart is hammering and I can barely breathe. I am, in fact, terrified.

One of the scariest parts of what is happening is his complete openness in harassing us. His colleagues stand by, one looking lazily at his fingernails, another scratching his head, both well within earshot. I can certainly imagine a similar scene happening at a United States border, but there, I'm pretty sure the bully would lean into the car and speak in hissing whispers. He wouldn't want witnesses. This guy at the Slovenian border is not worried in the least about being overheard.

He holds our two passports in his hand and continues with his heated stare. Am I supposed to hand him some cash? What if I do and he takes offense at my thinking he can be bribed? And bribed for *what*?

Thank god we found the missing passport before reaching the border. I can only imagine how he would respond to our telling him, sorry, we really do both have passports, it'll just be a few moments while we root around under the car seats.

He steps into a kiosk with our two passports in his possession. I try not to look but can't help it. He holds the passports in one hand and slaps them, over and over again, against the countertop. As he does this, he glares out the window, into the distance. It is perfectly clear to me that he's trying to figure out how he can fuck with us. Eventually he slips my passport under the scanner—I can tell it's mine by a couple of white stickers on the cover—and then pulls it back out. Next he slips in Pat's. He pulls hers back, looks at the passport picture carefully, flips through all the pages, once, and then again. He slips it back under the scanner. Shakes his head as if he's seen something there, maybe arrests for terrorist acts, and slips it back in again. I can't tell if the machine isn't working, or if he's just hoping that multiple attempts will eventually yield a negative result. Maybe the entire display is a charade.

By now I fully expect to be pulling the car over for a complete inspection. I'm already wondering if we'll be put into the same or separate rooms for interrogation. I'm not worried in the least about my hotheadedness, but I'm starting to worry about Pat's loquacious circuitousness. "Don't tell them our entire itinerary," I whisper. "Just say 'Venice,' if they ask where we're headed. One word."

"Of *course*," Pat says, as if she ever did differently.

Most of all, I'm wondering what exactly is the problem. Tourism is burgeoning in the region. The economic boost of tourism always comes at a high price to a country, usually a cultural one, and resentment is a common accompaniment. Is that the problem? Or perhaps a *lack* of tourism in Slovenia is the problem: everyone driving through this border has just spent loads of money in Croatia and is shooting through Slovenia to spend the rest in Italy. Possibly he's angry that we do in fact have the vignette and he can't exact a fat "fine" for not having it. Or maybe our U.S. passports, and everything they stand for, including our country's involvement in their war, could be the problem. I used to expect anger from the people in countries where the United States has fueled, or started, conflicts. But it rarely happens. I've come to understand that most people in other countries are better than Americans at realizing that a country's citizens are not the same as the government and corporations that rule that country. In fact, this once was explained to me and Pat by a couple of Spaniards we met in Argentina. "Americans are still shocked by what their government is capable of," they told us, without trying to hide their feelings of fatigue at having to explain something so obvious. "You're only 250 years old. You're still starry-eyed. Corruption still unhinges you."

None of this helps explain the Slovenian border guard's ire. Nor does any of it answer his fundamental question: What, exactly, means go?

When I was young, I believed that authentic travel—*going*—meant traveling alone. I considered companionship a cultural crutch, a distracting mirror of self. A true traveler, a pilgrim, maintained a pure view by looking through the lens of loneliness. When I was twenty years old, I turned down an excellent job as a National Park Service ranger so I could wander around Europe and northern Africa by myself. As it turned out, loneliness blunted, rather than sharpened, my experience. So I sometimes hooked up with other lonely, barely post-adolescent waifs I met along the way, never more disastrously than the time in Malaga, Spain. I was trying to catch the ferry over the Straits of Gibraltar to Tangier, Morocco. Unfortunately, the ferry dock in Malaga was deserted, the ticket kiosk unmanned, and the posted times of the crossings weren't accurate. Every time I showed up for the boat, it wasn't at the port. No one could tell me when it *would* be there, or when it would sail.

At this point I was a couple of months into my pilgrimage as a solo traveler and pretty much felt like a complete failure. My solitude dulled rather than inspired me. I'd hoped for nonstop philosophical inspiration and instead felt blank-headed most of the time. My observations, dutifully recorded in a handwritten journal, were banal even to myself. I was desperate to get to Tangier, where a real friend—not some guy picked up in a train station—awaited me. To make sure I didn't miss the boat, that had to come into the port at some point, I felt like I had to sleep on a bench at the ferry dock.

That's where I met a young man, an off-duty American soldier, who said he knew the schedule and that a boat was leaving that night. He was absolutely certain about his information and convinced me to join him and his girlfriend for drinks while we waited. The mention of a girlfriend relaxed me and I went with the soldier into town. The girlfriend sat at a café table, an untouched coffee before her, nodding out. He tenderly brushed back her dirty hair and urged her to drink the coffee. I wondered if she was sick, but mostly just felt relief in having a plan for getting to Tangier.

Shortly after sitting down, the soldier jumped up from the table, hauled his rag-doll girlfriend out of her seat, and urged, "Come on! Come on! We have to go. Hurry!"

What can I say? I was twenty years old. I followed them. We walked as quickly as we could with him nearly carrying the girl, through the streets of Malaga. When I asked where we were going, he said to get a drink. Then he told me, speaking breathlessly because of the effort in half-dragging and half-carrying the girl, that he had to keep moving because of the heroin he had hidden in the soles of his shoes. I don't know why he told me this. Perhaps he was stupid. Or high himself. Or just plain desperate.

From that moment on, my primary mission was to dodge them until it was time for the boat. But I'd been too friendly and Malaga was too small; ditching the couple became next to impossible. He was determined that I'd help him care for his nodding out girlfriend. I eventually took refuge with a group of Brits who were drunk on mint juleps, of all things, and I bought time in their shelter by sipping one of the sickly sweet concoctions.

Miraculously, the soldier was right about the time of the sailing. When I showed up at the dock at the appointed hour, there was the boat! A man in the kiosk sold me a third-class ticket, and I stepped aboard. Third class was comprised of a few rows of wooden benches in a small, cold cabin. No sooner had I settled my behind on one of the benches than the heroin smuggler and his girlfriend came along and of course sat next to me. These were my companions as I crossed from Spain into Morocco, throughout that long night at sea, sitting up on the wooden third-class bench, the small boat rocking hard, him chatting amicably as if we were the best of friends. I was afraid to move away from him, and anyway, there were no other available seats. So I stayed with my drug-trafficking soldier, pitching about miserably during that rough crossing, seasick and cold, imagining the insides of a Spanish or Moroccan prison.

It took me years to admit that traveling alone is miserable. I eventually figured out that I don't particularly like to *go* alone. Nor had picking up random companions along the way worked out for me.

I also realized that I don't care for aimless wandering. For me, going means having a pursuit. Not just a destination but a reason for getting to that destination. Every worthwhile journey is a pilgrimage, a search, or in service of research, which is why writing and traveling are perfectly symbiotic. I never know if I'm a writer so that I can travel or if I'm a traveler so that I can write.

I go to discover something specific: the details of a setting, a certain person's story, the meaning of home in extreme landscapes. I always have a question I'm trying to answer, or something or someone I'm trying to find. And yet, on many journeys I never reach my goal.

I once spent five weeks driving a tin can with a spiderweb for a windshield all over Tierra del Fuego searching for Lago Blanco. I never got there for a myriad of reasons. But I did see other extraordinary lakes, topped by ethereal ventricular clouds. I saw a Fuegian fox; the Patagonian gray fox; the lovely and strange black-necked, white-bodied swans; giant rheas with flocks of enormous chicks; and guanacos, lots of munching guanacos. I stood awed looking up at the stone pillars of the Andes, rising out of beech forests, amid the swirling clouds. I witnessed herds of wild horses running full speed at dawn, steam billowing out their nostrils. The whole while I was making my way, looking for routes, to Lago Blanco. I desperately wanted to find and see it, which is the most important trick about pilgrimages: for any payoff, you have to care intensely about getting there, even while knowing you may not.

Traveling with a purpose can definitely lead to problems other than never fulfilling the purpose. I'll never forget the angry man in McMurdo Station, Antarctica, who confronted me in a bar (yes, there are three bars in McMurdo Station), where I was admittedly taking notes. He sneered, "Do you have enough *material* yet? Should I do something weird so you can *write* about it?" His unsubtle message was that being an observer in his territory was supremely rude. He also wanted me to know that as an outsider, it was beyond arrogant for me to believe I could understand the inside of this place, the culture of a science station in Antarctica.

Earlier in the Adriatic coast trip, I'd had a similar encounter with a twenty-year-old waiter. He told me and Pat that Americans are terribly naïve (echoing the message of my Spanish friends in Argentina). He cited the way we all go on about the friendliness of Croatians. Indeed, I made statements to that effect earlier in this piece. The young—and very friendly—fellow had taken a seat, uninvited, at our table and stayed to talk, despite it being his work shift, for a good thirty minutes. We discussed Barack Obama; gun control; healthcare, theirs and ours; and the Croatian Homeland War. He said Americans didn't understand that Croatians were nice only because they wanted our tourist dollars.

As someone who travels a lot, all over the world, I'm well aware of what my dollars mean. No thinking traveler can ignore complex questions of culture mixing and border crossing, what it means to hold a passport and a bank account that allows for lots of freedom of movement, allows *going*. Our presence in other countries is always some mix of visiting and trespassing, and our dollars are always part of the relationship.

In other words, crossing borders can be illusory. Travelers may think they're seeing the inside of a place when they almost never are. I believe this is true. Nothing is more embarrassing and cringe-worthy than listening to some American talk about being "off the beaten track" or relating a story about an "authentic" encounter.

And yet the relationship between outsiders and insiders is more complex than the young waiter was insisting. For one thing, in Croatia, people *are* super friendly, often in situations where money plays no part. Economics does not, in fact, rule every interaction between travelers and local residents. All over the world, I've experienced so many acts of extreme kindness: a woman in Punta Arenas who cut our huge rental car bill in half, for no reason; the restaurant owner in Ushuaia who sent us free drinks all night; the B&B owner in Zagreb who tried to stuff a twenty-euro note in my pocket because she overheard me saying I had no cash. That same B&B owner, Tanya, wrote Pat after we'd left Zagreb, opening the e-mail with "I think of you all day." We're quite sure the comment was an error in her limited English, that she probably meant something like "I've been meaning to send you a note all day." She wrote that she'd ordered one of my books and one of Pat's CDs. She attached pictures of the hike that she and her husband Ivo had taken that weekend.

This is precisely why I *go*. For these moments when my expectations are broken, these physical and cultural border crossings. I go to pry open my limited worldview, to connect with people in surprising ways, to blow up stereotypes, including ones about Americans. The most exciting thing about borders is that by stepping over them, they stop being barriers and become gateways. A border that can be crossed is a border that is no longer successful at containment and separation. That, to me, is addicting. It means go.

None of this, however, can be explained to the Slovenian border guard. He doesn't care in the least about what I think. I recognize his particular style of rage, and I strongly suspect our female independence rubs him the wrong way. Here we are in a region where borders have quite recently been redrawn, as the result of a brutal war; where there are freshly triumphant winners and, more importantly, smarting losers; where an entire economy and maybe even culture are being remade by tourism. Here come two women who think they can drive blithely through all that in their rental car.

Perhaps I was crossing his border without enough gravitas. All that sense of freedom and entitlement may well have been in my body language as I inched past the Slovenian guard, glancing at but not *seeing* him, at least not seeing him well enough. *Are you blind? Is it dark?*

If I insulted him in some way, I'm sorry for that. But I'm grateful to him for providing me with the opportunity to think more deeply about what means go, about why I travel, about the meaning of crossing borders.

In the moment, though, I can't think. The uniform, the gun, the border, the feelings of powerlessness (perhaps his as well as mine), all of this trips a switch in my head. Even as it happens, I understand that I've lost the ability to make rational decisions, that I am about to take action without due calculation or planning, but I can't talk myself down.

The guard steps out of his kiosk and stands, with our passports in his hand, just out of my reach. He leaves his hand at his side, the two passports against his thigh. He doesn't speak, nor does he look at us.

I lean out the car window, stretch my arm to its fullest reach, and grab hold of the passports. His fingers grip so I have to pull hard. I do and the passports come loose. He's still refusing to look at me.

I go. I drive slowly forward into Slovenia. A policija car, parked in the bushes just beyond the border, gives me a fresh rush of fear. Surely my border patrol guard has radioed him to pull us over. But he doesn't.

I *keep* going.

The Chevra

Goldie Goldbloom

chevra kadisha (*Hevra kadishah*) (Aramaic: חברא קדישא,
Ḥebh'ra Qaddisha)

Jewish "holy society" for the preparation of the dead for burial

1

I want to write about my mother's life as if she is alive again, as if she never died. But I have not seen her in over twenty years. I have forgotten the way she used to hold her lips, the way she bent to retrieve small items from the floor, the way she looked at me when I had done something wrong. She's been dead a long time.

She was very tall, more than six feet. By the end of her life, she weighed no more than eighty pounds, but even in the good years, she was thin. She could run faster than anyone I knew. She smoked cigarettes. She had long fingernails and wore stilettos, and she made all her own clothing, including the bras.

When I wrote to the man with whom she had had a long-term affair, several years after she died, he denied ever knowing her. When I confronted him with photographs, with his nickname, Fishface, he admitted knowing her just a little. She led a "very alternative" lifestyle, he said. He said he liked the mini dress she wore that had large lime green spots on it.

My mother made that dress for my grandfather's funeral. Everyone else came dressed in black. My father would have *loved* this dress, she said. She was barefoot. Her black hair touched her bum.

She was angry that her father died so young. I am angry that my mother died so young too. At least *she* got to go to the funeral.

I have put in my order, with God, to live until I am ninety-seven.

2

I work for the Chicago Chevra Kaddisha, washing elderly Jewish women who have died without relatives, getting them ready for their burial. I think of this as my pact with God. I've got your back. Make sure You've got mine.

The time in the rooms with the dead is quiet time, without minutes. The clock never moves. In those rooms, the presence of the dead hangs like a swollen purple midsummer cloud, ready to burst at any moment. I look up as I work, expecting to see raindrops coming down in huge wet splats on my face, but instead there are those appalling industrial tiles, the kind with thousands of dusty holes that are said to absorb unwanted sounds.

The dead make sounds. They don't mean to. But the processes of the body do not need a brain to tell them what to do.

Sometimes, when I work, I do not need a brain to tell me what to do either.

For a long time after my mother died, my brain lay down and went to sleep, even though I continued, on the outside, to look like an ordinary teacher or a librarian or an artist or a mother or whatever it was that I was being (not knowing) at that moment.

3

The phone rang in the middle of the night. Never answer a phone that rings in the middle of the night. That sorrowful screaming on the other end of the line is not meant for human ears.

My brother was a teenager. He lived in a drug house at the edge of the city. His property had been repeatedly stolen from him. He forgot to pay whoever needed paying. The house was demolished soon afterward, to make way for a highway, but at that time, at the time when he called me in the middle of the night to tell me that my mother was dead, the house wore a condemned notice, and the boys who lived there lifted a corner of the iron sheet that had been stapled over the back door and slipped inside.

I said NO. I said No and no and no no no, but it didn't change anything, this disagreement of mine, because my mother didn't stop being dead.

4

The Chevra Kaddisha does not get paid for their work. The phone call comes in the middle of the night or first thing in the morning or just as you are about to give birth, and an anonymous voice on the other end of the line asks you if you are available to help and if you are, if you aren't pregnant or menstruating or divorced or generally otherwise occupied, the voice tells you where to go and what time to get there and then it hangs up and now you have a dead person to take care of, someone you have probably never known and definitely, now, will never know.

Two other women meet you outside, and you all look sheepish, because you are about to do this thing without words, and knowing that, it's hard to say anything at all, even before.

You put on plastic coats and gloves and booties. You fill buckets with water. You find combs and orange sticks and makeup remover and rubbish bins. You glance at her paperwork:

No known relatives

You glance at her arm:

Blue numbers

5

I don't go to Australia when my mother dies. I sit on the floor and cry every day. I miss the funeral. My brain is asleep so I don't care that no one writes to tell me what the funeral was like. It's less than three weeks since I returned from Australia. I was told that my mother had at least six months to live. I have her ethical will in my pocket, and it says that I should choose kindness over beauty, pain over deceit. Seven months after she dies, my brother will send me her diary and there will only be one entry in it, on July 16. The year isn't indicated.

In Katanning, the locals thought I had an affair. I was boarding in a home in the town while I did my student teaching. They thought I was screwing the husband. It wasn't true, but you can't convince small towns of anything.

Twenty years after my mother dies, my brother will casually tell me, as if I have always known, that the love of my mother's life was a woman who had a home at the edge of the glittering Swan River. I will be sitting outside, in my car, on a moonless spring night, and I will have just told my brother that I am seeing a woman who I think might end up being my wife. In the tender velvet darkness, I will remember going to the river with my mother, every Tuesday evening, and feeding the swans with stale bread while she went inside to talk with her friend.

I would like my mother's love back. There has only ever been one person who knew all of me and loved me anyway.

6

On May 5, 2000, I give birth to my daughter Chana. It is the tenth anniversary of my mother's death.

It was hot in my bedroom as I was laboring. My husband was away in Spain. The midwife sat in the second rocking chair, saying nothing. Time didn't pass. At one point, I said I was exhausted. I said I don't want to do this anymore, and Kay, the midwife, said, *Excellent. Looks like we are having us a baby.*

The phone rang and it wasn't my husband. It was the Chevra Kaddisha, looking for a third woman, to help at a Tahara. I was engaged in my own struggle with death/life/breaking/opening. I said no, because I say no to almost anything that comes over the phone.

I wanted my mother to be there with me. I wanted her to meet her eight grandchildren and love them. I thought about her story of how I was born, on a Saturday afternoon near a football field, and how she had thought the cheering was for her efforts to push me out. I had not been home in ten years. I had never visited her grave. I was afraid of it.

7

Once, it was not an old Jewish woman lying on the wooden boards, but a young girl, a child, with black and blue marks around her neck. The Chevra do not speak. We cannot. If we need something, we indicate it with our hands or our eyes. But that time, with that child, we spoke, because our eyes were full.

Sometimes people die holding things in their hands and their fingers close over whatever it is. We do not bury people with anything except their naked skin and simple linen shrouds. If they die with something in their hands, we warm up the flesh with a towel soaked in hot water, and then gently uncurl the fingers and remove the item.

My mother died with a photograph of me under her nightgown, clutched against her heart. They took her down to the morgue, not knowing the photograph was there, but somehow, the photograph fell out of her hands and cracked on the floor. I wouldn't have known this except my cousin, who was a medical salesman, went into the morgue at that hospital and saw my photograph, with a crack running across my face, on the wall. That's Goldie, he said. What's she doing here?

My daughter Chana was born with the cord around her neck twice and a true knot that threatened to strangle her. Her neck was black and purple before it faded to green and then to yellow. Pant, said the midwife, while I get the cord off her neck. No bloody way, I said. You're not getting this train to stop.

8

My Auntie Roz called me from Australia to wish me mazal tov on Chana's birth. Oh and by the way, she said at the end of the conversation, you are going to have to come and pick up your mum. She's been out in my shed with Rob, but I'm planning on moving. Don't blame your brother, Roz said. Pete wasn't up to burying her. I haven't found a place for Rob yet either.

Uncle Rob died a few months after my mother, also of cancer.

Roz lived up on the Darling Range, outside Perth, in a house Rob built with his own two hands. Once, the bath he'd installed fell through the floor with Roz inside it. It fell down about twelve feet, landed on the rocky mountainside and skidded down to the waterfall at the bottom of their block. Roz was forty-eight when that happened. My aunt was forty-nine when my mum and Rob both died. Her best friend, who was also my mum's best friend, Bev, died the same year, a horrible year, also of cancer.

What do you mean, my mum's not buried?" I asked. I worked for the Chevra Kaddisha and one of the principles of Jewish burial is that we get people into the ground within about twenty-four hours of the death. At the time, my mum had not been buried for over ten *years*.

Your brother is a procrastinator, Roz said.

9

I went to Australia then. The place my brother lives is considered to be the farthest place in the world from Chicago. It's famous as the most isolated city in the world, and after I arrived, I was planning on driving out into the bush for another three hours, to bury my mum.

I put your mum under some roses, my auntie said, and though I pictured a beautiful garden with wisteria overhead, and the scent of lemons on the wind, mum was actually out in an old shed in a box underneath dozens of shattered roses that must have been there the entire ten years. Uncle Rob was in the box on the trestle next to her. He'd have had a slightly more advantageous view of the loquat tree if he still had eyes.

I tried not to think that in that box was my mum, because, of course, my mother wasn't really in that box.

10

We start at the head. The woman is covered, always, with a clean sheet, and the Chevra lift only enough of the sheet to gently wash the body. The water is warm. The cloths are soft. The movements are slow and quiet. I wash the woman's hair and comb it out. Each hair that becomes tangled in the comb is removed and put into a cloth bag. If there is blood on her body, we will remove it with a small piece of damp cotton fabric and this too will be placed into the bag and the bag will be put into the *aron*, the plain pine box that stands in one corner of the room, waiting.

A Tahara begins, though, with a wish. I wish that everything I do will be done with kindness and respect. When this thought leaves my mind, I stop whatever I am doing and refocus my intentions.

Her right side is washed first and then the left. Head, arm, hand, torso, leg, foot. Each small section of her body is dried with squares of cloth before being covered again. When I come to her hands, I hold them within my own, for a moment longer than necessary. This is the last time someone will hold these hands. When I lift the body for the purification, I become the last to hug this woman, the last person who will know the exact shape of her in this world. The dead are as light as birds. They almost lift themselves and fly up to the ceiling.

The last time I held my mother's hands was in Perth airport, on Sunday, April 16, at 10:20 in the morning. I had been told it was safe to fly back to the United States, that my mother would live for another six months. She had pushed me to go spend the Passover holiday with my new husband and yet, even then, I *knew*. I was completely certain that I would never see my mother again.

Her hands were large. Her skin was soft, as soft as a warm summer night. The bones within her body felt like old roses and they were as fragile. I held her hands for many moments longer than necessary. I could not make myself let go. The flight attendant called my name again and again. My brother touched me on the shoulder and said, *You can come back.*

My mother put a letter into my pocket. She told me it was her ethical will. She told me not to read it until the plane had passed Adelaide. Good-bye, she said. I love you, she said. I will always love you, she said.

11

The midwife told me that if I ask my children what they remember from before they are born, sometimes, if asked young enough, they say extraordinary things. I asked my son. He said he remembered a warm beach and a beating red sun. He was three. I asked my daughter and she said she remembered her twin kicking her. She was two and a half. I asked Chana, when she was three years old, and she said, *I was your mother and you were my little girl and I used to take you down to see the boats.*

Until that moment, I had forgotten that my mother used to take me to watch the ocean liners leaving Fremantle Harbour. They come back, she said, but I only ever saw them leave.

12

My brother, Pete, met me at Auntie Roz's house, to load Mum into the back of the car. You are angry at me, he said. No, I'm not, I said. I am sad. So very very sad that Mum has been here all this time and I didn't know.

My brother picked loquats for us to eat while we waited for my uncle to bring the small piece of marble he'd carved for Mum's grave. He held the fruits out to me in his big scarred hands. *Nespole*, I said to my brother, because I could think of nothing else to say. In Italy, these are called *nespole* and you can buy them in the open-air markets in the south. The juice, sour and flesh-colored, ran down my chin and small droplets fell onto my shirt, saturating the fabric. I wiped my chin with my hand and then I wiped my hand on the back of my thigh. I did not have gloves. I did not have small squares of clean soft cloth for this process. I did not have my book of prayers. All I had was my intention to remember, the wish to do everything with kindness and with respect.

Mama. In Italy, the small children cry *mama mama* in the streets and women come out of their houses and kiss these children and lift them up and hold them. In Italy, when a death is announced, the newspapers have a thick black border, and in the rural cemeteries, fresh candles are placed on the graves and lit, every evening, and they burn through the night, illuminating the graveyards with the most mysterious and shifting of lights.

13

When my mother died, I stopped calling her mum and began to call her *mama*.

Mama mama mama

14

We fill three buckets with warm water. We pour the water in a single, continuous stream, from the head to the foot, first on the right, then on the left, and then in the center. The woman on the wooden boards, briefly, looks as if she has just been born, fresh and wet and new, and then we dry her again and she returns to being a dead person. We dry from her head to her feet, from the right to the left. When she is fully covered, we lay out the *tachrichim*, the shrouds in which she will be dressed.

The dead wear the same garments as the High Priest. They wear the same fine linen pants and the same fine linen shirt and the same apron and the same hood. The best linen, when you touch it, is cold.

15

Pete and I drive in silence on the way to the Wongan Hill Cemetery. My brother's car cannot be put into reverse or it blows a fuse that controls the air-conditioning, the power windows, the radio, the lights, and all of the engine gauges. When we stop for petrol in New Norcia, Pete forgets and reverses away from the pump. Fuck, he says, and he hits the steering wheel. I am so fucking sick of this bloody car. He pulls out the ruined fuse and tosses it onto the floor where there are at least a hundred other blown fuses, but then he can't find a replacement. Well, that's the air-con, he says. Carked it. Shame we can't even roll the windows down, he says, though the bloody temperature has got to be in the nineties.

In the heat, the box in the back begins to emit an odor, and now we are both sure that we can hear something that sounds like chopsticks, the faint tap of bones, one against the other. *Jes-us*, Pete says, and then he looks at me. Sorry, he says. It's your fault, I say. Why didn't you bury her?

In response, he stops the car, yanks open my door, and breaks out my window with mum's marble headstone. There you go, he says. Fresh air.

He's not a violent man. He does all this quietly. Calmly. Respectfully. I really am sorry, he says. Mum hated getting hot, he says. I know, I say. In the back, the bones continue to click together and now, more than anything, it sounds as if someone is knitting back there. Neither of us wants to turn around.

16

My mother said that human lives are divided into three sections. The first twenty years are the years of learning. The second twenty years are the years of family. And the third twenty years are the years of exploration.

She said that when she retired, she would get a ticket to China and she would walk, barefoot, from one end of the country to the other. For a woman who prepared for everything, it is strange that she did not have a Chinese phrase book in the bathroom, a map of the Great Wall above her bed.

Right before she was diagnosed with lung cancer, she sold her business and went to live in the far north of Western Australia with a man who had one eye. He mined for gold. She planted tropical palms and wrote letters to me, with drawings of parrots around the edges. When I called home, I had to first radio the Royal Flying Doctor in Port Hedland and ask for Nine Whiskey Echo Victor.

She didn't get twenty years for exploration. She didn't get twenty years to walk across China. She got less than a year of drawing parrots and planting palms. And then she got ten years in a shed at the bottom of a garden with my very shy uncle.

17

When the Tahara is finished, the chevra stand next to the coffin, and they silently ask the dead woman for forgiveness.

I didn't mean to forget you, we say. I didn't mean to hurt you or shame you or be unkind.

Please forgive me.

18

We take turns digging a hole in the hard red dirt for my mother's box. We can't dig deeper than three feet because below the red dirt there is hard red rock. There are no trees to shade us. Blood-colored ants scuttle across the disturbed earth. A magpie sits on the top rail of the cemetery gate and says something that sounds like *quardleoodlardloo*. My uncle's marble stone has been engraved with the wrong date, or maybe it's the wrong name. Something is wrong about it, and we stand there and stare at the stone for a very long time before Pete jams it into the dirt. What a fuckup this has been, my brother says.

Typical bloody mum, he says. Terrorizing us in the car. She'd get a kick out of that, I say. Knitting the whole way up here, she was, he says. Another blanket, I say. For when the weather drops into the eighties. You reckon this grave thing will be orright, Pete asks. We're screwed if she doesn't like it, I say. Remember when she said she'd prove to us there was a world to come, remember? That's all we need, an angry spirit chasing us down the track. Flinging bloody knitting needles after us.

Before she died, my mother said that if she could, she would prove to us that there is a world after this one. She said she was smarter than average, and she'd leave us a sign and Pete and I had both laughed. Yeah, we said. As if.

But then there was one morning soon after she died when it was raining, and I, in the United States, was walking next to the river, feeding the swans some bread, and talking about how my mother loved to walk next to the river and fish, and there was a bush covered in honeysuckle and that was my mother's favorite flower, and then a cloud of hummingbirds flew out of the flowers. Oh, I said! Oh! My mother would be so happy to be here this morning. When I got home from the walk, Pete was calling me from Australia. I just had the most beautiful walk, he said. Next to the river, feeding the swans. It was raining, he said, and I talked about how mum loved to fish. And there was a bush, he said, covered in honeysuckle, and a cloud of hummingbirds flew out of the bush, and oh! Wouldn't Mum have loved that?

We told that story standing at the edge of a fresh pile of dirt with a bit of marble stuck into the top. One edge of the box stuck up out of the ground and Pete mashed it down with his boot. He bent and patted the crushed box. Sorry, Mum, he said. I'm so bloody sorry. Ten years, I said. Can you believe she's been gone for ten years? *She was a good mum*, Pete said, and we both started crying. And of course the wind picked up and pelted us with tiny sticks and bits of bark and tattered leaves from the years before, and then the wind dried our tears to salt tracks on our dusty faces. Yeah, I said. She really was.

The End of the World & Its Beginning

Rachel Jamison Webster

here does a trip begin and end? And why do I feel most awake when I feel that I am being guided, both making something and being made by it, following a deeper river as I paddle doggedly with my own intention?

This particular journey began a week before we left. I hadn't planned to travel—I was a single mother and money was scarce—but I woke one morning in the middle of December just knowing that my daughter and I needed to go *somewhere*, and soon. That morning I was checking my e-mail when I saw a Groupon for an eco-resort in Belize. I knew nothing about Belize but felt drawn to the little thatched huts up in the mountains. But when I called the owner of the resort and asked about availability after Christmas, he said, "Why don't you come next week? Then you could be here with the Mayans for the Mayan New Year." It was one of those conversations that seem to happen on a deeper sonic register. There was no static between us, as if we knew each other already. "Let me look into it," I said and hung up.

"You have to go!" my friend said when I told her. "You have been talking about the Mayan New Year for months." But if some people were stockpiling weapons and bottled water in preparation for the end of the world, I was thinking, instead, of the shifts in consciousness being mapped by mystics and New Age writers, an age to usher in more trust in the intuitive, more harmony with the earth. Change was happening, and it seemed to me that people were responding either with fear or with hope. From my urban, Pentecostal students reading the Left Behind series, to the self-described rednecked friends I grew up with carrying guns, to my yogi friends talking more overtly about energy, healing, and peace, it seemed we were all anticipating a shift—and admitting that reality was becoming wider, deeper, and more mercurial than we thought it would be.

It turned out that the days he suggested were also the only days for a free award ticket on American Airlines, and my daughter's passport expired the day after we would return, and I had a research grant I had yet to claim. And so even planning the trip felt like traveling, following the next good hunch, noting instinct and coincidence as I kept switching direction to find a truer direction. Synchronicities, coincidences, all those unlikely alignments in time are to me like breadcrumbs, little signs that I am on the right path. Sometimes I think of them as openings through which I can see time as something whole, patterned, and not just a line.

❖

Invented around 2000 BC, the Maya's intricate and remarkably accurate system of timekeeping is based on three interlocking calendar wheels. The largest wheel, the Haab, or civil calendar, is divided into 365 days and twenty 18-day months; this calendar tells secular, quotidian time, the time that we in our culture think of as time and try to outrun or make good use of. The smallest wheel, consisting of 260 teeth, keeps the Tzolkin, divine time or "The Sacred Round," which cycles through 13-day periods of ritual. So as each quotidian day of the year interlinks with an ever-changing sacred day, time exists in more than one dimension, in an ever-cycling conversation between the ordinary and the mystical. Like the gears of a clock, or like our own planet spinning as it makes its longer spiral around the sun, these double circles rotate as they complete the largest cycle of all— the Long Count, which tracks the five-thousand-year increments of what the Maya called "the universal cycle."

The excitement about the end of the Mayan calendar was all about the Long Count, because the winter solstice 2012 was said to mark the completion of an epoch or cycle, according to the Maya's calculations, and according to just one of the three calendars that survived their mass destruction by Catholic missionaries. From what scholars and astrologists can gather, Mayan calculations did not attest that the world would end in 2012, however, but that one epoch would give way to the next, and the solstice—the day people were calling the end of the world—would exist as a portal between the ages. I picture the little wheels in my bike lock—when the proper combination is reached, the teeth release, the shaft slips out, there is an opening.

And while I have long noted the variability of time in my own life, the way time's textures and depths can change depending on the quality of my attention, I have never experienced time with as much elasticity as I did in that week before going to Belize. Somehow I edited the page proofs for a book in a half hour, completed all my grading in a day, made cookies for my daughter's holiday parties, and was packed and ready for the trip five days early.

Two days before we were supposed to leave, my friend texted me that she had missed her train from work and asked if I could watch her kids. I got the children situated and began making dinner, but her little boy, who is very sensitive and still young enough to know a lot of things before they are said and made manifest, was unsettled, asking questions.

"I miss Uncle Jeff," he said, although he had never actually met his Uncle Jeff, his dad's brother who was shot a decade ago with a dozen others by a lone gunman. And then, "Can I just talk to my mom for a minute?"

"Sure," I said and stopped chopping carrots to call her back.

"It's funny that you called just now," she said to me when she answered. "Our train just came to a screeching stop because a kid jumped onto the track and was hit. I heard it, and it sent a shock through my body, like I just knew he was dead. And the weird thing is, I have been in this reflective mood all afternoon because I realized that today is Jeff's birthday."

She arrived hours later after the trains got running again and took her children home. We put our kids to bed in their own beds and walked them to school in the morning. We kissed them good-bye and watched them go in—a little sleepy, wobbling beneath their big coats and backpacks. We chatted a minute just like the parents in Newtown, Connecticut, before going off to work or yoga or errands. And then, a couple of hours later, Adam Lanza entered that Newtown school and gunned their children down—twenty-one of them—before he shot himself.

⚜

It is the end of the world, I kept thinking as we lifted off into the sky the next morning, bound for Belize and the culmination of time. For all of those parents, all of those families, it is the end of the world. And if we needed a sign that our old way of life—our mythology based on individualism and violence, our culture of video games, materialism, alienation—needs to shift into a new worldview, this is it.

We took three flights just to get into Belize City and then boarded a hopper flight that would take us into the mountains north of Punta Gorda. And then we lifted off into one of those moments that seem designed to remind you that there is more to the world than its human pain. Sun showered through portals in the clouds, mountains glowed bluish in the distance and undulated below us, thick with tufted trees. The forest was dense, healthy, with just the occasional road—a dirt scar running through green. And I could see little tassels of smoke rising from the forest, gray as the trunks of the cottonwood trees. They were the wood fires the Maya have cooked with for thousands of years and cook with still. We were seeing the world before the colonizers came, before money, mining, and industry.

We landed and I felt like I was being healed just by breathing. I could smell the cleanliness of the air, the health of the trees, and that ancient, warming woodsmoke. "It's so beautiful," I said to the attendant. He had unloaded our bags and was just standing there, looking back at his own mountains. He nodded, silent. There was no need to say it. No need to say anything. There was just the deep peace of the earth, and it was in him.

Another Mayan, Sebastian, had come from the resort to pick us up. He was short in stature with his people's regally straight nose and front teeth covered in gold. He had a clipped rhythm and eloquence to his speech that I took to be Quiché but sounded like a brogue, maybe picked up from Irish or Scottish missionaries.

"I don't really like the town," he told me as we drove through Punta Gorda, a tiny town by our standards, a major one by his. "Children go bad in the town, they start buying and selling and getting dangerous. I like our villages more. We all help each other out. We work together to plant the crops we need; we grow the food we need.

"When the hurricane came, the whole region was half destroyed. And the half that was destroyed went and moved in with the villages that stood, and then we all worked together day and night to rebuild the new thatch huts. In three months, just three months, our whole village was rebuilt."

From the plane, I had seen one fire that looked alarmingly large. We passed near it, and I asked what was going on. "Oh, a white man named Robert bought up all this land," Sebastian said. "Five hundred acres, and when he first bought them, he bulldozed the forest. And then, because he had ruined the topsoil, he could not grow anything and could only raise cattle." The burning smell in the air was choking and seemed sinister amid such beauty.

"Our grandfathers used to burn," Sebastian said, "but now we learn better. We take corn or plants from the river and let them rot and go back to the land, and then we have better land, better crops.

"You see now, you can't plant a seed on sand or on a rock," he went on. "You have to plant on good soil with other things in it."

It was like listening to the Bible, and I wondered for the first time about the literal life of parables. A parable works because it uses the recognizable language of the practical to describe the moral or spiritual. But it only works, I realized now, if what you are saying about the practical world is actually true. Sacred time has to be understood in the moments of daily time, because daily time is *important*.

We drove almost an hour, deeper into the mountains, the forest, before we parked and got out to begin making our way on raised wooden walkways gently lit by solar-powered lamps. And then Sebastian stopped and said, "That there is the Cotton Tree. Look up." And there was the most enormous, magical tree I had ever seen. Its bark was smooth, clay gray and animate somehow, and the crooks between its raised root system were so deep you could build a cabin there. It was the mystical Ceiba tree, which the Maya believe connects the spirit world with the earthly world and brings them into conversation.

❧

We went to bed in our thatched cottage beside the river and woke to glowing green, a little lap of lawn and a beach with a canoe and kayaks.

I thought maybe I would feel connected to some ancient ancestors there, but I woke thinking of my own grandparents. When I was a child, we had stayed at a place called "Paradise," a little campground beside a lake in central Florida, before that area was mostly razed for strip malls and cattle grazing. My brother and I had learned to walk in Paradise—on little patches of grass grown over white sand, thin bearded droppings of Spanish moss and the shining leather-colored leaves of the pin oak—the same leaves my daughter was walking on now.

"I wish if Grandma and Grandpa were here," she kept saying. "And Uncle Douglas and Aunt Lindsey and Gwyneth." It seemed strange to be in such beauty and abundance and not be sharing it with anyone. We were just getting back to our cabin after breakfast when a beautiful Mayan woman came by with her cart of cleaning supplies.

"Oh, you don't need to clean!" I said. "We just arrived." We talked for a while, and I told her we wanted to go out in the canoe.

"Are you going upriver?" she asked, the kind of gentle question that is actually a suggestion.

"Yes," I said, looking up toward the mountains, into an even deeper, more mysterious landscape.

"Then you must visit my village," she said. "There will be people bathing, so you know where to stop. And you can walk up to the green, look around, get something to eat."

"Wonderful!" I said. "Thank you!" So I grabbed my wallet, picturing little stands with handcrafted items and some small café.

In Florida as a child, I had always taken our canoe farther than allowed and had dreamed of being back in the wild, where no one would see me, where I could watch the alligator and the heron unobserved. My whole life, it seemed, I had been turning my face from the bridges and power plants, trying to imagine what the land had looked like before the settlers came. And here we were. The river was brownish green, winding and deep, and the mud banks were lush with vines, shrubs, and trees. Best of all, there was no hum of machines, no buildings or cars to remind me of our time, or our colonizing, commercializing civilization that seems to me increasingly misguided.

It could have been one hundred, one thousand, or two thousand years ago. We could have been moving back and back in time, and when I hit a rhythm with my paddles I felt that I had done all of this before somehow. I had set off from the known world over slithering brown water. I had paddled upstream, far from anything I recognized. And the farther I went, the more I felt like myself, or the self I was becoming.

It was an hour before we saw the first person, and I imagined that I remembered that too—the relief early explorers must have felt when they saw another human, some evidence that a land was habitable. The man we saw was Mayan, sitting by the river with a fishing pole. "Excuse me," I called out.

He looked up, silent, not wasting language.

"How much farther to Santa Ana?"

"You are going to Santa Ana?" he asked, surprised.

"Is that crazy?" I said, and he laughed. "Is it possible?"

"Isn't the baby scared to be in a boat?" he asked.

"No," I answered. "But she is hungry, and we would like to get something to eat."

He laughed again and told me it was about a half hour more.

"Forty-five minutes for me because I am slow!" I said, laughing with him.

"The river will wind around this way and then that," he explained, "and then you will be on the other side of the land. You will know the village because there will be people there, bathing."

I remember this, I thought, the way you would press on toward a village hoping it was safe but not knowing, hoping that your trust that the people were safe would make them—and you—safe.

So I kept going. And going. A half hour later I grew afraid because I realized that no one in the world knew where we were. On a remote river in the south of Belize, with no one else even on it. I couldn't even remember the river's *name*.

What should I do? What should I do? I began asking, and then, almost as an afterthought, *thank you, thank you,* the way the prayers of the Mayans were said to go, continually, with every pull of the paddle. And the answer I kept sensing was, Whatever you want. You can go on or turn back. You are already here. In the middle of your life, which is strange to you.

I saw myself from another angle then, with embarrassment, even shame. How could I have imagined that I was on some kind of quest, implying that I am a hero, that a place like this could have *called* me? I was just some silly, earnest woman paddling her daughter deeper into the mountains in search of lost time. We were just two breathing beings inching up the flowing vein of a larger breathing being who knows she *is* and needs nothing.

However deeply I need nature, nature does not really need me, I realized, especially not me as an *individual.* And my own reading of the journey will be just that—idiosyncratic, even arbitrary. In a city, choices have been made, roads have been laid, and we live within a shared social-historical vision. But in the wild, everything exists in multiplicity, equality. Do I notice that pink flower, shining with dew, or that pod, dead and dangling from the branch of a tree? Which holds the message for me? And is it my primitive, poetic sensibility asking for a message, or my narrow, whining ego? Am I only asking out of fear that I am not, in fact, necessary? How can I see life as not only symbolic, but whole, complete outside of me?

This wincing reckoning of my humility went on for a long time, maybe an hour, before something cleared—maybe *me*—and I began to love and see it all more deeply. So many layers of green. Birdsong and birds lifting off—shapes of trees from the trees—when they saw our little movement in the water. At one point, two young Mayan men saw us coming and pulled in their dugout canoe and scampered up the banks, hiding. I remember this too, I thought. To be watched, appropriately distrusted. To be the *other*.

I just kept paddling, trying to see, and through all of this, my adventurous little five-year-old was getting increasingly hungry. It had been two and a half hours now, and it was only fair to give her the choice. "We can turn back and go to the lodge," I said finally. "Or we can continue on to try to find the town."

"Keep going," she said with a kind of taciturn resignation, very much like a Mayan, and then she lay down in the front of the boat. I covered her with a towel, and she went to sleep. And I thought, not for the first time, that it seemed we had been together before, doing this kind of thing.

So I kept going, and then I began to see things, little signs and communications—as if, as I was watching it, the land was watching me. A red bird just up ahead, flying along as if to urge us forward. A dugout canoe on the bank, painted the same sky blue of my grandparents' canoe. And then a small corn field, just like the fields my grandfather had tended behind the house, the ribboned tops of the stalks a deep and waving green. So I knew we were getting to cultivated land, which I figured would have to be walking distance from the village. And I felt myself entering that paradox again—that when I sense the future or the past speaking through the moment I am in, I become more *present*.

Eventually, up ahead, I noticed a glinting in the trees, and I told myself, either that is the village, or we are turning around. And as we got closer, I could see that someone had thrown an old cassette tape up into the branches of a cottonwood tree, so it made a faint, twinkling garland across the water—almost invisible, but just enough to mark the spot.

There were two women and two children in the river, washing their dishes. Their washed clothes were laid out and drying on the rocks.

"Hello," I called, waking my daughter. "Is this Santa Ana?"

"Yes," the younger woman answered.

"Would it be okay if we came ashore?" I asked.

"Sure," they said, smiling. So I pulled us onto the muddiest possible spot, and my daughter stepped out and her flip-flops came off a foot under the mud, and then I got out and mine came off too, and we were sinking up to our knees and writhing around, completely inept and clumsy. Then the older of the two women came over with a pan full of water for us to wash, and then they both went back into the mud to help me to dig out our shoes. We were all cracking up, laughing about my skills in docking a canoe, when they motioned that there were solid banks all around us, which made it even funnier.

After we washed and stopped laughing, I pulled out my last granola bar and offered it to the mother. Then I asked if it would be okay if we walked into the village to get something to eat.

They were silent. "Well, we don't have any place to eat." The younger woman smiled. "There is no restaurant or anything."

"Oh," I said.

And then after a pause, she asked, "You came alone, all the way from the resort?"

"Yes, Rebecca told us to go upriver and see her village. She told us we could look around, get something to eat."

They both started laughing again. "Rebecca is her sister," the mother said. And I realized that they did look alike.

"I will cook for you," the daughter said then, nodding in her slow, sweet way. "My name is Elizabeth."

I asked if I could help with the washing, and they said that's okay, they were just finishing. And then after a few minutes Elizabeth put the big plastic tub full of washed pans on her head and started up toward the village. She was barefoot and I took off my flip-flops too because it was so much easier to walk that way, gripping the bank's mud and hearty grasses.

The village was well tended and very neat. It had a cleared lawn in the middle and maybe ten to twenty thatched structures around it, and a single community building. It was framed by mountains in the background and a brightly painted school bus parked evenly at one end. Elizabeth led us diagonally across the green, and by this time, many of the town's children we running along with us, wondering about this strange white woman and little girl. We met Elizabeth's youngest siblings—Lily, a little girl of four with gold earrings and newly washed white clothes, Adam, six, with a big smile and saintly heart who was always trying to keep up with his older brother Leon, who was nine. Skinny, fierce-looking hogs were running around everywhere, and my daughter was in her bathing suit, bravely walking ahead of me. "I think that is the daddy pig," she said when we saw the biggest one of all, and I was proud of her for continuing, for not looking away.

We got to their little compound of buildings—a kitchen building, a sleeping-living building, an outhouse, and a coop for the chickens and turkey. They all had thatched roofs and walls of scrapwood of many colors with bare openings for windows. You can sit in here, Elizabeth said, leading us to the living room. It had a packed dirt floor, three hammocks, and one little couch that must have been used as a bed. We sat together in a hammock and my daughter cuddled up to me. Then the kids came in, Leon swaggering with an armful of sugarcane they had gathered at the river. He had a big knife and began cutting the cane, scoring the top and slicing off strips. And then the three kids were sucking on the cane and proudly offering strips to my daughter, who was devouring them happily.

"Look at that beautiful girl," my daughter said then, and a stunning young woman came in and started scattering water on the floor and sweeping out the dust. Then another beautiful girl came in—her sister or twin—with a bundle that she leaned down to show me. "Oh, a baby!" I said. He was wrapped in a white sheet turned into a sling, and the girl gave him to me to rock and hold. We talked for a while about the baby, and about his father, who had left her to go back to Guatemala. I understood it was really hard. She was young, scared, and tired, a single mother.

There was a treadle sewing machine in the room, one of those black and gold singers from the late 1800s set into a wooden piece of furniture, and across from that, a television. After she swept, the one sister plugged it into a generator and put on a National Geographic VHS about the ancient Mayans. The special began with loud, melodramatic music, and then an exaggerated voice-over introducing a lone white researcher, Richard something, who seemed to be acting out the Celestine Prophecy, looking for some portal point, a cavern that would introduce us to this lost civilization.

Who were the ancient Maya and why were they wiped out? The grim, apocalyptic voice was saying. *We have discovered a tomb that will explain the demise of these people who were some of the most advanced timekeepers the world has ever known.*

Leon had pulled up a plastic pail to sit on and Adam was crouched beside him. "This is about the Maya," he kept saying, pointing to the television and then patting his own chest proudly, "Us, the Maya." The self-important voice was going on and on about their demise, but here we were with them. I was rocking the baby, who liked to look at his hand in mine, the two shades of brown, and sitting beside my daughter, who had entered another world with me, but who understood and loved it, because she was human.

The kids couldn't watch for very long, with so much life and beauty outside. Soon the boys went to climb their grandfather's tree to get some oranges, and my daughter followed them. "Oh, they do my trick!" she said when she saw Lily gathering the fruit in her skirt. "That is your trick?" I asked.

"Yes, they fill their skirts with oranges and it helps them to carry them. I showed it to my friends at school, but they didn't know what I meant."

And soon she was gathering up oranges as the boys climbed the trees to drop them down to her. And I thought that, in some ways, she looked more comfortable, more herself, than she ever did at school.

Then lunch was ready. We went into the kitchen building, where one of the two younger sisters was sitting by the fire making tortillas. She was taking bits of corn dough made from ground corn, kneading it down with the heel of her hand into a circle, and then baking them on the broad, circular stone over the fire. Elizabeth had set the table with tall tumblers of cacao, the raw chocolate drink made from the cacao seeds, and soft scrambled eggs from the chickens outside. I was embarrassed by all they were giving us, and shy to be eating without them, but then the kids came in to eat too, and Leon was eating ten tortillas, and Adam was trying to catch up, and we were all talking. And it felt almost as if we had known one another, but only because of humility, I think, because I never forgot how much we did *not* know.

Eventually, it was time to leave. I knew we needed to make it back to the lodge before dark, but I also knew that the river would be with us now, making it all go faster. I gave Elizabeth money—an amount I hoped would pay her well for her trouble but not insult her, since she had made us their guests—and then we all started walking back down to the river. The children were making whirligigs out of palm fronds and showing my daughter how to run with them so they spun. Some of the young men of the village came out of their homes to walk alongside us and then helped me to put the canoe in a section that was not muddy, and we settled in with the bag of oranges and cacao pods they had given us. And we were off.

As I paddled back, I was grateful, and in awe of their kindness. "I wish we lived like that," my daughter said, "with sugarcane and an orange tree right outside our door. And Grandma and Grandpa beside us."

"Me too," I said. They were our friends, real friends, but I had never taken a picture or gotten an address. I couldn't have, because to pull out my iPhone in that world would have hoisted us out of its timelessness. It would have othered us, or othered them, and the beauty of the day was in its connection.

Later, I learned that the Mayan greeting, the one they had given us, means, essentially, "You are another of me."

❖

The Maya had their own mythologies around the long count. Some say that the first age of man was the age of mud, and the second was the age of corn. "And the third age? What is the third age?" I asked of the hotel manager, who was setting up programs in honor of the end of the Mayan calendar, including a talk by his father, a Mayan elder.

"I don't know," he said, ticked off by the question. "I don't think there is a third age. This way of life can't continue. This is the *end* of the Mayan age."

"We keep looking for endings," explains the archaeologist William Saturno, who recently discovered an ancient Mayan calendar painted in the caves of Guatemala. "But the Maya were looking for a guarantee that nothing would change. It's an entirely different mindset. The ancient Maya predicted that the world would continue seven thousand years from now, that this was just one shift in a continuing process."

This difference in thought is even apparent in language. The "End of the World" was set to happen on the winter solstice, and "solstice," in our Romance languages, essentially means "sun stand." And yet the Maya call the solstice the "rakan k'ij," which means "change of road." Where the Western mind sees a delineated moment, an event or an end, the indigenous mind sees a path, an ongoing circle through the stars.

❖

Our tour package at the resort included one excursion to meet the real Mayans, so we decided to learn about forest gardening and permaculture from cacao farmer Eladio Pop. We set off walking through his land, a mountain forest rich with some of the most nutritional and healing plants of the earth—from the fragrant allspice tree to turmeric roots and cinnamon bark; banana, orange, grapefruit, and lime trees; and several varieties of cacao. And as we walked through the little winding paths beside his mountain stream, he fed us, showing my daughter how to crack the cacao pods and chew their pulp-covered seeds, then pulling out pale green spirals from the hearts of palm for me to eat. And while he talked about the fruits of the land, he told us about its spirit also.

"I tried to read the Bible once, but all those black words didn't make sense to me," he said. "So I wake up every morning and talk to Jesus and he tells me, go here, take care of that plant there, plant this sapling here, weed up a little around this tree so it gets more air. So every day I just come out and work like this and talk to God, and I am happy."

We were filling up on bananas and cacao—everywhere—and seeing the way the forest sustains itself with just a little help. And it was clear that decay and creation are inextricable, that the healthy tree that yields the fruit grows best from the one that has fallen into mulch and bugs.

"I thought I would have a different kind of life," said Mr. Pop. "I thought I would go to the town and school, become a big man." He laughed. "But my mother took sick, and I came home and married my wife and began to get to know our land. And now this is my life. My wife and I have nine children, and none of them have ever been sick. I come out and make medicines and care for the plants, and every day we eat the good food we grow."

"You live in Eden." I smiled.

"Yes, we live in Eden," he said. "And my wife and I, we have the river of life between us."

At one point, someone on the tour asked Mr. Pop what he thought about the end of the Mayan calendar, and he said, "I don't really know about all that. I think life is always beginning, always ending, every day."

"But—it is a funny thing. In all of my years of farming, the weather of this year, 2012, has been the best."

❖

Back at the resort, the manager was planning for the big event: the end of the Mayan calendar. And I felt that tinge of cynicism that infects most tourism, the way the tourist never really leaves his or her comfort zone to become a student of the other, or to remember that he *is* the other. They'd rather make a little fun. The owner had come up with a new drink—a Mai Tai for the End of Time—featuring a triple dose of rum, and most people sat drinking it, while a few of us came over to listen to the elder talk about Mayan history. He told us about the advancements of their calendar, the sophistication of their early civilization, and, especially, the ways the Maya have been persecuted and maligned by European colonizers.

"And as for this idea about the end of time," his son, the manager, said, "It is all hoopla. It is just another marketing ploy by the West imposed on indigenous people, another way to use us to make money."

"Do you think it may also be expressive of some underlying feeling we have," I asked after a while, "that the way we are operating in Western culture just cannot continue?"

I could tell that he thought I was some New Age missionary, full of shit. "The way of life of these people is so connected and wise," I tried to go on, "and we have so much to learn from them. What do you think we can do?"

"Nothing," he said bitterly. "One culture will take over the other. It is the oldest story in the world."

He was right, I realized. It is the oldest story, older even than our delineations of colonizer and colonized, and changing it now would require deep inner changes, the first being that the more technologically advanced people would have to know that we are *less* advanced in terms of relationship—with other humans, and with the earth itself. And we would have to know that these relationships matter— that is, if we want to survive.

As I listened to the history and justified anger these men were expressing, I thought of my friends back at home, holding their own solstice ceremonies for healing, renewal, and bringing in the New Age. The cost of their yoga mats and latest pedicures could permanently change the life of one of these families. And I thought, yes, it is unfairly appropriative and foolish to co-opt an idea from a culture we do not even know. But isn't it also evidence of our longing for the kind of wisdom and connectedness that the Maya—those who survived—have never lost? And isn't there something sweet about it, hopeful—all of these people gathering for healing, for a new, very different kind of world?

We went to bed and woke on the last day of time. It was a sparkling morning, with sunlight filtering through the trees, like the very first day. But we had to leave quickly because our flight was set for 11 a.m., precisely the time of the astrological shift, the apocalypse. "I tried to stay longer," I said to the manager, "but there were no seats open."

"Maybe you are meant to be bridging the worlds," he said then.

In a few days, we had gone from the end—because what culture that sees the murder of its children by its children doesn't sense in that an end?—to the beginning, to the basic, gentle cultivation of an earth that produces enough to feed its beings. It was all wondrous and nonlinear, and it convinced me that time is, indeed, subject to the quality of our attention, and progress does not move forward in only one way.

Contributors

John Beckman is the author of *American Fun: Four Centuries of Joyous Revolt*. His writing has appeared in the *New York Times*, *Wall Street Journal*, *Washington Post*, *Granta*, *McSweeney's*, and elsewhere. His novel, *The Winter Zoo*, was a *New York Times* Notable Book. He lives in Annapolis, Maryland, with his wife, the journalist Marcela Valdes, and their daughter.

Lucy Jane Bledsoe is the author of five novels, including *The Big Bang Symphony* and *A Thin Bright Line*. Her fiction has won a Yaddo fellowship, the *Saturday Evening Post* Fiction Prize, a California Arts Council Award, an American Library Association Stonewall Award, and two National Science Foundation Writer Fellowships. Her stories have been translated into Japanese, Spanish, German, Dutch, and Chinese.

Brian Bouldrey is the author, most recently, of *The Peasant and the Mariners* and *The Sorrow of the Elves*. He is the editor of several anthologies and the author of four nonfiction books, including *Honorable Bandit: A Walk across Corsica*, and four novels, including *The Boom Economy*. He is the North American Editor of the Open Door literacy series for Gemma-Media. He teaches writing and literature at Northwestern University.

Charles Coe is the author of two volumes of poetry, *Picnic on the Moon* and *All Sins Forgiven: Poems for My Parents*, and the novella *Spin Cycles*. He has been designated a New England "Literary Light" by the Associates of the Boston Public Library and is an artist fellow at Boston's St. Botolph Club.

Jonathan Monroe Geltner was born in Newton, Massachusetts. He holds degrees in Classics and English from the University of Cincinnati and the University of Chicago, and is currently pursuing an MFA from Warren Wilson College. He and his wife reside in southeastern Michigan.

Goldie Goldbloom is the author of *The Paperback Shoe* and *You Lose These*. Her writing has appeared in the *Kenyon Review*, *The Best Australian Short Stories 2015*, *Prairie Schooner*, and *Narrative*, among other publications. She has been a recipient of the AWP novel award and fellowships from the National Endowment for the Arts and Dora Maar House. She lives in Chicago with her eight children and teaches creative writing at the University of Chicago.

Miles Harvey is the author of two books, *The Island of Lost Maps: A True Story of Cartographic Crime* and *Painter in a Savage Land: The Strange Saga of the First European Artist in North America*. He teaches creative writing at DePaul University. "At the Grave of Sadie Thorpe," which originally appeared in *New Ohio Review*, received a Notable Essay citation from *Best American Essays 2015*.

Trebor Healey is the author of three novels, a short story collection, and a book of poetry. His most recent short story collection, *Eros and Dust*, will be published in 2016. He has received a Lambda Literary Award, two Publishing Triangle awards, and a Violet Quill award.

Raphael Kadushin is an award-winning food and travel writer. He has served as a contributing editor to both *Bon Appétit* and *National Geographic Traveler* magazines, and his work has appeared regularly in a wide range of outlets, including *Condé Nast Traveler*, *Wall Street Journal*, *Travel & Leisure*, *National Geographic Traveler*, *Bon Appétit*, *Epicurious*, and *Out*. His fiction and journalism has been widely anthologized, appearing in such publications as three *Best Food Writing* collections and *National Geographic's Through the Lens*. He is also the editor of two travel anthologies, *Big Trips* and *Wonderlands*.

David Stuart MacLean is a PEN/American award-winning essayist. His essays and stories have appeared in *Ploughshares*, *Guernica*, *Gulf Coast*, the *New York Times*, the *Guardian*, and on the radio program *This American Life*. He was a Fulbright scholar in India, a cofounder of the popular Poison Pen Reading Series in Houston, and now lives in Chicago. He is the author of the memoir *The Answer to the Riddle Is Me*, named by *Kirkus* as one of the best books of 2014.

Marta Maretich is the author of a novel about the Tiepolo family, *The Merchants of Light*, and two novellas, *The Possibility of Lions* and *The Bear Suit*. Her short fiction and nonfiction have been published in many journals, including *Boom! A Journal of California* and the *Harvard Review*. Born in Nigeria, raised in California, she now lives and works in London.

Kimberly Meyer's work has appeared in *The Best American Travel Writing 2012*, *Ploughshares*, the *Kenyon Review*, *Ecotone*, the *Oxford American*, the *Georgia Review*, *Agni*, the *Southern Review*, and *Third Coast*. She teaches in a Great Books program at the University of Houston's Honors College and is the author of *The Book of Wanderings*, a memoir about the journey she and her daughter made by retracing a medieval pilgrimage route to the Holy Land and St. Catherine's Monastery in the Sinai Desert.

Jivin Misra is a composer, musician, and writer. He wrote the music and libretto for *The Loop*, a one-act chamber opera that premiered in the spring of 2014. He teaches creative writing to international high school students in New Haven, Connecticut.

Susan Fox Rogers is the author of *My Reach: A Hudson River Memoir* and the editor of twelve book anthologies, including *Antarctica: Life on the Ice* and *Solo: On Her Own Adventure*. She traveled to Antarctica on a National Science Foundation award for artists and writers. She teaches the creative essay at Bard College.

Sharman Apt Russell teaches at Antioch University and Western New Mexico University. Her *Diary of a Citizen Scientist: Chasing Tiger Beetles and Other New Ways of Engaging the World* won the 2016 John Burroughs Medal for Distinguished Nature Writing. Recent fiction includes the award-winning YA *Teresa of the New World* and the science fiction novel *Knocking on Heaven's Door*. The topics of her nonfiction range from *Standing in the Light: My Life as a Pantheist* to *Hunger: An Unnatural History*. For more information, go to www.sharmanaptrussell.com.

Russell Scott Valentino is a scholar, editor, writer, and translator based in Bloomington, Indiana. He is a professor of Slavic and East European languages and cultures at Indiana University and a senior editor at Autumn Hill Books. He currently serves as president of the American Literary Translators Association.

Rachel Jamison Webster is the author of the books *September* and *The Endless Unbegun*. She has published poetry and essays in many journals and anthologies, such as *Poetry*, *Tin House*, the *Southern Review*, the *Paris Review*, and *Blackbird*. She lives in Evanston, Illinois, with her daughter and teaches at Northwestern University, where she directs the Creative Writing Program.